St. Helena Library

D1555325

B
CHAPLIN

Chaplin, Saul,
1912-

The golden age of
movie musicals and
me.

$24.95

DATE			

The
Golden Age of
Movie Musicals

and Me

The
GOLDEN AGE of
MOVIE MUSICALS

and ME

by
SAUL CHAPLIN

University of Oklahoma Press : Norman and London

My thanks to
Michael Mindlin
for his invaluable
editorial assistance.

Library of Congress Cataloging-in-Publication Data

Chaplin, Saul, 1912–
    The golden age of movie musicals and me / by Saul Chaplin.
        p.   cm.
    Includes index.
    ISBN 0-8061-2652-3 (alk. paper)
    1. Chaplin, Saul, 1912- . 2. Composers—United States—Biography.
3. Musical films—United States. I. Title.
ML410.C4177A3 1994
782.1'4'092—dc20
[B]   93-48198
                                                                      CIP
                                                                      MN

Text designed by Cathy Carney Imboden.

1   2   3   4   5   6   7   8   9   10

This book is for my wife, Betty,
who insisted that I write it
for my grandchildren,
Charles and Daisy Prince.

Contents

Illustrations

The
GOLDEN AGE of
MOVIE MUSICALS

and ME

■ On Wednesday, March 30, 1955, the Academy of Motion Picture Arts and Sciences presented its yearly awards at the Pantages Theater in Hollywood. The nominations for Best Scoring of a Musical were *Carmen Jones, The Glenn Miller Story, A Star Is Born, There's No Business Like Show Business, Seven Brides for Seven Brothers.* The winners were Saul Chaplin and Adolph Deutsch, for *Seven Brides for Seven Brothers.*

It was the second of three Academy Awards I was to win (the other two were for *An American in Paris* and *West Side Story*),

Prologue

but it's an evening I will never forget. Sammy Cahn, who received the award for the category that followed mine, Best Song, was responsible for my being there that night— despite the fact that we hadn't worked together for fourteen years. That we both should have won the Academy Award on the same night is ironic.

But all of that happened a very long time ago, so in the parlance of musicians, "Let's take it from the upper left-hand corner."

Chapter 1 ■ On April 23, 1940, Sammy Cahn and I arrived at the El Jardin apartments in Hollywood, California, having driven across the country from New York. My wife, Ethel, and I had agreed that she and Judy, our ten-month-old daughter, would join me as soon as I could find a suitable place for us to live. Young songwriters—Sammy was the lyricist; I was the composer—we left behind a trail of over thirty published songs, more than half of which had been on the popular weekly network radio show the "Lucky Strike Hit Parade." The ten most popular of our songs were "Rhythm

Hollywood

Is Our Business," "Shoe Shine Boy," "Rhythm in My Nursery Rhymes," "Until the Real Thing Comes Along," "If It's the Last Thing I Do," "Dedicated to You," "Posin'," "Please Be Kind," "Joseph, Joseph," and "Bei Mir Bist Du Schoen."

The only friend Sammy and I had in Hollywood was Phil Silvers, the comedian, who subsequently became known to the world as Sgt. Bilko. We had met Phil when we played together as teenagers in a band at a hotel in the borscht belt. Phil was under contract to MGM, but he was miserable. Not only wouldn't they cast him in a film, but they never acknowledged his existence. Although we hadn't a clue what the future held for us, we spent most of our time consoling Phil.

Sammy and I had begun thinking about Hollywood a year earlier, right after we had written the score for the *Cotton Club Revue of 1939,* starring Louis Armstrong and Maxine Sullivan, who had become famous for her hit recording of "Loch Lomond."

We came up with one of my favorite songs, "You're a Lucky Guy," for Louis, but it never achieved the popularity we felt it should have because the publisher was not plugging it sufficiently. We were then under contract to Warner Bros. Publishing Company, and not only were our songs being ignored, but we were reduced to writing lyrics for some piano novelty standards they owned—things like "Porky the Porcupine." We were

4

becoming increasingly unhappy. Finally we'd had it. Sammy found an ingenious solution for us.

We made an appointment to see Herman Starr, the executive in charge of the Warner Bros. music publishing companies. We told him we wanted to be sent to Hollywood to write for Warner Bros. features. Starr said he had no objection so long as we sent him any new songs we wrote. We had two additional requests: a $50 raise each to make ends meet in Hollywood and a letter of introduction to the person who was in charge of the music at the studio. He granted both requests and gave us a letter to Leo Forbstein, the head of the studio's Music Department. It told him who we were and offered him our services gratis since we were already being paid by the publisher.

When we got to Hollywood, we sent Forbstein the letter. We never heard from him or anyone else at Warner Bros. They wouldn't let us on the lot. They didn't want us—even for free.

We were greeted in Hollywood by the Orsatti Agency people as if they had been waiting for us for years. It had all been arranged by Phil. He, as well as almost everyone else who worked at MGM, was signed by the agency. The Orsatti brothers were close friends of L. B. Mayer, the head of the studio, and there were rumors that Mayer was part owner of the agency. From their effusive greeting, we expected to be doing the score for a movie by nightfall, certainly by the end of the week. We never heard from them again. We couldn't even get them on the phone. Several months later, after Phil had been dropped by MGM, he went with Al Kingston, a young, hustling agent. We joined him.

A month after we arrived, I found a newly furnished two-bedroom house in West Los Angeles with a front lawn and flower garden, for $85 a month the first year and $75 the second year if we chose to stay. It was a palace compared to our three-room apartment in Brooklyn. Ethel and Judy left to join me on May 23, 1940. The details of their departure from Grand Central Station are a tale often retold by my family. You would have thought they were leaving the earth forever. There was such sobbing and wailing that it prompted a bystander to inquire, "Who died?" As someone once said, "Among the Jews there's no such thing as a stiff upper lip. They let everything hang out and play every emotion to the hilt."

Through Phil Silvers, Sammy and I met Garson Kanin, a very successful young film director at the time with a vast background in the theater. We spent several evenings a week at his home. His other guests were primarily writers who were among the brightest and wittiest people in town: Dore Schary, Fred Finkelhoffe, John Monks, Leonard Spigelglass (later the chicest major in the U.S. Air Force), Mike Kanin (Gar's brother), Fay Kanin, and transients like Marc Connelly, Burgess Meredith, and others.

At some time every evening, I was at the piano playing Broadway show tunes, some of which Gar taught me, and doing new songs Sammy and I had just written, or improvising new material with Phil and Sammy. We did a song for anything and everything that happened to members of the group. We created long biographical cantatas for birthdays, new jobs, new girlfriends. Often the most innocuous events were our inspiration.

One night Freddie Finkelhoffe mentioned that he was going to New York. Phil suddenly said, "You're going to New York! Do you know what it's like? Solly, give me a vamp." I played a big-city, New York–type vamp. Sammy began intoning "Manhattan, Manhattan" over it. Against it all, Phil sang "New York City, New York what a town!" He then went on to describe the hustle and bustle, the grime, the filthy subways, and all the other depressing aspects of New York life—most of it in rhyme, with suitable scoring. Somewhere in the number there was a tour of the nightclubs of Manhattan that included takeoffs of the shows at the Hawaiian Room of the Hotel Lexington, the Bublichki, the Persian Room, and a dive up in Harlem. The last part of the number dealt with Finkelhoffe's eventual return to Hollywood. None of his friends would remember him—his favorite restaurants would no longer accept his reservations—the Hollywood

Legion Stadium (where everyone ritualistically attended the prizefights every Friday night) would no longer hold seats for him—everyone would ask, "Freddie who?" Phil was absolutely brilliant.

Later we extricated the "nightclub section" from the number and it became a very important piece of material for Phil. It had a curious history. He first performed it with Rags Ragland when they appeared together at Charley Foy's Supper Club in North Hollywood later that year. They did a terrific act and were an immediate sensation. One of the biggest laugh-getters was our number "Manhattan" (not to be confused with the Rodgers and Hart song of the same name).

Now, to narrate the odd events that followed I have to describe the Harlem section of the number. In it Phil emulated a marijuana-smoking "hepcat" who explained the lyrics of a song to an innocent bystander:

SINGER: I'VE BOUGHT YOU GIFTS GALORE.
PHIL: Dig this! The cat lays a gang of fancy goods on his chick.
SINGER: I'VE PARKED OUTSIDE YOUR DOOR.
PHIL: He stashes his frame outside her pad. Are you latchin' on to his jive?
SINGER: I'VE BEEN RATED A GENIUS ON AN I.Q. TEST, BUT STILL YOU ARE NOT IMPRESSED.
PHIL: Will you dig this? He spends righteous loot on her, he shadows her pad, he's got a solid murder noggin' that just won't quit but the chick is *bringing him down.* [as he pushes the imaginary joint into the bystander's mouth]. Here—take a little air with it. Light up and *be* somebody.

The entire chorus continues in this manner.

Cut to the Samuel Goldwyn Studios. Goldwyn is preparing a Brackett and Wilder film called *Ball of Fire*, starring Gary Cooper and Barbara Stanwyck. In it, Cooper is compiling a dictionary of slang. He thinks he's finished when he happens to see Stanwyck performing in a nightclub where she uses a kind of slang he has never heard before. He goes to her dressing room to learn more about it and thus starts their relationship. Someone told Samuel Goldwyn (it could've been Billy Wilder) that Phil Silvers was doing a number at Charley Foy's with lots of "jive-talk" that would be perfect for Barbara Stanwyck and would fit the film's situation. Goldwyn came to Charley Foy's, saw the number, liked it, and bought it from us. Also, he hired Phil Silvers to do the number with Barbara Stanwyck.

Now someone got the notion that to make the number even more entertaining, they should hire a name band to play it for Stanwyck and Silvers. They engaged Gene Krupa and his orchestra, who were playing at the Hollywood Palladium at the time. Sammy and I began teaching Barbara Stanwyck her part while the Goldwyn legal department went about obtaining the rights to use the song from the publisher. Much to everyone's shock, the price quoted by the publisher for the one use was enormous. So enormous that Goldwyn decided it was too expensive to do it. So it was out, but he wanted to retain the idea.

Sammy and I told him we'd write a new song that would be all jive-talk and would accomplish the same purpose that "Manhattan" did. He gave us the OK, and in several days we were back in his office doing our new song. The title was "Coppin' A Plea," and the lyric went:

> You sure solid sent me for fair
> When you dug me so righteously,
> You're lookin' at
> A beat-up cat
> Who's Coppin' A Plea for a he.
>
> It turns out that I'm just a square
> An ick with the old one, two, three.
> My one stale dream
> Is off the beam,
> I'm Coppin' A Plea for a he.
>
> I'm just a chick
> Who's sick in the ticker,

He's got me up on the shelf.
I stay at home
And rockin' in my wicker,
Bustin' a hole in myself.

If he'd only collar my jive
I wouldn't be just half alive.
I'm like the bear, I ain't nowhere.
He's givin' the puller to me
I'm Coppin' A Plea for a he.

We finished, having given it our best shot. There was a moment of silence, after which Goldwyn said in a squeaky tenor, "I don't understand it."

SAMMY: Right. That's the way Gary Cooper is supposed to react.
GOLDWYN: But I don't understand a single word.
SAMMY: Well, isn't that what it's supposed to be?
GOLDWYN: But I don't even know what the title means.
SAMMY: That's impossible. Everyone knows what "coppin' a plea" means.
GOLDWYN: Let's see.

And with that he pressed half a dozen buttons on his desk. A steady stream of people now started filing into his office. He asked each one, "What does 'coppin' a plea' mean?" To our utter astonishment, not a single person knew. We were about to admit defeat when in came a chubby gray-haired lady in her late fifties. Certainly she wouldn't know. Well, she launched into a detailed explanation of the phrase, including its early usage by prisoners and lawyers. Of course, she came too late to help our cause, and with the preponderance of evidence against us, the song was turned down.

But now they still had Gene Krupa under contract. They settled for an instrumental number of theirs called "Drumboogie." In it, Krupa drums on everything in sight, winding up with using matches as drumsticks and drumming on matchboxes until the matchsticks ignite. The song had nothing to do with advancing the plot of the picture, which was supposed to be its purpose in the first place. In fact, Barbara Stanwyck wasn't even in the song.

That wasn't the end of the saga of "Manhattan." Later that year, Phil did it with Ella Logan at a Sunday Celebrity Night at Ciro's. These evenings were very special and attracted the most important stars and executives in town. While they were performing, Ella kind of inched forward slightly. Phil stopped the orchestra. The room became silent. He turned to Ella and said, "Ella, please get back. Mr. Zanuck can't see me. You're blocking his view."

His ad-lib spread over town like wildfire. No one ever mentioned executives' names in those days. They were as inaccessible as gods. Nevertheless, two weeks later Phil Silvers was put under contract to Twentieth Century–Fox by Darryl Zanuck. And it all started in Garson Kanin's living room when Freddie Finkelhoffe happened to mention that he was going to New York.

About two and a half weeks before our contract with Warner Brothers music publishers ran out and we were planning to return to New York, our agent, Al Kingston, arranged an audition for us with Albert J. Cohen, a producer at Republic Pictures. He was impressed with our songs but later told Kingston that he didn't need songwriters, he needed stories. Kingston told him we could write anything—stories, screenplays, name it. We had never written a story, but we weren't about to let this opportunity slip by.

We concocted a tale that included some vaudeville sketches and burlesque bits we remembered and invented a central character who was a songwriter about to be drafted. I'm glad I don't remember any more than that. As luck would have it, Cohen, a big vaudeville and burlesque fan, was crazy about our story. So our first assignment in Hollywood was a film for Republic called *Rookies on Parade,* starring Bob Crosby and his Bobcats, for which we did the original story, words, and music. I don't recall it very vividly, but I'm sure it was no better or worse than the other B musicals that were being made at the time. It did, however, provide an entree for Sammy and me into the film business.

One of the surest ways to land a job in Hollywood is to be unavailable. While we were still at Republic writing the score for *Rookies on Parade*, Al Kingston arranged for us to do our songs for Morris Stoloff, the head of the Music Department at Columbia Pictures. He was impressed and wanted us to start immediately on the score for a film they were planning. When he was told that we were still busy at Republic, he assured us that Columbia would wait until we were available. They did. I'm convinced that what made us irreplaceable was that we were busy on another project. Stoloff, who became a very good friend, was a talented conductor, administrator, and teacher.

While we were writing the score—the film was called *Time Out for Rhythm*—Columbia placed us under term contract for a year, with yearly options after that. It was several months before we met Harry Cohn, the ironfisted ruler who reigned single-handedly over all that was Columbia, at a party given by the producer we were working for. It's a particularly memorable evening to me because it was the only time in my long relationship with Cohn that I found him most charming.

He listened to our score and grunted, which I took as approval. For the rest of the evening he extolled the virtues of Irving Berlin's score to a World War I show called *Yip, Yip, Yaphank*. The only song I knew from it was the hit "Oh How I Hate to Get up in the Morning." Cohn had worked as a song plugger for the publisher of the Berlin score. That, of course, made him an authority on all pop music.

The entire guest list consisted of employees of Columbia. The kowtowing to Cohn was shameless. It wasn't then, nor is it now, that unusual, but today it's done with considerably more finesse. Cohn demanded subservience and reveled in it. He was your boss, responsible for your economic existence, and he never let you forget it. If he said something that wasn't funny but that he thought was funny, you laughed! It's called "playing the game."

He undoubtedly felt he deserved this obeisance by virtue of the fact that he had labored at many jobs to earn his present position.

He once revealed that when he was young, he quit one job after another to better himself. Then suddenly one day he had a job from which he was fired. The trauma was so great that he vowed right then and there that never again would he be in a position where "I could be fired next Wednesday. If there's any firing to do, I'll do it." That somehow led him into the film business as a salesman, and he later became a producer of short subjects. From this he created Columbia Pictures in 1924. He was true to his word. Never again was he in a position to be fired. He could now do the firing and intimidating of others—especially me.

I lived in mortal fear of his disapproval. It wasn't so much his physical presence (he was medium height and stocky) as his manner. To me, he even walked angrily, as if he were on his way to give someone a tongue-lashing for some goof. I found no joy even in his smile. To me he looked snide. He spoke in a loud, gruff voice and never indulged in small talk. Even when he said a casual hello or good-bye, it sounded threatening. All I can say on his behalf, and it's a small kudo indeed, is that he treated his contract players, including his stars, with no more consideration than he treated underlings like me.

Rita Hayworth was at the height of her love-goddess, pin-up popularity when she starred in one of her most memorable films, *Gilda*. The company was shooting on a large nightclub set with about 150 extras. Rita was about to sing the ballad from the picture when Harry Cohn exploded onto the stage, ever-present riding crop in hand (it always reminded me of a slave master's whip), two sycophants trailing behind him. He stormed through the nightclub tables menacingly to where Rita was standing alone in the middle of the floor. The tension on the sound stage was staggering. He bellowed at her, "I just ran the dailies [the film shot the day before]. You got a big fat ass! You look awful!"

Rita stood for a long moment fighting back tears as he ranted on. Then she ran into her dressing room, sobbing. What Cohn had accomplished by his tirade was the loss of a day's shooting because it was impossible for Rita to continue working after such a humiliating experience.

Our first assignment under our term contract was to write the score for a film called *Eadie Was a Lady,* starring Rita Hayworth. Until that time, Rita's voice had always been dubbed by a professional singer. But Ed Judson, Rita's domineering husband, decided that there was no reason why she couldn't sing for herself—all she needed was some singing lessons. He engaged Al Siegal to work with her. A dark, heavyset man with crossed eyes that gave him a sinister, Svengalian look, he was well known as a vocal coach, having been Ethel Merman's arranger-accompanist in vaudeville. As a matter of fact, it seemed to be common knowledge at the time that he had discovered Merman. She always denied it.

When Siegal thought Rita was ready to display her singing talent, he gave a dinner party to which he invited my wife, Ethel, and me; Sammy; Mr. and Mrs. Stoloff; and, of course, Ed Judson. Siegal and Judson reasoned that if we thought Rita could sing well enough, we would then convince Cohn that she be allowed to sing for herself.

It was the first time I saw Rita Hayworth in person, and I was dumbstruck. She was truly a glamorous movie star. It was impossible to reproduce her beauty on the screen. There was no way I could keep myself from staring at her, to the point where it was almost embarrassing. Everything about her was striking. Her face, her figure—the delicacy and grace of her hands and feet, which were surprisingly small. To complement her beautiful physical appearance, she was soft-spoken, gentle, and gracious.

The dinner was ghastly. Not the food, which I don't remember, but the conversation. *Filibuster* is a more appropriate word. Ed Judson considered himself the world's foremost authority. Whenever any of us tried to interject a sentence, he ignored us, condescendingly. Except for Rita. He insulted her with "What the hell do you know about it anyhow?" It was a most uncomfortable hour, after which he ordered us all into the room with the piano and commanded Rita to sing.

She obeyed like an automaton. Siegal had made her several very attractive arrangements, but they couldn't hide the fact that she had a very small voice, not good enough to do her own singing. Her voice could never match the energy with which she danced in her films. (She did her own singing once. In *Gilda* she sang a soft, intimate version of "Put the Blame on Mame," accompanying herself on the guitar.) I was sincerely sorry that the audition turned out that way because I felt great sympathy for her. To have to contend with Harry Cohn during the day and come home to Ed Judson at night was the kind of emotional torture no one should be expected to endure. She divorced Judson shortly thereafter, but I always wondered what the extenuating circumstances were that made her marry him in the first place.

Eadie Was a Lady was shelved. It was later rewritten and made with Ann Miller.

Sammy and I were next assigned to a B musical, starring Lupe Velez, to be made by the Briskin unit. Irving Briskin was a tall, amiable, rather gruff man who supervised a half a dozen producers. They turned out about thirty B pictures a year. The number of films was more important than their quality. It was during wartime, before television, and the picture business was booming.

Sammy and I went to Briskin's office. He handed us a script and told us the nature of the songs required. Then suddenly the door burst open, and there she was: Lupe Velez, looking every inch the Mexican spitfire she played in all her movies. She was shorter than I expected, extremely attractive, with piercing dark eyes that were her most dominant feature. She was constantly in motion and wore the kind of jewelry that jangled every time she moved. After the introductions were made, Briskin said, "Lupe, tell the boys what you'll do if they write you good songs."

"I fuck everybody!" she answered.

She and Briskin howled while Sammy and I sat there in shock. No one talked that way then. Especially not glamorous movie stars. This was at a time when our song "Please Be Kind" was banned by NBC because the first line had the word *affair* in it ("This is my first affair, so please be kind").

In our usual manner, we finished the songs in three days. We played them for Morris Stoloff and were about to make an appointment to play them for the producer when Morris stopped us and gave us some invaluable advice: "Don't play the songs for them for at least two weeks. Otherwise they'll expect you to be this fast always, and someday you may need more time and they won't let you have it. The other thing to remember is that most people think that if you wrote something this quickly, it can't be any good. So wait."

After the songs were approved, an appointment was made for us to go to Lupe's house to rehearse with her. We arrived at her house, rang the doorbell, and waited. After about five minutes, Lupe, wearing a silk robe wrapped around her obviously nude body, opened the door. She was surprised to see us. She had forgotten about the rehearsal. She led us into the living room and said she'd be ready in a few minutes. As we entered the house, we saw a nude man run into one of the rooms upstairs, slamming the door behind him. While we waited, we could hear loud voices arguing. One was Lupe's, the other definitely a man's.

Eventually she reappeared, and we began rehearsing. Shortly after we started, we heard another door slam. A few minutes later the front doorbell rang. Lupe went to the door and let in a bleary, bloodshot-eyed, fully dressed man—an up-and-coming actor. Everything now became clear. We had come at an inopportune moment. They couldn't be sure whether we had recognized the actor, so to convince us that he wasn't the upstairs guest we had seen, he quickly dressed, left the house through the back door, came around to the front, and entered like someone dropping in on a friend. The reason for all the machinations was that he was married and had a rising career that a scandal could stop in its tracks. Little did they know how little we cared what they did privately.

Sammy and I had an office in a small apartment house across the street from the studio. The advantage of being in this building was that our friends could visit us at will without having to get a studio pass. They could just walk in off the street, and did. Skitch Henderson, then a pianist much in demand by the radio networks, was a constant visitor between broadcasts (NBC and CBS were within walking distance). At the time, he seemed more interested in being an airplane pilot than a pianist. All kinds of out-of-work actors and musicians we knew from New York dropped in. They all served as a tryout audience for our new songs.

Frank Sinatra was then the male vocalist with Tommy Dorsey's band, appearing at the Hollywood Palladium. Frank was a good friend from New York and a frequent visitor. His personality was no different then than now, except that he has acquired a little more polish and tact. Not very much. He was intensely loyal, generous, arrogant, insolent, and a fierce battler for the underdog. This sliver-thin Sinatra once punched Tommy Dorsey, who was at least four inches taller and thirty pounds heavier than he, because he heard Dorsey make what Sinatra construed as an anti-Semitic remark.

It seems Dorsey had referred to one of his musicians as a "Jew bastard" because he hadn't shown up for a recording session. I knew Dorsey well enough to know that he fell into a group who consider musicians either good or bad—regardless of their height, weight, color, religion, sexual preference. This was particularly true of Dorsey, who if anything was overmeticulous about the sidemen he hired. Watching Dorsey rehearse a new arrangement was like watching a sculptor create a masterpiece. He fashioned the ultimate sound from his orchestra just as fastidiously.

Frank was a takeover guy even as early as his Dorsey period. If he showed up for a rehearsal and it was late getting started because Dorsey hadn't yet appeared, he would insist that one of the arrangers rehearse the band so that he could run through his numbers. Frank attributes his early singing style to Dorsey, who was famous not only for his gorgeous tone on the trombone but for playing extremely long phrases on one breath. Frank would sit on the bandstand, listen to Tommy, and then emulate him when he did his vocal. It was a stunning device for Frank's caressing, velvet voice. The wonder was, where did Frank get all the breath required? He had virtually no chest cavity. He learned something else from Dorsey: the importance of tempo. There is one perfect tempo for every song. Dorsey instinctively found it. Later, so did Sinatra.

During Frank's many visits to our office, just one subject was discussed: Should he leave Tommy Dorsey? The kids were already crowding around the bandstand when he sang, and the "oohing" and "ahing" had already begun. He was becoming increasingly restless sitting on the bandstand waiting for his vocals. And he disliked always having to sing them in tempo so as not to disturb the dancers. The question was, could he make it alone? We decided it was a little too soon. He should make a few more hit records with Dorsey—he had already made "South of the Border"—which would attract even more fans than he had then. He agreed. About six months later (he did "I'll Never Smile Again" during this period) he finally did leave, without consulting us, taking Axel Stordahl, Dorsey's fine arranger, with him. Together they made history.

During our time at Columbia, Sammy and I wrote all kinds of songs for low-budget musicals. For the A musicals, they got Cole Porter, Jerome Kern, and Johnny Mercer. While they were busy doing the scores for *You'll Never Get Rich* and *You Were Never Lovelier,* we were doing pictures with titles that included a place or the color of the star's hair: *Two Latins From Manhattan, The Redhead From Manhattan, Two Blondes and a Redhead, Blondie Goes Latin, Go West Young Lady, Honolulu Lu,* and so on.

Combining them all makes it two redheads, three blondes, two Latins, and Lu go to Manhattan, Honolulu, and West.

Lumping them together that way is not as farfetched as it may seem because in most cases the plots were the same. One, two, or three blondes or redheads pretend to be wealthy South Americans or heiresses in search of wealthy husbands in Manhattan. During the first four reels, our heroine pretends to fall in love with a handsome young millionaire (in the middle reel she does fall in love with him), and the rest of the film is taken up with his trying to devise a way that she can let him know that she is really Sadie Glutz from Manhattan. As far as he is concerned, he either knew it all the time or doesn't care. On the way, they visit at least one nightclub where a Latin, Hawaiian, or Western production number is done, and they sing a romantic ballad to each other while they're dancing. The only element that was occasionally changed was the locale. Instead of Manhattan it was sometimes Rio, a ship, or as previously mentioned, Honolulu, where Lupe Velez played a Hawaiian.

We had a much larger obstacle to overcome than writing songs for the banal films we were working on. The radio networks refused to pay the American Society of Composers, Authors and Publishers (ASCAP) performing-rights fees, so ASCAP prohibited any songs written by its members from being played on the air. Nothing but songs in the public domain, like "Jeannie with the Light Brown Hair," were heard on the radio during this period. It eventually led to the networks forming their own performing-rights society, Broadcast Music Incorporated, more commonly known as BMI.

This situation continued for a year and happened to coincide exactly with the time Sammy and I were at Columbia. Since we were ASCAP, no matter how good the songs we wrote were, there was no way they could become hits because radio performances were needed to accomplish that. Columbia had originally hired us because we had a long string of hits behind us. Now that that seemed no longer possible, they saw no point in keeping us, so our option was dropped. Several weeks before, I had been told by our manager that Sammy was going to go out on his own when our contract expired.

A reasonable person would have anticipated the split, but I didn't. Unconsciously I was hoping it would never happen because I dreaded the consequences. It turned out to be every bit as horrendous as I had anticipated.

Chapter 2 ■ Sammy and I had met on a snowy night in 1933. I was all of twenty-one and he was not quite twenty. I had been called to play a club date on the Lower East Side of Manhattan with a band called Saxey and His Music. Saxey turned out to be an untalented alto saxaphone player whose equally untalented twin brother, Al, was on drums. They did manage, however, to get a lot of club dates in that area. Playing the "hot fiddle" that night was a medium-size skinny kid named Sammy Kahn. He was not a topflight musician, but there were

Sammy Cahn

two compelling reasons for hiring him: He got most of the club work on the Lower East Side that Saxey didn't, and he could entertain, which is not to be underestimated. Sammy became a star in the neighborhood and thus an extra attraction for the club to advertise when they hired Saxey and His Music.

Sammy sang rhythm songs in a rather cloudy not-very-good voice, but he performed them well. In fact, he loved performing so much that his enthusiasm was irresistible to his audiences. His act varied, but his opening and closing numbers were always the same. For his opener he did a song he had written himself, "Shake Your Head from Side to Side." It referred to a head movement that was part of a dance popular at the time.

His closer, however, was the real blockbuster. He circled the room and improvised lyrics about members of his audience to a tune called "One More Time." His lyrics were always very funny and quite personal because he would arm himself with club gossip from the head of the entertainment committee and include this information in his rhyming couplets. Everyone he sang about felt flattered, even when he wasn't being complimentary. Those who weren't lucky enough to have been immortalized by his rhymes looked forward to the next time when maybe they would be noticed.

At one point during a rest period, Sammy told me that he liked the way I played and asked, "Do you ever make up tunes?"

I replied, "Sure, all the time."

"Well, I got a lot of ideas for lyrics, so why don't we write some songs together?"

It was the simplest of questions, yet it altered my life completely. I have often speculated on what my life would have been like if Sammy hadn't steered me into songwriting. After all, I was an accounting major at NYU. Although I'm certain music would always have been part of my life, I'm equally certain that I would never have done anything practical about it, like organizing my own band. That required a certain aggression I didn't have. Actually, during my entire career as a musician I had never called anyone about a job. In fact, I never initiated anything. Anyone who wanted me somehow found me.

From the moment Sammy and I began writing together, it was clear that this was meant to be. We simultaneously discovered that we had at last found the thing we wanted to do most. At that first session, about three or four hours, we wrote five songs. We would have continued writing far into the night, but Sammy had to be home at a reasonable hour so that his folks would not find out he had taken the afternoon off from the United Dressed Beef Company.

He began meeting me more and more frequently, which meant he was away from work more and more, which led to the inevitable result: He quit his job before he was fired. Since he knew his family would never tolerate that, he moved out of his parents' home and moved in with an old friend, Edward Traubner, who lived in a rather spacious house in the Bronx. After that he was usually waiting for me when I got home from school.

We wrote dozens of songs and looked forward to the day when we would, with luck, have them published. Of course, we hadn't a clue how to get a publisher to listen to our efforts. But even after our first meeting Sammy never had the slightest doubt that we would someday be successful songwriters. Confidence and determination were two qualities that Sammy always had in abundance. And when you add *chutzpah* to that, it's an unstoppable combination. Being talented doesn't hurt either.

What was most important for Sammy and me at this point was to stick together and continue writing so that when summer came, we would get jobs in the same band in the Catskills. It turned out to be a wise decision because it was during that summer of 1934 that we started writing special material. We began by making special arrangements for the singer on the social staff. At first it was just introductions and special endings. Later it included new words and music for special verses and patter. It never occurred to us to charge her anything. We didn't even charge her for the manuscript paper on which I was writing her orchestrations.

In a rather short time we built up a small clientele among singers in the surrounding hotels. At this point we decided we should be paid something. But how much? We didn't want to make the price so steep that we would lose any customers. After much discussion, we hit on what we thought was a fair price— $5.00. FIVE DOLLARS!! For that staggering amount, the singer got new words and music, a special introduction and ending, new orchestrations, as many rehearsals as necessary—and Sammy usually helped them in their performance of the new arrangement. In addition to special arrangements for singers we began writing comedy songs for comics, for the same lofty fee of five dollars. Needless to say, we became very busy.

The following winter we rented a tiny triangular office in Manhattan from the Resort Entertainment Bureau, an agency that booked acts and bands for hotels in the Catskills. We continued writing for all the acts we had written for during the summer, and we picked up more business among entertainers who came to the Resort Entertainment Bureau looking for summer jobs. At the prices we were charging, we did a land-office business.

I had the old familiar problem. Because of college (it was my last year at NYU), I never got to the office for rehearsals until one o'clock. That didn't matter; no one in show business at that time even breathed before noon. The problem was that I had to spend nights working with Sammy. This left no time for studying or homework, which now became more boring than ever. I could hardly wait for that last year to be over so that I would fulfill my obligations to my parents. This was when I finally knew for sure that I was never going to be an accountant.

The following summer, Sammy and I put a band together and accepted a job at the Hotel Evans in the borscht belt. One day at lunch, the girl who worked in the office and sat behind me at the next table handed me a folded piece of paper. I found that she had written out the music for the first eight bars of "When I Grow Too Old to Dream." I was very impressed. Who ever heard of a girl writing music? And a very pretty girl at that. Her name was Ethel Schwartz, and we started going steady from that moment on.

The head of the social staff was a loathsome character, a former vaudevillian with a mammoth ego and absolutely no talent whatsoever. In the middle of the summer he had the comedian fired. Our feeling was that he resented the laughs the comedian was getting. For a while we were without a comic. One night during a show he introduced the new man, who made his entrance from the audience.

He was tall, rather thin, and wore tortoiseshell glasses. No sooner had he gotten up on stage than the MC began bullying him and for about fifteen minutes made the new man his stooge. Suddenly the new guy interrupted and flattened him with one line—something like "Don't go too near the lights because I can smell ham burning." The audience howled.

The new man was Phil Silvers. From the moment he uttered that line until the day he died, we were close friends. I always thought of him as one of the most creative comedian-actors of all time.

When we returned to New York, we moved into larger quarters right next door to our triangular office of the previous year. We raised the price of our arrangements to $15. Our phone was the pay phone on the wall. We expanded our organization by the addition of two "salaried" members. First there was Lou Levy, a boyhood friend of Sammy's already in show business, part of a dance team called Lou and Lee. They donned dark makeup and danced the Lindy Hop as part of the Jimmy Lunceford Orchestra act. Not exactly a headliner, but he was in show business and knew people. He became our manager. He was not overworked since there was virtually nothing that required managing.

We offered Ethel a job as our secretary. She could make her own hours. She was delighted with that arrangement—no more so than I. Of course, we had to pay her, which brings me to the matter of finances. Our payroll was as follows: Sammy and I each received $12.50 a week; Ethel's salary was $10.00; Lou's, $8.00. The only member of the organization who was paid regularly was Ethel. We always managed somehow to scrape together the $10.00 for her, and the rest of us often settled for a lot less.

Actually, things weren't easy for us, but we were having too much fun to notice it. It was much tougher for Sammy and Lou than for me. I went home to Brooklyn every night, but Sammy and Lou had both run away from home, so they often slept on the couch and the floor of our office.

Regardless of anything else we did, Sammy and I never stopped writing songs. Periodically we invaded the publishers in the Brill Building to get the songs published. The invasions were usually repulsed. Most publishers wouldn't even see us. We continually demonstrated our wares for the few who would, and they continually turned us down.

After a while I started wondering why we kept going back. It took years, but I finally figured it out. We did it because Sammy enjoyed performing our songs, even if it led to nothing. Just give him an audience of any size, and he would get into his "battle" position, rear back, and let loose. He was such a superb demonstrator of songs that in later years on more than one occasion a publisher impressed by one of our lesser efforts agreed to publish it. The rude awakening would come later when he had his staff pianist play it for him. He would then realize that he'd bought a good performance, not a good song.

In most cases the "dogs" were never published, but unfortunately for us, sometimes they were. Incidentally, all songwriters have such skeletons in their closets that they prefer not to talk about. I'll never bring it up again.

Our first song was published through one of Lou Levy's connections. Because of his former affiliation with Jimmy Lunceford, it was simple for Lou to arrange for us to do our songs for him. We did two, and he accepted both! The first was a song called "Rhythm Is Our Business," which we had written for our own band the previous summer at the Hotel Evans in the Catskills, and the second was "Rhythm in My Nursery Rhymes," which we wrote with a performer named Don Raye. Finally! We had broken through. A professional orchestra was going to play our songs. And what an orchestra! One of the best in the country. It was truly thrilling.

Several months later, a friend of ours rushed into our office waving a copy of *Variety* opened to the Music and Record section and yelling, "Hey, look at this!" There in fourth place on the Best Selling Records list was "Rhythm Is Our Business" by Jimmy Lunceford and His Orchestra on the Decca label.

We had no idea that he had recorded the song. We called Decca Records. We were greeted by "Where the hell have you guys been?"

"Right here in New York."

"We've been looking for you. We owe you money, and we've got contracts for you to sign. How soon can you get here?"

We were out the door before he hung up. We were ushered into the office of Dave Kapp, who was in charge of recording at Decca and the brother of Jack Kapp, the president of Decca Records. He asked to hear other songs we had written.

He liked what he heard and before we left we agreed to play any new songs we wrote for him before we went to the publishers with them. It was advantageous for both of us. It meant that if the song was a hit, Decca would release the first record of it before the other record companies could, and it made it easier for us to get our songs published if the publisher knew that we already had a record promised. That proved to be true of the two songs we had given to Lunceford. No sooner had we returned to our office than we received a call from Lester Santly, who with Georgie Joy ran Select Music Publications, Inc. Obviously, Dave Kapp had advised him to call.

The first song to be published was "Rhythm Is Our Business." Seeing the sheet music made us feel like Irving Berlin and Cole Porter combined. There it was—a copy of a song we had written that could be bought in a music store for thirty cents. The fact that nobody might want to never occurred to us. After the excitement diminished, we noticed something on the front cover of the song: our names, Sammy Kahn and Saul Kaplan. Clearly Kahn and Kaplan didn't sound like a songwriting team. Changes were in order.

In Sammy's case it was easy. He just substituted C for K. I tried that, and it still came out like a manufacturing firm. Cahn and Caplan. So now we worked on my name. We came up with Chapson—sounds made-up. Capson—no better. Chapman. Before we could even consider that, Sammy said, "Chaplin." We all liked it and said "Cahn and Chaplin" out loud several times. It sounded right to us, so that was it. In subsequent years I suppose I've derived certain benefits from people's assumption that I was related to the great Charlie.

We put our new name on everything: the front door of our office, new stationery, and score paper. We even had cards printed. When Ethel answered the pay phone, it was "Cahn and Chaplin." One day the voice on the other end said, "Hello. Is Mr. Cahn or Mr. Chaplin there? I'm calling for Glen Gray and the Casa Loma Orchestra."

Ethel replied with exasperation, "Oh, Jimmy. Stop it. I haven't got time to talk to you now." She hung up. Jimmy was a friend of mine who always used the name of a star when he called.

The phone rang again. Again the voice said, "This is Glen Gray and the Casa—" Ethel hung up again. It rang once more. This time the voice said, "Don't hang up! Is there anyone else there whom I can talk to?" The call was from an agent who represented the Casa Loma Orchestra, which was about to launch a tour of theaters and wanted a piece of musical material the band could perform. We wrote the piece that very night. Two days later, we demonstrated it for them. They were very happy with it and turned it over to one of their staff arrangers, Glenn Miller.

Our success with the Casa Loma Orchestra led us to a new phase of operations. It was the beginning of the era of "name band" presentations in theaters, with rising pits and simulated starry skies for ceilings. Bandleaders, their soloists, and their singers were quickly becoming household names. Tommy and Jimmy Dorsey, Benny Goodman, Artie Shaw, Harry James, Gene Krupa, Bob Crosby, Sammy Kaye, Guy Lombardo, and many others became as famous as movie stars. Their presentations were all essentially the same. They played their obligatory theme song as they were being hoisted into view on a rising pit. The rest of the act consisted of playing their hit records featuring their most famous musicians and singers. To show their versatility, they searched for new material that enlisted the band as a glee club, doing funny lyrics, playing toy instruments—anything that would be a change from playing the pop tunes.

Enter Cahn and Chaplin. We became the unofficial "writers-in-residence" for many of the most popular bands of the swing era.

At about the same time our careers got a terrific boost when we were hired to write the score for a nightclub show called *Connie's Hot Chocolate,* an all-black show staged at Connie's Inn, which had been one of the flourishing hot spots in Harlem during the early thirties. The glamour of Harlem had begun to tarnish considerably, so Connie Immerman moved his club downtown to West Forty-ninth Street. Connie was a tall, balding, rotund jovial man in his forties who seemed so affable that it was difficult to reconcile his personality with his involvement in the cutthroat nightclub business.

Imagine my reaction when I was told that the star of the show we were writing was to be Louis Armstrong. Louis Armstrong! I couldn't believe it. I was in my teens when I heard my first Armstrong record, and I was immediately hooked. It was instant hero worship. Other kids had Babe Ruth, Lou Gehrig, and Dazzy Vance as idols. I had Satchmo. While they were memorizing batting averages, I was memorizing Louis Armstrong records.

They had an advantage. If they wanted to see one of their heroes, they had only to buy a ticket for a ball game. That was not so with Armstrong. He hadn't been seen in years. There were rumors galore. He was in Europe, afraid to come home because he had crossed a mobster. He was a dope fiend. He was in a hospital somewhere, slowly dying. And many more I don't recall. The mystery that surrounded him heightened my unbounded admiration. Would I ever meet him? The thought never crossed my mind. Why would it? To me, he wasn't even real.

I didn't sleep for nights before the fateful day arrived. Of course, the meeting was nothing like what I had anticipated. I did manage to blurt out a garbled sentence about what a fan of his I was. He responded with a slightly embarrassed "Yeah?" in that incredible voice of his. He was not only real, alive and well, but the gentlest, kindest, easiest-to-talk-to person I had ever met. I worked with Louis many times in the years that followed, and my opinion never changed. If anything, it intensified. He was truly nature's nobleman. He loved life, the world, and everybody in it. I don't think he ever had an enemy.

It's safe to say that in his entire life Louis never said an unkind word to or about another musician. To him, there were no bad musicians. As a result, he sometimes fronted inferior bands. Such was the case at Connie's Inn. Instead of organizing a group of his own, he used the Luis Russell orchestra, which was mediocre at best. They might have played better under a more demanding leader. One afternoon I was listening to a rehearsal of a radio program they were to play that night. In the middle of a number, the first trumpet player hit a series of clinkers that was hair-raising. Instead of stopping and rehearsing that section again, Louis continued on to the end of the arrangement. He then addressed the trumpet player: "Tonight on the broadcast, don't do that." Unfortunately his request didn't help the trumpet player's technique.

Connie's Hot Chocolate usually consisted of a series of acts interspersed with production numbers. The latter were done by chorus girls and led by one of the performers or stars. All in all, the score usually consisted of about eight songs. But not with Cahn and Chaplin. We wrote twenty-three! Everyone in the show who could carry a tune had a special song. We thought that was required.

Rehearsals went smoothly until the finale in which the cast was usually presented one by one, reprising sections of the songs they had introduced earlier in the show. We had so many songs and so many performers that the finale would have been endless had we followed that formula. Instead it was decided to present them in pairs. It turned out that the last pair was Louis Armstrong and a small boy in the show. The problem was that there was no song to fit them. Pressed for time, we went to our files and found a song we had written for a black vaudevillian years before, "Shoe Shine Boy." It was perfect. We had the little boy come out carrying a shoe-shine box and ask Louis to play for him. Louis said he would if the boy would give him a shine. As he did, Louis sang "Shoe Shine Boy" to him.

The show opened to excellent reviews that unanimously singled out Louis's rendition of "Shoe Shine Boy" as a "must-see." As I mentioned, we had written twenty-three songs for the show, yet the one we inserted almost as an afterthought turned out to be the hit. Then out of the blue came a letter from a lawyer who represented Jessie Cryor, the black vaudevillian for whom we had originally written the song, claiming his client was entitled to one-third of the royalties.

To go back for a moment: When we had raised the price of our material to $25.00 we felt that our clients weren't getting enough for their money. So I drew up a contract that gave them a one-third interest in the material should it be published. What we wrote was always so special, we felt we were making a safe deal. We were safe until "Shoe Shine Boy." I never thought that the contracts I had drawn were really legal. What did I know about contracts? I used to sleep during my commercial law classes at New York University. However, when we took a copy of the paper we had given Cryor to a lawyer, his answer was quick and to the point: "He gets one-third of the royalties." Cryor eventually settled for less, but to this day he or his estate still shares in the royalties of "Shoe Shine Boy" on a total investment of $25.00.

We were paid nothing to write the score but were promised $50 a week for as long as the show ran. It didn't quite work out that way. We were paid for several months until Lou Levy went up to the Connie's Inn office to pick up our regular payment and was met by Red Murray, one of Big Frenchy's lieutenants.

"How're the boys doing?" he asked as Lou was handed the check by the secretary. "We got ten percent of them, you know."

"No, you don't," said Lou, more than a little surprised.

"Oh yes we do—that was part of the deal."

"No it wasn't—I made the deal—nothing like that was even mentioned—even I don't have a piece of them, and I'm their manager," Lou replied.

"Okay. Then don't come up here for your checks anymore" was Red Murray's final word.

Lou came back to the office looking white as a sheet. We were being gypped, but what could we do about it? We knew that no logical solution would do it. We had to find another way. We finally came up with the only plan we thought might work.

Ethel, much to her terror, was a particular favorite of Red Murray's. Whenever he knew she was in the club, he would seek her out. He showered her with gifts, prizes you'd win at penny arcades—obviously a sideline of theirs. She wasn't aware of

Lou's conversation with Murray, so we blithely sent her for our check the next time it was due. They gave it to her as if nothing had happened. We sent her the following week. Again she came back with it. The following week, however, she returned empty-handed. The message had apparently finally filtered through that we were not to be paid anymore. We then told her what had happened. She was livid.

Chapter 3 ■ Louis Armstrong's record of "Shoe Shine Boy" was on the Decca label, with which we had had an ongoing relationship since our first meeting with Dave Kapp. We were writing songs for their artists, and they were pleased with the results. On the strength of this, Jack Kapp arranged for us to meet Herman Starr, the head of the Music Publishers Holding Corporation, the name of the three music-publishing companies owned by Warner Bros.: Harms, Witmark, and Remick.

On Jack Kapp's recommendation, Starr arranged for us to be hired as staff songwriters by Vita-

Vitaphone

phone, in Brooklyn, another sub-sidiary of Warner Bros. Shorts were produced there for ten months of the year. The other two months, from June 15 to August 15, the entire studio was closed, and all employees took vacations or layoffs. Since air-conditioning was unheard of, it was a very sensible arrangement. Financially, the studio was a bonanza because of "block booking": if an exhibitor wanted a Warner Bros. feature film, he was required to book and pay for two shorts whether or not he ran them.

When we began working at Vitaphone, we gave up our office on Forty-sixth Street and rented an apartment on Fifty-seventh Street and Sixth Avenue. It served not only as our office but a place for Sammy and Lou to live. I still went home to Brooklyn every night. Ethel did not move with us. She got a job at the Resort Entertainment Bureau, our landlords on Forty-sixth Street.

The first song Sammy and I wrote for a movie short was called—are you ready?—"You Don't Need a Fire to Keep Your Wig Warm." That's a perfect example of the kind of songs that were written for production numbers. There was a short about two life-size cutouts of movie stars in a theater lobby who come to life and sing another of our memorable efforts, "You Were Cut Out for Love." Another was "If It's Got Something Spanish, It Gets Me," written for a band short in which all the musicians wore sombreros.

One of the expensive items in many Vitaphone shorts was the

cost for the use of published music. All the acts that were hired used the most popular hits of the day, and getting the rights would come to a tidy amount. One of the shorts for which we were writing the score included a dance number to "Bye Bye Blues." When I saw the routine, it became clear to me that they didn't really need "Bye Bye Blues"—they needed the structure of "Bye Bye Blues." So I rewrote it, matching their original orchestrations exactly. Where they had stops in the orchestration so that their taps could be heard, I duplicated the stops. Where there was a key change, I matched it. In other words, what I had written had the exact structure of their "Bye Bye Blues," but a totally new tune.

Everyone was enormously pleased with it—Vitaphone because they didn't have to pay for a pop tune; I because I had such fun doing it. Before long I was rewriting everything, from the smuggler's dance from *Carmen* for a dance team to "The Doll Dance" for a marionette show. The only time music had to be paid for was when a band played a song it had made famous.

When Vincent Lopez and his orchestra made a short, the use of his theme song, "Nola," had to be paid for, but instead of "Old Man Mose," which was usually done by his eighteen-year-old singer, Betty Hutton, we substituted a new song Sammy and I wrote that demanded the same kind of energy. Best of all, it was free. I rewrote "Bye Bye Blues" at least a dozen times. It was the national anthem of tap dancers, and we had at least one tap dance in every short. My biggest problem was finding titles. So I named them after my friends. I had "Irving Blues" and "Hy Blues." I even had "Sadie Blues," named after a secretary at the studio.

It seems to me now that every entertainer, known and unknown, in the environs of New York worked in a short at Vitaphone. And we wrote for all of them. And we wrote fast, because we were still pursuing our other life—writing pop songs and material for our old clients. In fact, most of them did their acts in shorts at our instigation. Our close friend Phil Silvers, who was then appearing in burlesque and beginning to build a reputation as a creative comedian, was signed for a series of four shorts. We became friendly with a comic who was eking out a living entertaining during the ten-minute rest periods at marathon dances. We got him a series of shorts. His name—Red Skelton. We arranged for a new band, Woody Herman and His Orchestra, to make a short.

We had the distinction of being the only songwriters who ever wrote a hit song for a short, "Please Be Kind." It was on the Hit Parade for many weeks despite the fact that in the beginning it seemed it would never see the light of day. It was slated to be introduced by Guy Lombardo and his Royal Canadians as the "hit of the week" on his Sunday-night coast-to-coast radio show. That would immediately ensure its popularity because all the other bandleaders rushed to play the new song he featured each week.

The preceding Thursday, Martin Block, a very influential disc jockey, broadcast his annual anniversary party. All the singers and songwriters whose songs he had featured on his "Make Believe Ballroom" radio program appeared and talked about their careers and their recent activities. Block was very well liked by everyone, so it was always a pleasant, relaxed afternoon. During our chat with him, he said, "I'm sure you must have a new song you can do for us." Without giving it a second thought, I went to the piano, Sammy to the mike, and we did "Please Be Kind."

As fate would have it, Guy Lombardo was home ill that day and heard the program. He immediately canceled the song from his Sunday-night show because he could no longer claim that he was playing it "for the first time on the air" inasmuch as we had already done it. Our publisher was frantic. He was losing a sure hit. We tried to point out to Lombardo that our performance had been on a local station (WHN) with a limited audience. He wouldn't buy it.

In desperation and to reestablish a good relationship between the publisher and Lombardo, we offered to turn over all the royalties the song earned to Lombardo's favorite charity. He still refused. The Guy Lombardo Orchestra never did play "Please Be Kind," but all the other orchestras did, so it became a hit anyhow. It just took a little longer. Lombardo never introduced any of our songs after that, but we managed to have quite a few hits without him.

The years from 1938 to 1940 were the most successful for Sammy and me. There was rarely a week when we didn't have at least one song on the Hit Parade. In fact, one week we had four of the ten. It was a record. Almost every song we submitted to our publisher was accepted.

Our biggest hit was "Bei Mir Bist Du Schoen." There are countless myths about how we happened to write it. My favorite was a piece that appeared in the New York *World Telegram* when the song was at the peak of its popularity. It informed its readers that the song was written by two gentile songwriters from the Bronx who paid two poor Jewish songwriters "thirty pieces of silver" and had so far earned $90,000 in royalties.

To begin with, no matter how drastically we changed our names, we could never be gentile. We weren't from the Bronx. And until we wrote our version of the song we had never even met Sholom Secunda or Jacob Jacobs, writers of the original Yiddish version. The $90,000 figure was ludicrous because it hasn't amassed that amount of royalties for us in the forty-five years since it was first published.

No one would consciously sit down and decide to write an English version of "Bei Mir Bist Du Schoen." It happened completely by accident. Sammy, Lou, (our manager), and I attended the Apollo Theater in Harlem regularly. It was the black equivalent of the Palace. One night two black performers did "Bei Mir" in Yiddish. It rocked the place, stopped the show cold. Sammy said something like "Imagine how much more the audience would enjoy it if they understood the words."

On the way home we decided that an English version would

be a great piece of material for Tommy Dorsey, who was about to open at the Paramount. Our English version was submitted to Dorsey, who not only turned it down but was almost insulted that it had been suggested. What made us think that he, who was obviously not Jewish, would do a Jewish song just because most of his audience at the Paramount would be Jewish? No way. So we put the manuscript on the top of the piano in our apartment, and there it remained. For a while.

Now I must go back for a moment. At one of our early meetings with Dave Kapp of Decca Records, he had asked us to be on the lookout for a girls singing trio that might be good for records. He knew that we were writing for all kinds of acts, not only privately but also at the Vitaphone studio, where we were working at the time. In fact, several hours were set aside every Thursday at Vitaphone to look at new acts. At one of these auditions a girls trio appeared. They looked rather odd in their garish print dresses and large picture hats. They sang well, though. They were the Andrews Sisters. They had been traveling across the country with their parents in a large touring car, picking up dates wherever they could. An agent had brought them to Vitaphone, who was not interested in them.

We immediately thought of Dave Kapp. We called him, and he said to send them right up. We arranged for Lou to meet them at Decca. They sang for Kapp, who was impressed but would record them only if a fresh piece of material could be found for them.

We began a search. In the meantime, Lou got them a job singing with Blue Barron and his orchestra at the Edison Hotel. During the day they hung around our apartment. They had it to themselves most of the time because Lou was usually out hustling our songs and looking for something the girls could use for their first record. Sammy and I were at Vitaphone in Brooklyn. The Andrews Sisters inevitably found the manuscript of "Bei Mir" on top of the piano and, I suppose out of boredom as much as anything else, made themselves an arrangement and learned it.

Lou took them back up to Decca, where they sang it for Dave Kapp, who liked it well enough to record it. It was done without our knowledge, and we were unhappy about it. If the song had any potential, we would have preferred that it be recorded by an established artist like Ella Fitzgerald, who made a hit out of everything she sang. Giving it to an unknown trio was taking too much of a gamble. We never figured that this particular trio and this particular song would be a perfect mating, like Jolson and "Mammy" and Judy Garland and "Over the Rainbow."

The record was released and the sheet music hit the music stores about a week before Christmas 1937. Over New Year's weekend the avalanche struck. It was the most played song on radio. On New Year's Eve, a Friday night, it was played over a dozen times on the "Milkman's Matinee" on WNEW, the most influential disc-jockey request program on the air. It was requested over and over again at all the hotels and ballrooms, not only in New York but all over the country. It still enjoys a fair popularity all over the world.

"Bei Mir Bist Du Schoen" changed our lives in several ways. It gave us a nationwide reputation. Its popularity created a demand for the rest of our catalog. The phrase "a Cahn and Chaplin song" suddenly took on new meaning. Who knew? It might be another "Bei Mir Bist Du Schoen."

That was the good news. The bad news was that the song caused an extremely unsettling change in our lives. When we first earned our reputation as top material writers, we began to sign managerial contracts with certain performers. We would not only write their acts but see to it that they were booked in the proper places, attend their opening nights to make certain that they were getting as much out of their material as possible, and so on. For all of this we took a percentage of what they earned.

When the Andrews Sisters came on the scene, Lou Levy was spending all of his time trying to further their career. While we were in Brooklyn at Vitaphone, we naturally assumed that Lou had signed them to one of our managerial contracts. We were deeply shocked to learn that he had instead signed them to a personal contract and that we were excluded. It was at best unethical. He claimed he did it because we hadn't signed anybody for a long time and we seemed totally disinterested in the Andrews Sisters' career. Neither of his arguments was valid, but since he refused to rewrite his contract with the Andrews Sisters to include us, we had no recourse but to end our relationship with him. It was a very sad moment for us. We had been through all the lean days together. It seemed a shame that we were parting just when we were starting to make it.

Postscript: Lou married Maxene Andrews, the one on the right.

We expected a much bigger reception in Hollywood than we got, considering that "Bei Mir Bist Du Schoen" was our first song to be performed in a feature film, *Love, Honor and Obey*.

When we returned to New York, my romance with Ethel blossomed, and we decided to get married. It was a joyous decision, but not for Sammy. From the day Sammy and I started working together, one thing became clear: We preferred entirely opposite lifestyles. I was a morning person, and he was a night person. He often wanted to work late at night, and I simply didn't function well at that time.

Sammy always attributed the difference in our working-hour preferences to external causes. In the beginning, before Ethel, he thought I preferred spending evenings with my family. He was wrong. I spent those evenings with friends. When we hired Ethel, he thought it would keep me working later. Wrong again. I didn't go home as early because I took Ethel to dinner or a movie or whatever entertainment we had planned. Even on those occasions when we did work late Ethel and I would go off to dinner by ourselves while Sammy and Lou went elsewhere. Now he was faced with the prospect of my marrying someone he thought would hinder our working relationship even more.

During all the years we worked together, Sammy never gave me credit for being anything more than a terrific accompanist. He never acknowledged that I had anything to do with writing our songs, even the bad ones. It was always "Do you want to hear a song *I* wrote?" "I played *my* song for him," and so on. It wasn't true, but I didn't object. I had convinced myself that since he was out every night meeting Tommy Dorsey, Woody Herman, Benny Goodman, and all of the other potential hit makers, it was easier for him to say "I." Otherwise they would ask where I was, and the answer might be embarrassing to him. I was home in Brooklyn. I was miserable about the whole situation, but I accepted it.

Not so Ethel. She didn't accept it for one minute. She was constantly goading me to insist that my contributions be recognized. I could never get myself to tell her of my fear that Sammy might break up the team. Had I told her, she would have pointed out that that would be better than our present situation where he took all the credit. She also would have assured me that I could find another collaborator.

So with Sammy and Lou berating me on one side and Ethel on the other, I was between a rock and a hard place. Time, of course, has proved Ethel right. In truth, I knew her to be right at the time, but I didn't have the guts to do anything about it.

Chapter 4 ■ After Columbia dropped us and Sammy and I split up, the first thing Ethel and I did was move from our comfortable house in Westwood to a less-expensive apartment in West Hollywood. We were not poor since I was still receiving royalties from my songs as well as ASCAP royalties, but the mere thought of having to economize was depressing. For months I sat around doing nothing because I didn't know how to get started again.

It never occurred to me to call another lyricist and ask him to write with me. And if I had thought of it, whom would I have called? I didn't know any other lyric

Columbia

Pictures

& Harry Cohn

writers. I was also apprehensive about writing with anyone but Sammy. He was the only lyricist I had worked with, and his chutzpah made our operation go. I was in a hopeless situation and I knew it.

Finally the day came when I got back to the piano. I wrote a piano solo that required no lyrics. I took it to the only publisher I knew, who turned it down because it was "too difficult to play." He didn't play the piano, so how could he know? Even so, I thought he was probably right. I took it home, put it in the piano bench, and that was the end of that.

I then wrote the words and music for two songs. One of them was a kind of blues that I thought would be perfect for Woody Herman, whose original band Sammy and I had helped finance some years earlier. I sent it to him. He, or his representative, wrote back a most complimentary letter telling me what a terrific song it was. Unfortunately he couldn't use it because it was too "special." I had now written a piano solo that was too difficult and a song that was too special. That discouraged me from doing anything with the other song. I was down in the depths again.

Some months later, ASCAP had a meeting to report its settlement with the networks. I went only because Ethel insisted. I arrived after the speeches had started. I slipped quietly into an empty chair at the nearest table and listened to the speaker. After a while I looked around at the other men sitting at the table. I couldn't believe it. There were Aaron Copland, Igor Stravinsky, Arnold Schoenberg, and Roy Harris. If a bomb had fallen on that table that night, it would have meant the end of modern music. That was clearly no place for me, so I left the table and stood in the back of the room until the speeches were over.

After the business of the meeting was finished and everyone was milling around, I realized I knew more songwriters than I had thought. During our entire year at Columbia, I had never gone to an ASCAP meeting, so I wasn't aware that many of the writers I knew in New York had emigrated to Hollywood. I was chatting with one of them, Walter Samuels, about the reports we had just been given when he suddenly said, "Is it true you're no longer writing with Sammy?"

"Well . . . I guess so." I still wasn't facing it.

"What do you mean?" he asked.

"It's just that we decided that we should be free to write songs by ourselves . . . or maybe even with other writers if we wanted to."

"So what've you been doing?"

"I've been writing my own lyrics."

"So have I. Why don't we try to write a couple of songs together? If it doesn't work out, what have we lost?"

Here was a professional songwriter asking me to work with him. I was flattered but still uneasy. "I don't know. I got this song I sent to Woody Herman . . ." I trailed off as I searched for a way to say no. Instead, I heard myself saying, without enthusiasm, "I guess it's okay. Like you say, what've we got to lose?" So we made plans to meet the following week.

I approached our first meeting like a child going to a new school—excited but a little frightened. He arrived at the appointed time, and we spent at least an hour talking about everything but songwriting. It was during World War II, so there were lots of subjects to choose from. In the middle of a sentence he abruptly asked me to listen to a song he had just written.

He played and sang beautifully. I liked it and suggested a lyric change. He accepted my idea, which gave me the courage to play my two songs for him. He thought they were fine and had an idea about improving the ballad by changing the tune in one place. He then told me about an idea he had for a song, which I liked. I immediately found a tune to fit his title.

We continued writing the song together. We worked on the words and music. We didn't finish it at that session because we didn't work as quickly as Sammy and I had, but I was elated. I was writing songs again. And with a guy I liked.

I was writing out the piano part of one of our songs when the phone rang. It was Morris Stoloff. I was delighted to hear from him. While I was at Columbia, we had become good friends, and I always enjoyed talking to him. He asked how we were getting along. He was fond of Ethel and our daughter, Judy, whose musicality amazed him.

Morris asked me what I had been doing. I told him about the songs I had written with Walter, and he asked to hear them. Walter and I decided that I would play and he would sing. For the second chorus, he joined me, and we played four-handed piano.

Morris heard our songs and enthusiastically approved of the new writing team. He immediately picked up the phone and called the producer of a new B musical they were preparing, *Cowboy Canteen* (another inspired title). They bought a song from us, "Boogie-Woogie Choo-Choo," about a train whose wheels made the sound of a boogie-woogie beat and a conductor who was "on the beam," and more along the same lines. How that could have anything to do with a cowboy canteen I don't know, but very often songs were inserted into those films only because producers liked them. They never let lack of logic stand in their way. What was of prime importance to me, however, was that I had sold my first song without Sammy. It was possible after all.

Columbia had no songwriters under contract at the time, so Walter and I, as well as other teams, continued to sell them songs for their B musicals. We had two advantages over the others: I already knew the producers in the Briskin unit and Morris, although he tried to be fair, would occasionally tell us in advance the kinds of songs they were looking for. In addition, he permitted me to attend the scoring sessions of dramatic pictures. A set of conductor parts was prepared for me to look at while they were rehearsing and recording. I was being educated.

There was a great demand for films during the war period, so Columbia increased its feature-picture program. Unfortunately they didn't increase the Music Department commensurately, and things quickly became frantic. Morris asked me to make vocal arrangements of two published songs they were planning to use in one of their films. The trend had changed. They were using more published material than original songs. I found myself doing more vocal arrangements than original songs. Gradually Walter and I drifted apart. He went on to work with other songwriters. I remained at the studio where I was working steadily, so steadily, in fact, that I was given an office in the Music Department.

After I had done several films, Morris made an appointment for me to see Harry Cohn about making a deal to become a permanent member of the Music Department. Why Cohn and not Morris? Because as a former song plugger, Cohn fancied himself an expert at dealing with songwriters. I had the misfortune of always having to deal directly with him.

The appointment was for ten o'clock, but I, of course, arrived fifteen minutes early. I identified myself to one of his two secretaries, who showed me to a chair and asked me to wait. I waited and waited. Ten-thirty, eleven, eleven-thirty. I read every magazine in the place. All kinds of people came and went, but I still sat there.

At twelve-thirty, Cohn came out of his office, walked right past me without acknowledging my presence, and presumably went to lunch. A relief girl now replaced the secretary I had approached that morning. I asked the relief girl, "Would you please check whether Mr. Cohn is scheduled to see me today?"

She looked at a piece of paper containing a list of names and couldn't find mine. Then she said, "Oh yes. Here you are. You were scheduled to see him at ten this morning."

I went back to my seat. I was getting very hungry and thought if he'd gone to lunch, then I suppose I could. I asked if Mr. Cohn had gone to lunch.

"I imagine so."

"How soon will he be back?"

"That's hard to say. He sometimes has a very quick lunch. Other times it's longer."

There went my lunch. I was determined not to miss him. I was sure I would be his first appointment after lunch.

Wrong again. At about a quarter to three, Cohn stormed back into his office, again ignoring me and yelling back over his shoulder to one of his secretaries, "Get me Fier, that son of a bitch," and slammed the door.

Jack Fier was the head of the Production Department. A few minutes later he arrived, ashen-faced, and disappeared into Cohn's office. About an hour later, he reappeared—a beaten man.

Me? I still waited.

"Mr. Cohn will see you now."

It was a quarter to six. I was tired, hungry, intimidated, and had an awful headache when I finally left my perch to enter Cohn's sanctum sanctorum. The Christians must have felt this way when they entered the Colosseum to fight the lions. The same kind of bloody, one-sided battles took place in Cohn's office. In fact, Cohn had an advantage over the Roman emperors. He used a technique that hadn't been thought of in ancient times: brainwashing. He used it on me by keeping me waiting outside his office an entire day until I was thoroughly demolished mentally, physically, and emotionally. It was a common practice with Cohn.

I opened the door, and there stretched before me was a large high-ceilinged, oblong room with comfortable-looking sofas along both side walls and a white baby grand piano on the left.

44

On the right side there were three windows overlooking the entrance to the studio. They reached from a foot above the floor to the ceiling. It was common knowledge that Cohn constantly checked the arrival and departure times of his employees. He also had a perfect vantage point from which to spy on their comings and goings from the parking lot directly across the street from the studio entrance.

The office was tastefully furnished, like a pleasant living-room set, but that was something I didn't notice until months later. The first thing that caught my eye was a raised platform at the opposite end of the room half a mile away. Seated in the middle section of an enormous three-sided desk on the platform was the malevolent potentate himself, lit by a bright spotlight that shone on him from above. Included in the spotlighted area were his dozen or so brightly shining gold Oscars displayed on shelves directly behind him.

There were no extra chairs on his platform. When he addressed you it was always from on high. Only when he wanted a favor did he deign to come down from his aerie to floor level. It is rumored that from his desk he could listen in on the activity on any of the sound stages by pressing the proper button. He is also supposed to have bugged many offices. I believe both rumors.

My meeting with him was very short.

"Are you the guy Stoller sent up here?" Another ploy. He pretended not to remember names because men of power can't be bothered with such trivialities. Also, it diminished your importance not to have your name remembered. He and Stoloff mixed socially quite often, and he knew his name perfectly well, but he couldn't depart from his usual practice.

"Yes," I answered meekly.

"I don't have time for bullshit. You get two-fifty a week, and that's it. Now get the hell out of here!" To impart this thrilling information and display his irresistible charm, he had kept me waiting almost eight hours.

"Yes sir," I replied, and got myself to the other side of his door as quickly as I could. I was so weary, I would have settled for five Mexican jumping beans and a potato sack. When you consider that the deal included my writing lyrics, music, arrangements, scoring, vocal coaching, and everything else that had to do with music, I wasn't getting much more than that.

Working in the Columbia Music Department during the forties was an education for me—thanks to my able tutor, Morris Stoloff. He introduced me to every facet of music in films: music editing, music mixing, recording, rerecording, preparing a film for scoring, tempo click tracks. I am not suggesting that I performed all these jobs myself, but I learned what to ask for to achieve a particular result I had in mind. And I got lots of experience. It was not uncommon for me to find myself working on as many as five pictures at the same time. For one, there would be vocal arrangements to make; for another, a song to be rehearsed; for another, a new song to be written; for another, scoring; and a fifth, rerecording.

We were preparing a musical called *A Thousand and One Nights,* starring Cornel Wilde, Phil Silvers, and Evelyn Keyes. I had written the songs with a talented lyricist, Edgar De Lange ("Moonglow," "Solitude"). Moss Hart's *Winged Victory* was playing at a downtown Los Angeles theater at the time, and Morris and I auditioned one of the members of the cast who, we were told, was a fine singer.

He was a nice-looking young man with a dark complexion and a short, stocky build. He nodded to his accompanist and started singing an operatic aria. From his first note, we were aware that we were listening to an extraordinarily talented singer, a glorious tenor voice. We kept him singing for about twenty minutes while we sat there with goosebumps. Morris then asked him to wait outside his office for a moment.

After he left, Morris turned to me and said, "His name is Mario Lanza. He needs money because he has a family, but more than that, he has to get his voice on a record so that more people can hear him while he's traveling with *Winged Victory*. We'll use him as a voice double for Cornel Wilde."

"But, Morris, he doesn't match Cor—"

"Never mind."

Mario recorded our songs beautifully, but even before the film began shooting, his voice was replaced by a proper double for Cornel Wilde. Lanza now had a little money, and Morris sent his record on to Frank Sinatra, who helped launch Lanza's career.

The main problem with being involved with multiple projects was the constant pressure of time. If I had to write a new song, I never had the luxury of being able to read the entire script, study the situation that included the song, formulate ideas concerning its content, then write it. The best I could do was read about five or six pages before the spot where the song occurred and the same number of pages after it. For a film called *Kansas City Kitty* I was told that a new song was required on page 51. I read from page 45 to 56: "The setting is a publisher's office. A tall Arab, dressed in full desert regalia enters. He sits on the floor, pulls an ancient instrument from under his robes, and plays a boogie-woogie number." The suggested title is "The Arab Boogie-Woogie."

The humor stems from the incongruity of an Arab playing this wild piece of music—in case you haven't figured it out for yourself. By this time, we had already had "The Run Boogie," "The Samba Boogie," "The Chopin Boogie," "The Boogie-Woogie Bugle Boy from Company B," and dozens of others.

Partly as a revolt against all these titles and partly because I didn't know how to write "The Arab Boogie," I wrote a song called "The Nothing Boogie-Woogie from Nowhere." The song referred to a spot that was "east of the Atlantic," "west of the Pacific," and "south of where the River Shannon flows," where

> They take the good old ordinary boogie bass,
> The same old bass that no one has been able to replace

47

And they add nothing to it.
They simply do it.
It's called The Nothing Boogie-Woogie from Nowhere.

And then to prove their rhythmic education is complete,
They take the Cuban rhumba and Brazilian samba beat
And then they just ignore 'em.
They don't go for 'em
They like The Nothin' Boogie-Woogie from Nowhere.

They've got nobody to conduct them
Or to instruct them
In choreography.

And yet they never are dejected,
They're unaffected
By their nonexistent geography.

In case someday you should decide to visit there,
And so you save your pennies so that you will have the fare,
You're headed for a rip-off,
'Cause here's the tip-off—
You'll lose your mind because you'll find
The Nothin' Boogie-Woogie is from Nowhere!

I taught it to the "Arab," and several days later we went to the scoring stage to record it with a Dixieland group. We rehearsed it for about an hour, then made a test recording. We were waiting to hear it when Morris appeared on the stage with Sammy Cahn. It was a rather awkward moment for me because I hadn't seen Sammy for a long time and he was about to hear a song I had written myself—words as well as music. After the playback, he came up to me and was most complimentary about the song. I was extremely pleased that he was so friendly. As for his opinion of the song, I didn't take it seriously because out of courtesy there was nothing else he could say. He left the stage, and we resumed recording.

Sammy reappeared about an hour later with two men and introduced them to me. They were from Capitol Records. He wanted them to hear my song because he thought it would make a terrific record. Unhappily, they didn't agree, but it's a typical example of how Sammy operated. He did things *now*. He had heard my song, liked it, ran over to Capitol, about three blocks away, and convinced two of their executives to return to Columbia with him to hear it. I was very touched by his gesture, and we have been friends ever since.

Chapter 5 ■ Ira Gershwin and Jerome Kern wrote an outstanding score for *Cover Girl.* "Long Ago and Far Away" is certainly one of the most beautiful songs ever written. There are others in the score equally distinguished that never achieved popularity: "Sure Thing," "Make Way for Tomorrow," and "Put Me to the Test."

Ira originally wrote the latter with his brother, George, for *Damsels in Distress,* but the lyric was not used, so Kern wrote a new tune for it. Toward the end of the film, where the plot became semiserious and there were

Cover Girl

no songs indicated, it was decided they could use a piece of comedy material to be performed by Gene Kelly and Phil Silvers, who starred in the film along with Rita Hayworth. The number was to be a satire on the Fred Waring Glee Club, which was all the rage at the time. Since I had been cowriting material for Phil for some years and was the vocal arranger at the studio, I suggested to Morris that I do it. He agreed and sent me to see Gene and Phil, who were in rehearsal on one of the sound stages. He warned me that it probably wouldn't be easy because Gene had definite opinions about everything, wasn't reticent about expressing them and was very articulate.

As I entered the sound stage, I heard gales of laughter. It was coming from Gene, Phil, and Rita rehearsing on the far end of the stage. At first I thought they must be rehearsing a funny number, but I later learned it was their usual behavior. Phil and Gene teased Rita mercilessly, particularly about her relationship with Orson Welles, whom she later married. I overheard Phil say, "Orson's gonna do to you what he did to Hearst in *Citizen Kane.*"

It was quite a different Rita from the one I had met several years earlier. She was relaxed, happy, and enjoying what she was doing, despite the fact that her two costars never gave her a moment's peace. One of them always had his hands all over her, or when they were all together, they were constantly making what they called a "Rita sandwich." She loved every second of it. Their joy is reflected in the film.

Mind you, I don't claim that good relationships off-screen guarantee good performances on-screen. There are no rules. But because musicals have longer schedules than most other films, people have to work with one another for a longer time, and it's much more pleasant if they can manage to have some fun along the way.

Actually, they didn't *all* get along. There was Charles Vidor, the fine Hungarian-American director. He had never done a musical before, but that would not have mattered if he had not been so totally humorless. And there he was, up against Gene and Phil, who were trying to make the film as light and airy as possible. Vidor had no trouble with Phil, but Gene's latent towering Irish temper would get the better of him every now and then until he and Vidor had a fistfight. Cohn, the great peacemaker, had to be called down to the set more than once to settle their disputes.

At my first visit, I watched them for about a half hour until they took a break. Phil introduced me to Gene as King Gustav of Sweden, whom I resembled at the time. Phil then launched into a rather lengthy résumé of our friendship, leaving nothing out. He detailed our experiences in the Catskills; the mishaps at my wedding; the time he convinced a stripper that "Rhythm Is Our Business" would improve her act because he was plugging my songs wherever possible; the innumerable auditions I had played for him, including the one that resulted in his starring in the Broadway show *Yokel Boy*, which had brought him to Hollywood; and how Sammy and I had written material for him. In some instances he embroidered the incidents so much that I didn't recognize them, but that was Phil. Getting a laugh justified any exaggeration, even bending the truth when necessary. He had an ulterior motive for his monologue: He was using this means to give Gene a list of my credits so that it would make working with Gene easier for me.

Morris hadn't exaggerated. I had already become accustomed

to reading from page 49 to 52 and then writing the required material. No way with Gene. He laid out everything he thought might affect the number: the set, the other characters, the method of shooting, the plot to where the number occurs, his and Phil's attitude—everything. I recall thinking to myself, "This is impossible. I can't write anything that has to take all of those elements into consideration." I contributed very little to the discussion and was getting more and more concerned when Gene suddenly said, "Look—make Phil as funny as you can and don't worry about me. I'll take care of myself."

I was amazed. I had never met such an unselfish actor. He had obviously read more than his part and was interested in the picture as a whole. I've worked with Gene many times since then, and his attitude has never changed. He was always concerned with the entire project and was indeed able to take care of himself.

I set about doing the arrangement. The number to be used was "Put Me to the Test." I included every Fred Waring cliché I could think of during the first chorus. I made Phil as funny as I could, secure in the knowledge that he would invent a lot of his own schtick during the rehearsal. I then used the patter of the song Kern and Gershwin had written but hadn't been used during the film. To make it fit our needs, I found I had to change the tune in a few places and write some new lyrics. I was at a point where I needed just two more lines to finish it when it suddenly struck me that maybe it wasn't quite as funny as I thought. I decided to try it out on Morris with the two lines missing. He thought it would work but added, "Who are you to change Kern's music and Gershwin's lyrics? They're not bad, you know."

He decided that before we approached Kern for his approval, we'd better try Ira Gershwin. He would be easier to deal with. If he okayed what I had done, he could then write the two lines I needed. I entered Ira's living room and found the following people sitting around whiling away a lovely summer afternoon: Yip Harburg, Leo Robin, Johnny Mercer, Arthur Schwartz, Marc Connelly, and Oscar Levant. It was a formidable group for whom I had to demonstrate my "comedy material." I was so unnerved, I wasn't sure I could play. With a lot of stuttering, I explained the song and managed to get through it, adding that I needed two lines. They reacted favorably and were about to leave when Ira stopped them. "Please stay and help me get him the two lines. Otherwise I'll be up all night."

What happened after that was incredible. Lines started coming at me like buckshot. They were funny, tricky, clever—you name it. The biggest contributor was Yip Harburg. He spouted couplets like a fountain. This continued for about an hour. Finally, you know who wrote the two lines? Ira Gershwin.

I had occasion to visit Ira several more times during the filming of *Cover Girl,* and we became good friends. We saw each other fairly often but there was one particular period during the 1970s that I shall cherish forever. Ira phoned me. "I'm donating one of George's notebooks to the Library of Congress. I have to annotate the music on every page. You know I don't read music, so would you mind stopping by one day on your way home and going through it with me? It shouldn't take you more than twenty minutes."

There was absolutely nothing that Ira Gershwin could have asked of me that I would have refused him. He was known among his peers not only as an extraordinarily gifted lyricist but as the president of the mythical Sweetfellows Club. It's not even arguable that if there had not been a George Gershwin, Ira would have achieved even more fame than he has. But he was so modest that in the beginning of his career he used the name Arthur Francis, the names of his other brother and sister, not to detract from George.

I can't make a comparison between them because regrettably I never knew George. But Ira was affable, bright, and witty. When he said something funny, he chuckled quietly to himself. He loved to sing songs around a piano, and he was the quintessential homebody. On the other hand, George, I am told, was gregarious, outgoing, and egotistic. To see how different they were, one has only to look at their self-portraits. Incidentally, they were both fine painters. George presents himself nattily attired in top hat, white tie, and tails. Ira's self-portrait shows him standing at an easel dressed in shoes, socks, and underwear with a cigar in his mouth.

Ira's wife, Lee, was equally bright and witty, but with a sharper tongue than Ira's. She established their living room as a gathering place for the most talented people in the arts who lived in Los Angeles or happened to be passing through. Their salon was in full swing nightly.

I considered it a rare privilege to go through a George Gershwin notebook and went to Ira's at the earliest opportunity. George Gershwin was the most influential composer of American popular and classical music in the twentieth century. I once heard someone say, and I believe it, that every minute of every day, somewhere in the world, someone is performing Gershwin music. My first visit to Ira's led to several years of sessions at the piano with him, during which time we went through over a dozen of George's notebooks along with many pages of loose manuscript. It was an awesome experience.

In the first notebook I found a piano piece he wrote when he was seventeen in which each hand is written in a different key. The trick isn't as important as the fact that it's a wonderful piece of music. Equally fascinating were the notes he made while he was studying with a man named Schillinger, an eminent teacher of the time who developed his own method of composition, orchestration, and so on. There were many examples of early versions of George and Ira's most popular songs, in some cases just four- or eight-bar phrases.

The early notebooks also contained George's first attempts at *Rhapsody in Blue* and *Concerto in F* and how he gradually molded them into the pieces we know. Watching them take shape was a rare insight into the mind of a genius. There is a section of the concerto that is in a minor key in several early notebooks. In each case, a few notes were changed. Finally, in one of the later notebooks, it reappears in a major key, and that's

54

the version that is published. Among his unpublished works we found two charming contrapuntal waltzes he had written for the stage musical *Pardon My English* in 1930. Ira and I edited and adapted them, and they are published as *Two Waltzes in C.*

I was also impressed by how many notebooks and pages of loose manuscript there were. Gershwin apparently wrote down almost every musical idea he had on a sheet of manuscript or a notebook and saved it all. Ira had many of these pencil sketches. George and Ira's avocation was painting. They were both excellent, and quite a few of their paintings hang on the walls of art connoisseurs.

I saw Ira upset on only two occasions. The first was on a Monday after his usual Saturday poker game. I thought he must have lost a great deal of money to be so disturbed, but that wasn't the case. The problem was that he had won. I couldn't understand why that should bother him, but he explained: "I invite people to my home to play poker, and then I take their money. There's something wrong with that besides just being inhospitable." I didn't understand his explanation then, and I don't now. The fact is, he hated to win at poker in *anybody's* home.

On the other occasion he was as angry as I've ever seen him. After a hasty "hello," he led me to his record player. "I want you to hear something," he said as he put a record on the machine. A loud brass section blared out a jazzy introduction, and then one of our leading jazz singers sang, "Baby, it's wonderful. Baby, it's marvelous—" At that point, Ira stopped the record and turned to me angrily. "Why does he have to sing 'Baby, it's wonderful—baby, it's marvelous'? If I wanted the word 'baby' in the song, I would have used it. I know the word. In fact, I was one of the first songwriters to use it in a song: 'Of Thee I Sing, *Baby.*' Doesn't he understand that the charm of the title is that the word 'it' is left out and the song is 'S' Wonderful.'?"

I tried to explain that with certain jazz singers the lyrics were unimportant and that all they were concerned with was being able to improvise on the tune. His reply was "Then why don't they leave out the lyrics altogether and sing 'da,da,da,da'?" He had me there.

During one of my visits with Ira he handed me a white sheet of paper full of scribbles and said, "Look what I found." The page contained a lot of rhymed couplets, but that was clearly not the reason he was showing it to me. I had been looking at his lyrics for years. Then he pointed to one corner of the page where scribbled in pencil was the rhymed couplet he had written for the number I did in *Cover Girl*.

"I always have wondered," said Ira, "how you got that piece of material past Jerry Kern since you tampered with his music. Did he approve it?"

"Not exactly," I replied, and I recounted the events that had led to the number being included in the film: Morris Stoloff decided not to let Kern hear the number with Ira's new lyric, the couplet, and the musical changes I had made until it was rehearsed and recorded. The most important approval, of course, came from Gene and Phil, who, as I anticipated, made it much funnier during rehearsals than it had been originally.

It was then recorded, and we could no longer postpone the fateful day—Kern had to hear it.

Before I go any further, I must tell you that I consider Jerome Kern one of the greatest composers of light music for theater the world has ever known. He could have written everything that Franz Lehar, Johann Strauss, or Victor Herbert wrote, but they never could have composed his range of music. He ran the gamut from operetta songs like "Old Man River" to a dance craze called the "Shorty George."

His reputation as a collaborator, however, was another thing. He was difficult to work with because he was so inflexible about his music. It is not uncommon for a lyricist to ask a composer to add a note to a phrase so that it will fit a particularly good line he thought of. Kern very rarely cooperated. It's understandable why we were so apprehensive about his hearing an arrangement of one of his songs where not only was his music changed but new music, not his, was added.

He came to a projection room at the studio where the sound track of the number was played for him. The entire routine lasted only about three minutes, but that day it seemed to go on for hours. He sat motionless with a noncommittal expression through the entire number, which we had all thought was funny. When it mercifully came to an end, there was a dead silence. After what seemed like an eternity, Kern said, "If it works at the preview, keep it in. Otherwise throw the damn thing out!" What a relief that was! I'm sure he didn't like it, but at least he didn't have it thrown out, which he could have done easily.

Ira was amazed that we had so little difficulty. "You know," he said, "when he first showed me the tune for 'Long Ago and Far Away,' he had titled it 'Midnight Music' because Gene Kelly sang it to Rita Hayworth at midnight. It took some convincing to have him accept my title. And that's not even about music."

I was then assigned to "Cover Girl" as the assistant musical director, along with whatever else I was doing. I had occasion to visit Jerome Kern at his house one afternoon in connection with *Cover Girl.* To my surprise, Artie Shaw, the bandleader and an old friend from New York, answered the door. Artie, who was on leave from the navy, was married to Kern's daughter Betty. He immediately pulled me over to a piano and had me play several songs he had just written.

The fact that Kern was waiting for me in the next room was of no importance to Artie. His songs were all right, but they were what I call arranger's songs. Any decent arranger can write a passable song. In most cases the harmonic structure is more important than the tune. These songs are rarely successful. There are several exceptions, the most notable of which is David Raksin's "Laura." Artie's were not exceptions.

I finally met with Kern. After we discussed the purpose of my visit, he said, "Artie made you play his songs, didn't he? Aren't they terrible? That's nothing. He keeps telling me what's wrong with some of my biggest standards. I can't wait until his furlough is over."

With the exception of the problems between Kelly and Vidor, which really didn't affect me, working on *Cover Girl* was great fun. Rehearsals were very serious, but the general atmosphere was relaxed and because of Phil, often very funny. He resented having been required to dance alongside Gene and Rita, who were professional dancers.

But when you're Phil Silvers, you don't express your feelings as other people do. As an example, there was the time he gave a party and his guests stayed longer than he thought they should because he had an early shooting call at the studio the following morning. If he had explained the problem to his guests, they would have understood and left gladly. Not Phil. He went to the window, stared out at the black night, and said wistfully, "All my neighbors are sleeping. *I* got company."

It was in *Cover Girl* that Gene first established himself as a super talent and cinematic dancer to be reckoned with. He created the highly original and innovative "alter ego" number. Gene shot the number himself while Vidor went off to Palm Springs. It was all for the best because no one could have shot it as well as Gene. It was his concept from start to finish, and he knew exactly what he wanted it to look like. In it, his alter ego tries to make him face the reality of a situation. Gene keeps attempting to remove his alter ego by first chasing him and finally throwing an ashcan into a store window that is reflecting the alter ego's image. As the glass shatters, the alter ego finally disappears.

The number was shot on a rather long street that stretched over two of Columbia's stages. Gene danced both parts, which made rehearsals pretty tricky. In addition to having to devise choreography for both characters, he had to learn both parts himself, then teach them to two assistants so that he could see what it would look like when it was filmed. His assistants were Alex Romero and Stanley Donen. Alex, a sweet, gentle man, has been Gene's assistant on every project involving dancing since that time.

Stanley Donen, who had been a chorus boy in New York, owes his entire career as a director to Gene. As Gene became more influential, many opportunities opened up for him, and when he was given his first picture to direct, *On the Town,* he insisted that Stanley be his codirector. As co-choreographers (*Take Me out to the Ball Game, Anchors Aweigh*) and codirectors (*On the Town, It's Always Fair Weather, Singin' in the Rain*), they revolutionized and reshaped the American film musical. In every case, Gene was the prime mover and Stanley an eager and talented pupil.

Stanley had a problem, however, during the rehearsal of the alter-ego number. He played the alter ego while Gene played himself. During the chase section, Gene had to run after Stanley so that he could judge just how close he could come without actually catching him. The problem was that Gene could move a lot faster than Stanley, so the air was constantly filled with "Stanley, move your fat ass!" Then there was the slide down the telephone pole. Stanley would start his slide, but Gene was so much quicker that he would wind up sitting on Stanley's head by the time they both got to the ground.

It was an extremely difficult number to shoot. The camera was locked into a stationary position. Gene danced as himself on the street set. Then the entire set was covered with black material, and Gene danced the part of his alter ego. Eventually this was superimposed over the film of the "real" Gene. There were innumerable technical problems that hadn't been anticipated because nothing like it had been attempted before. For instance, when the two Genes were supposed to be dancing alongside each other, if the alter ego danced behind the other character, when the superimposition of the two figures was done by the special effects Department, it would seem he was floating. Also, they each had to be meticulous about not invading the other's dancing area, or it would look as if two bodies were occupying the same space. There were many other problems, all eventually solved. The number took two weeks to shoot and cost over $100,000, a sizable sum for that time. With today's technology, it could be done in half the time but probably for more than twice the cost.

Cover Girl finally finished shooting—over schedule and over budget. By that time, everyone loved everybody. Even Gene and Charlie Vidor were civil to each other. There was a "wrap party" at a Hungarian restaurant on the Sunset Strip. I wrote a long piece of material for Phil in which I not only recounted the problems of making the picture but good-naturedly insulted everyone connected with it. No one was offended because they were flattered to hear their names mentioned in a song and because of something lyricists have known for years: The mildest jokes become funnier and the harshest insults are softened when they're rhymed and set to music. The next day there were about fifty requests for copies of the lyrics. Even Harry Cohn asked for a copy.

The evening turned out to be a minor triumph for me. I even hoped that my relationship with Cohn would ease a bit. I didn't have to wait long to discover how naive I was. The Stoloffs gave a party to which my wife and I were invited, along with the Gershwins, Kerns, Cohns, and the stars of *Cover Girl*. It was a pleasant enough evening, and after dinner I was at the piano as usual. Morris asked me to play "Long Ago and Far Away." By now, it had become one of my favorite songs, and I played it very well.

As I hit the last note, Cohn blurted out "You stunk it up." Without missing a beat, Kern said, "You played it beautifully, Saul. Thank you." Cohn was profoundly embarrassed, and he wasn't about to overlook it. His opinion had been challenged by an irrefutable source. To him, it was my fault, and he held it against me. Part of the fallout was his refusal to give me screen credit on *Cover Girl*. He later gave it on subsequent films in lieu of a raise in salary, a not uncommon practice with him.

The postproduction period on *Cover Girl* involved long hours of hard work. Cohn had decided on a preview date that was at least two weeks earlier than it should have been. Everyone worked virtually around the clock to get the film ready. That was not unusual. The postproduction people always asked for enough time to do the best work possible, and the front office never understood why it should take them so long. (Years later, Eddie Mannix, an executive at MGM, wanted a picture ready in a ridiculously short time. When I told him it couldn't be done and was about to explain why, he stopped me with "Don't explain it to me. If you're right, then I'll never ask again, and I want to continue asking.") Needless to say, the picture was ready on the date Cohn had chosen, but everyone worked eighteen-hour days, with no overtime pay. It was also the time of the six-day workweek.

Morris, Carmen Dragon (the arranger), and I studied the picture, then planned the scoring, picked places where the singing could be improved, chose sections of music to be redone because they no longer fit what had been shot. Gene, for example, had changed his mind several times during the shooting of several of his numbers. The music now had to be made compatible with what was on the screen. We finally wrote, arranged, and recorded it all. The music tracks were then ready for rerecording. (Rerecording, also called mixing, is a process where all the sound tracks—music, dialogue, and sound effects—are properly balanced and rerecorded onto one piece of film.) It is often a tedious process and during the early forties lasted for several months. Now it's usually accomplished in half the time.

Early one morning, about two-thirty, we were busy dubbing when Cohn suddenly appeared with one of the picture's dancing girls in tow. He listened for about five minutes, stopped everything, glared at me, and yelled, "I can't understand the goddamn words. What the hell is that word they're singing? *Oldiers?*"

I answered meekly, "It's supposed to be *soldiers.*"

"It sure as hell doesn't sound like that." We played it again. Dammit! He was right! They were singing 'oldiers'!

"You don't know what the fuck you're doing. Fix it!" He shoved his girl ahead of him, and they left. I was extremely upset and at a loss to figure out how it could have happened.

The head mixer spoke up. "You know it's not your fault."

"What do you mean? Didn't you hear it? They're singing 'oldiers'!"

"That's because the music editor in cutting the tracks together cut off the letter *s* from *soldiers*."

Of course! That's the only way it could have happened. No chorus would have sung 'oldiers' instead of 'soldiers.' "If you knew that, why didn't you say something when Cohn was here?" I asked.

"Because with him I only answer questions. I don't offer information." Another loyal employee of Harry Cohn.

Stanley Donen and I attended almost every mixing session. Morris was there whenever his duties as head of the Music Department permitted. Finally the day of the sneak preview arrived. Cohn had rigorously enforced rules about sneak previews, which if disobeyed meant instant dismissal. It was like a CIA operation. The name and location of the preview theater was highly classified information. Those invited gathered in front of the studio at a designated time. They all got into a waiting limousine, and after they were under way, Cohn would whisper the name of the theater and the city to the chauffeur.

In the case of *Cover Girl,* it was the Crown Theater in Pasadena. The only people allowed to attend were the head of production, the producer, director, film editor, mixer (who adjusted the sound during the screening), and Morris. Stanley and I were obviously not invited, and it was driving us crazy. We had been with the picture so long, we simply had to see what the audience reaction was. At the same time, we knew that if Cohn spotted us, we would be looking for new jobs in the morning, and we weren't ready for that.

We devised a plan. We had Ethel drive our car while Stanley and I sat scrunched up on the floor behind the front seats. We drove to Columbia and parked down the block from the limousine. When it drove off, we followed it at a discreet distance to Pasadena. We parked across the street from the theater and waited until they all went in. Then we bought tickets and found seats on the side toward the middle. That way, the most they could see would be the backs of our heads since they always sat in the back rows.

The picture was already on by the time we took our seats. It was playing beautifully. The laughs were coming in the right places, and "Make Way for Tomorrow" even got a hand. Everything was going along fine until Gene's alter-ego number. The moment the image of the alter ego appeared on the store window, the audience burst out laughing. It wasn't meant to be funny. What could they be laughing at? It was particularly disturbing because we had been told that Cohn never liked the number and wanted to cut it even before the preview. Now it probably didn't stand a chance of being retained. With the exception of that one number, the audience response to the film was all anyone could have hoped for. Happily, my number did very well, so there was no danger of its winding up on the cutting-room floor.

Most of the next day was spent trying to convince Cohn to leave the troublesome number in the picture. Everyone pleaded with him, from the head of production to the assistant film editor, but he was adamant. It didn't work—out it goes.

Then the manager of the Crown Theater in Pasadena telephoned with an explanation for the audience's strange reaction. The film that they had seen before the preview of *Cover Girl* was called *Flesh and Fantasy*. There was a sequence in it in which Edward G. Robinson's image was reflected in a store window and he talked to it. When the viewers saw the same device in *Cover Girl,* they naturally found it funny, so they laughed. On the strength of this new information, Cohn consented to having another preview. This time the audience not only didn't laugh but chose the alter-ego number as one of their favorites on the preview-opinion cards they filled out after the screening.

Cover Girl went on to become very successful and one of the prime examples of the romantic Hollywood musical at its best.

Chapter 6 ■ At my very first meeting with Gene, when we discussed the material I was to write for *Cover Girl,* he invited me and my wife to a party at his home in Beverly Hills the following Saturday night. He gave me the address, told me to come any time after ten, and said dress was casual. We arrived at the house at about ten-thirty and rang the doorbell. No one answered. We tried the door. It was open, so we walked in. We were in a room packed with a lot of noisy people.

Gene was nowhere to be seen. We went looking for him. We were overwhelmed by the people

Gene Kelly

nodding and smiling at us as we squeezed our way through the room. The guest list that night included Judy Garland, Mickey Rooney, Johnny Mercer, Roger Edens, Kay Thompson, Hugh Martin, Ralph Blane, Frank Sinatra, Lennie Hayton, Lena Horne, John Garfield, Vincente Minnelli, and others, who looked familiar but whose names we didn't know. It seemed like a convention of all the young talents of Hollywood.

"This is your first time here, and you're looking for Gene, and you can't find him, right?" someone asked. We nodded. "The same thing happened to me a couple of weeks ago. It doesn't matter. You'll find him eventually. In the meantime, just introduce yourself to anybody. They're all very friendly."

Our savior turned out to be Norman Panama. He and his partner, Mel Frank, later became well known as writers and directors of many important and successful comedies. Norman and I have been close friends ever since that first night when he showed us the ropes. He even helped us find Gene, who introduced us to his pretty, energetic red-headed wife, Betsy.

We talked for a while, and then someone yelled, "Let's play the game!" Before we knew it, Ethel and I found ourselves on different teams—one captained by Gene, the other by Betsy—and we didn't even know what "the game" was. It turned out to be charades, but we had never seen it played this way. The teams were in separate rooms so that they could not hear each other. Between them sat a person with a list of names, book titles, movie titles, aphorisms, quotations, to be acted out simultaneously by both teams. The team that completed the list first was the winner.

Games are usually played for fun, but not at the Kellys'. Both teams were going at it desperately, as though it were a matter of life and death. Friends who had been chatting and laughing amicably five minutes earlier were now snarling at each other because of a missed word or phrase. Soon the reason for the hostility became obvious: the savage competitiveness of Betsy and Gene. Games are played only to be won. Losing takes all the fun out of playing and is unacceptable.

It was scary watching our easygoing hosts turn into veritable storm troopers right before our eyes. The time between games was taken up with postmortem recriminations. Gene would yell, "If it weren't for [name of person who was right there], we would have beaten you easily!" It was as if we had suddenly been transplanted to a house of horrors.

Several weeks later, we tried to find a way to blunt Gene's verbal abuse. It took a lot of conspiring, but a workable plot was finally hatched. We arranged it so that he would have to act out the song title "Tramp! Tramp! Tramp! The Boys Are Marching" to five of us on his team. He quickly imparted to us that he was doing a song title and then proceeded to stamp the floor. One of us said, "Stamp." Gene shook his head and began marching in place. Another said, "March." Now Gene, utterly frustrated, added a salute to his marching, and the answer came back: "Soldier." Gene was enraged and pounded the floor. We continued giving him the wrong answers.

Chances are that if he hadn't been so angry, he would have realized he'd been set up, because we should have guessed "Tramp! Tramp! Tramp!" almost immediately. Our opponents finally won the game, and Gene started berating us mercilessly. The difference in our reaction this time was that we laughed. We told him what we had done, and he took it very well—for him. He joined in the laughter, but not very willingly. Our moment of glory was short-lived. He reverted to his abusive attitude in the very next game.

It was remarkable how everyone's personality reverted to normal when the game-playing period was over. But the most amazing part of the evening was yet to come. Through the din we suddenly heard the unmistakable singing of Judy Garland. Gradually everyone became quiet and sat down, mostly on the floor. They all seemed to know what was about to happen. Ethel and I didn't.

Judy was doing "The Boy Next Door" from *Meet Me in St. Louis.* Hugh Martin, one of the writers of the song, was accompanying her. Then Ralph Blane, Hugh's cowriter, joined them, and they did the rest of the score from the picture. They were followed by Johnny Mercer, who sang his song "One for My Baby" from the Fred Astaire picture *The Sky's the Limit.* Lennie Hayton played for him. Johnny sang a few more of his tunes, and then it was Lena Horne's turn. Among other songs, she did her unmatchable version of "Honeysuckle Rose." Then it was Sinatra, then Gene, then combinations of all of them. Everyone who could perform did—not reticently but happily. New arrangements were created on the spot. I found myself accompanying Phil Silvers in a comedy song we were making up as we went along. It was the kind of memorable entertainment that could never be paid for or planned. It went on for hours—until dawn.

As soon as it was light enough, some of the men adjourned to the backyard, where they started a volleyball game. Suddenly the gaiety disappeared, and all the tension of the charade game returned. Volleyball was played with the fierceness of war. It was unbelievable that here were ten or twelve men who less than an hour ago had been crowded around a piano singing and laughing and now were reduced to hurling insults at each other. ("With you on our team, we couldn't beat the Marymount Girls School team," etc.).

The master of the merciless put-down was Gene. At the same time, he was the best athlete on the court by far. He was incredible. He didn't really need a team. He made the most impossible shots from all over the court. They played until seven or eight in the morning and then dispersed. Many times during the ensuing years I would drop by the Kelly household on Sunday afternoons about one o'clock to find a volleyball game in full swing. Gene would be playing with the same intensity with entirely new teams. Had he slept? I never found out.

There was a party at the Kellys' every Saturday night with changing guest lists. The front door was never locked, and sooner or later every talented person from both coasts dropped in. Or so it seemed. Just offhand, I can remember seeing Judy Holliday, Betty Comden, Adolph Green, Zero Mostel, Charles Chaplin, Fred Astaire, Noel Coward, Margot Fonteyn, Spencer Tracy, Louis Jourdan, and on and on. Nor were the festivities confined to Saturday nights. Since everyone was always welcome, there was usually some activity or other going on every other night of the week. Sometimes they were quite surprising.

There was the unforgettable night when Betsy, at the urging of her housekeeper, had consented to having a man demonstrate waterless cookers by cooking a meal for her and her guests. She had no way of knowing what the meal would be, so she invited only six of us, her closest friends. We all gathered in the living room. The demonstrator introduced himself, then launched into his lecture extolling the merits of cooking without water and the wonders he was going to perform when he finally got around to cooking our meal. He then asked us to join him in the rather small kitchen where he had set up his pots, along with plates of various foods he was going to work his magic on.

The doorbell rang. Betsy went to the door. It was George Cukor, the director. "Hi, Betsy. We saw lights on, so we thought we'd drop by and see what you were up to."

"I'm glad to see you. You can have dinner with us, but I must warn you, there's a guy from Long Beach in the kitchen demonstrating waterless cookers and preparing dinner for all of us."

"Fine," replied George. "Wait—I'll go and get my date." Betsy waited at the door while he went to his car and returned with his date, who was, of all people, Greta Garbo.

They introduced us in the kitchen. Betsy, grinning from ear to ear, introduced Garbo to us, as though anyone who looked like that could be anyone but Garbo. She perched on the tile counter alongside the sink. That was a little behind where the rest of us were sitting, which was unfortunate for our chef because he no longer had our undivided attention.

It was impossible not to stare at Garbo's fabulous face, so we all took unnoticed (we hoped) peeks. She, on the other hand, was fascinated with the waterless cooking demonstration and was very cooperative and friendly. I can still hear her first comment: "Vot? No vater?" During the entire ritual, she was the only one who gave her undivided attention to the chef.

After much talking and much cooking, the meal was finally finished. It was served to us in minuscule portions, which turned out to be a blessing. None of it was really edible. Had the portions been any larger, it would have been impossible to get the food down. As it was, we could just about finish each course before nausea set in.

Poor Betsy. Here she had Greta Garbo in her home for dinner, and she was forced to serve her that hideous meal. She needn't have been concerned, however, because the only person who seemed to be eating the dinner with relish was—who else?—Garbo. She bought a full set of waterless cookers. No one else bought even one. The amazing sidelight to the whole evening was that the demonstrator was never aware that he had Greta Garbo in his audience. I guess he just knew about pots.

There was never a dull moment in the Kelly household. There was the night when a French writer drank a martini, then ate the glass. For those who missed his first performance, he repeated it. By the time he was through, he had put away half a dozen martini glasses. Then there was the touching moment when Phil sang a song he claimed to have written for Betsy's birthday, "Betsy with the Laughing Face." When he finished, there wasn't a dry eye in the house.

Actually it was a cheat. He had originally written the lyrics, to

Jimmy Van Heusen's music, for Bessie Burke, the wife of Johnny Burke, the lyricist. At that time it was "Bessie with the Laughing Face." A year later, he sang it at Nancy Sinatra's birthday as "Nancy with the Laughing Face." Frank recorded it and made it a hit. It was Phil's all-purpose song.

The night before Gene left for the navy, of course there was a party. On that occasion, Phil and I improvised a forty-five minute cantata tracing Gene's life from his birth to his triumphant return from the navy. It was followed by everyone singing "Auld Lang Syne." It was very touching.

The Kelly regulars were remarkable in another sense. They performed all kinds of miracles. Their greatest achievement was accomplished when Gene's secretary, Lois McClelland, bought a new house. We all liked it but decided that in addition to more furniture it would be nice if someday she could break through the wall and have a pass-through window between her kitchen and dining room to make serving easier. Lois was thrilled with our reaction to her new house. As for the window, she wistfully said, "Maybe, someday."

About a week later, she left for the studio at her usual time, about 8:00 A.M. On the way home, she stopped at Gene's to pick up the mail and finally got to her house about 7:30 P.M. She opened her front door—and almost fainted. Not only was her house full of all her friends, but all the furniture she had lacked was in place and, wonders of wonders, a window had been cut through between the kitchen and dining room. It looked as if it had been there forever.

Under Betsy's leadership, the group had bought all the new furniture, stashed it away in various garages until the agreed-upon delivery date, arranged for construction people to break through the wall, carpenters to build the window frame, and painters to paint it. The logistics were planned like a motion-picture shooting schedule. All the workers were called for different times so that the painters, for example, would not arrive before the carpenters were finished, or there would be nothing to paint. The enormity of the operation can really be appreciated when you consider that it happened right after World War II when it was next to impossible to get a man to come to your house to fix a plumbing leak. And it was done within twelve hours. Until then, such things were possible only in movies.

It was around that time that Ethel, Judy, and I moved to West Los Angeles. Since I didn't drive, I took a trolley to Columbia every morning. The trip took the better part of an hour. To while away the time, I acquired Paul Hindemith's book on harmony, used for a course he was teaching at Princeton that year, and did harmony lessons. I found them endlessly fascinating. I then went on to his second book, which concerned itself with counterpoint. That was like solving math problems, which always appealed to me. My real problem was that there was no one to correct my mistakes. I must have made many. I nevertheless learned a lot about music I hadn't known before.

Several years later, I finally studied music formally with a fine Italian composer named Mario Castlenuovo Tedesco. Tedesco, a tall thin man with a shock of gray hair and a charming grand-fatherly manner, spoke slowly with a soft Italian accent and was the gentlest of men. His interest ranged far beyond music. He was knowledgeable about painting, classical literature, poetry, philosophy, and, much to my surprise, pop music. What really endeared him to me, in addition to his skill as a teacher, was that he was the only person I had ever met with eyesight as poor as mine. When we examined scores together, nose-to-nose, it must have been an hilarious sight.

He was a master orchestrator, and for the first time in my life, I found out that many musical devices I had been using for years by instinct were musically valid. Tedesco had endless tricks to make small orchestras sound larger. These were useful for scoring small pictures where the music budget never allowed a large enough orchestra. At least half a dozen Hollywood composers were studying with him when I was. He wrote quite a few symphonic pieces, some chamber music, and several pieces for classical guitar—solo and with orchestra—which had been commissioned by Andres Segovia, the genius of the classical guitar. But his real passion was composing art songs. He admired Shakespeare greatly, composing overtures for most of his plays and setting all of his sonnets to music. Dozens of his songs are published and frequently performed at recitals.

A simple description of an *art song* is a song in which the accompaniment is as important as the melodic line in expressing the lyrics. For example, a lyric about wind would probably have an accompaniment with motion expressing the sound and feeling of wind. It is not unlike the score of a film, the dialogue corresponding to the lyrics and the score accompaniment. Tedesco suggested that I try writing an art song. The idea appealed to me immediately because I had been employing one of its requirements for years. As an accompanist (I've always been considered an excellent one), I always try to enhance the lyrics without interfering with them. I chose a poem by Byron and set it to music.

I've never had so much fun writing anything. I didn't have to be concerned with the built-in restrictions of a pop tune. It didn't matter if it was too rangy, longer than thirty-two bars, the accompaniment was difficult, or the key it was written in had more than one flat or sharp. It was composing without compromise and without any thought of mass acceptance.

I finished it in a week and presented it to Tedesco at my next lesson. It was four pages long. He stared at those four pages for fully twenty minutes. He started by looking at all four pages. Then he looked at page 1 again, then 3, then 2 and 4, then back to the beginning. (Incidentally, he never played it.)

Finally he looked at me through his thick horn-rimmed glasses and said, barely above a whisper, "It's beautiful." He said it again: "It's beautiful. I set the same poem to music. I have a published copy here which I will show you. Yours is much more beautiful—more sensitive and more inventive."

I was never prouder! I felt like screaming! Approbation from the maestro! It was more than I had dared hope for!

Chapter 7 ■ *Tonight and Every Night,* an important musical I was assigned to at Columbia, was about the Windmill Theater in London, which never missed giving a performance during the endless bombings of World War II, the performers having to live in the basement of the theater. It starred Rita Hayworth, Janet Blair (originally signed as a voice double for Rita), Lee Bowman, and Mark Platt.

Because of its English subject, an English director, Victor Saville, was engaged. At least I assume that was the reason. In many ways, it turned out to be an

Tonight &

Every Night

ways, it turned out to be an unfortunate choice. Although he had produced a number of successful films (*Good-bye, Mr. Chips, Dr. Jekyll and Mr. Hyde, White Cargo,* and others), he hadn't directed a film for over ten years. That's the only way I can account for the destructive relationship he maintained with his crew. On the first day of shooting he gathered them together and spoke to them. Among his remarks was "I don't want cooperation. I want discipline."

Now, anyone who has ever had anything to do with an American film crew knows you can't talk to them that way. As a result, our shooting days were riddled with the most bizarre and unaccountable accidents. In the middle of one shot, suddenly all the lights went out. Another time, a large arc light came hurtling down from the flies up high, crashing on the stage floor below. Then the film buckled in the camera. Actually, it was the only film I have ever been connected with where several times an entire day would go by without a single shot being printed. Saville got his discipline, all right, but he also got about a month and a half over schedule.

I had my own problems with him. The score was by Sammy Cahn and Jule Styne. It was OK, but the title song was one of their lesser efforts—long, wordy, and definitely not a rouser, which is what it should have been. A long, five-minute production number was planned, which would end with a large singing chorus doing the song. Saville suggested to me that I make the vocal arrangement two choruses long. Because of the length of the song and the long production number that was to precede it, I thought a chorus and a half would be enough.

I got a call that Morris wanted to see me. "Victor Saville tells me you're giving him problems by refusing to give him what he wants."

"What problems?"

"He wants two choruses of 'Tonight and Every Night,' and you insist on doing only a chorus and a half."

"I don't insist. I'm not sure a chorus and a half will hold, but I can guarantee that two won't."

"It's his picture. Give him what he wants."

So I made a perfectly straightforward arrangement of two choruses. We recorded it, and the result was about as stirring as one could expect from that song.

Another call. Cohn wanted to see me. What could I have done? I gave Saville his two choruses. What else could he want?

I walked into Cohn's office to be greeted by Himself, Morris, and Saville. As I entered, Cohn hit me with "Chaple [he never got my name right], I want you to hear something." He went to his broken-down phonograph, matched in quality only by his out-of-tune, awful-sounding piano, and played the marvelous choral arrangement of 'Oklahoma' from the cast album. When it was over, he said, "You hear that?"

I replied, "Sure. It's terrific. I know it by heart."

His next line explained the purpose of the meeting. "That's what 'Tonight and Every Night' should sound like."

"That's impossible," I replied. "We don't have that kind of song." I confined my criticism to the "type" of song rather than quality.

"You mean you can't do it," he challenged me.

"No one can do it."

He ignored me and turned to Morris. "I told you he couldn't do it. Better get someone from off the lot."

73

I felt I was letting Morris down. I was now getting angry. "Okay. You want 'Oklahoma'—I'll give you 'Oklahoma'!"

"I still don't think you can do it, but you can have another chance." I'm sure Cohn was being magnanimous because he knew it would cost him money to bring in someone else.

I then made a new arrangement that was as close to "Oklahoma" as possible without plagiarizing. Where they sang the long "O-O-O-O-klahoma," I did "To-ni-i-i-ght and every night." Where they shouted "Yow!" my chorus shouted "Yay." In place of "Okla-homa—Okla-homa," we did "Tonight—and every—tonight—and every." By the time I was finished, I no longer had the Cahn-Styne song but an "Oklahoma"-type choral arrangement.

I regarded the whole thing as a joke and was sure that once Cohn heard it, even he would realize how ridiculous the whole idea was and we'd go back to my original arrangement. How could I have been so naive? He approved it, and that arrangement is in the picture to this day, much to my embarrassment.

Jack Cole was the choreographer. Someone—I can't believe it was Cohn—got the brilliant notion of hiring him as a staff choreographer and having him organize a group of twelve dancers who would be put under contract and always be available for the many musicals the studio was making. Cole gathered around him the most astounding group imaginable, six boys and six girls. For all-around dancing they were probably the best in the country. When they weren't busy filming, they were studying different types of dancing. They had lessons in ballet, tap, Spanish, East Indian—taught by Jack or a teacher who was brought in. Because of their familiarity with each other and Jack's style, numbers were choreographed very quickly. It's too bad that some of his best numbers are hidden away in B musicals long since forgotten.

For reasons I can no longer recall, I was invited to the sneak preview of *Tonight and Every Night* in Santa Barbara. The picture played well enough, but there were obvious problem areas that had to be fixed if possible. Cohn always held meetings in his office immediately after sneak previews to discuss changes, cuts, and so on. That way he didn't waste his employees' time on a meeting during a working day. Actually it was a bad idea because one never had time to digest the audience's reaction to the film. Snap judgments had to be made that were often changed.

The meeting started after midnight. His Imperial Highness sat on his spotlighted throne on his private dais. We lowly vassals sat below him. He went through the film scene by scene from a script that was spread out in front of him and discussed the audience's reaction to each of them. He was obviously not in the best of moods and was disappointed that the picture had not played better. There was general agreement about the cuts and changes needed, but there was a stifling tension in the atmosphere.

Then he came to the number "Tonight and Every Night." "That goddamn number is too damn long. How can we cut it?" No reply from anyone. "Jesus, ain't there anyone here who can shorten the number? What the hell am I paying you all for?" That was a favorite expression of his.

I finally said softly, "I know how to cut it."

"You! You don't know a fucking thing!"

More silence. Then he said, "No one else is saying anything, so I guess I'll have to listen to your schmuck idea. How would you shorten it?"

Because it had been a long tense day and I was weary and had finally had it, I heard myself saying, much to my surprise, "Figure it out for yourself."

A yell came from somewhere: "Good! Don't tell him!"

I suddenly had an ally! When I saw who it was, I was astounded. It was Joan Cohn—Harry's wife.

There was a long, long silence, then Cohn continued with the discussion of the rest of the picture as if shortening the number had been settled. The fact is, he was right. He knew I'd weaken, and several days later I did. Shortening the number was complicated because it meant cutting the picture in one place and the sound track in another. I had doped it out during many viewings of the picture because the song had been such a constant problem.

What was more important about that meeting, however, was that my attitude toward Cohn began to change. I suddenly realized that the worst he could do was fire me. While I considered that disastrous, it was preferable to what I had been going through.

That was when I came to the realization I mentioned earlier: If Cohn thought he needed you, there was no way he could be provoked into firing you. I learned that night that I fell into that category. Otherwise he would have fired me immediately when I refused to give him the information. As a result, I became more brazen in my conversations with him. Before meetings, I would try to anticipate what he was going to say and be ready with a corresponding insult. I wasn't very good at it, so it rarely worked, but I did get my licks in on several other occasions.

In 1945, Columbia was preparing a musical called *Tars and Spars*. Most of the cast was supposed to be chosen from the Coast Guard vaudeville unit of the same name that had been touring the country (Sid Caesar was among them). A stage was set up for them to audition for the producer and director of the film, Cohn and Morris, and me. Everything was proceeding smoothly until a girl singer wanted to do a song the pianist didn't know, Johnny Mercer's "Accentuate the Positive." I knew it, so I went to the piano to play it for her. She couldn't sing loud enough to be heard without a microphone. It was decided that we would break for lunch, during which time the mike would be set up.

When we reassembled after lunch, I went to the piano and was about to play an introduction when the singer suddenly said, "'I've Got You Under My Skin' in A-flat."

I unconsciously scratched my head, which prompted Cohn to snarl, "What's the matter. Don't you know the song?"

I shot back immediately, "No. My head itches. Do you mind?" It got a howl from the twenty or thirty people who were there.

When the auditions were over and I got back to my office, there was a message that Cohn wanted to see me immediately.

This time I wasn't kept waiting. "You shouldn't talk to me that way in front of people," he said.

"Then don't talk to me that way, and there'll be no problem," I replied.

"But I'm the boss here. I can throw you the hell out if I want."

"That still doesn't give you the right to insult me."

"Get the hell out of here" was his final order, as usual.

Nothing was resolved, and our insulting relationship continued.

I worked at Columbia for nine years, during which time I received infrequent and miniscule raises. Toward the end of that period, I was told that a new deal was going to be negotiated with me. "Negotiated" meant that Cohn would tell me what my new salary would be and what credit I would receive. I was proof positive of the old adage "A lawyer who represents himself has a fool for a client." I was never a good businessman and certainly no match for Cohn.

I was on my way to one of the dubbing rooms one day when I met Cohn, riding crop in hand and omnipresent entourage trailing behind, on his way to the other dubbing room. He yelled at me, "Hey, Chaple. Come with me." (How come he could remember Chaple and not Chaplin?)

I said, "Harry, I'll go with you, but I'm not working on the picture you're going to check out."

"Why not? For what I'm paying you, you should be working on all the pictures."

"I'm on four now. There are just so many hours in the day."

"If you're not on all the pictures, why the hell should I give you a new deal?"

I came back with "I'll tell you what, Harry. *Don't* give me a new deal."

Infuriated, he made a gesture as if to hit me, which of course he wouldn't do. I must add that I was brave only because I had a deal pending at another studio—if and when my contract ran out at Columbia. In any event, I again topped my adversary, and that gave me great satisfaction.

Chapter 8 ■ During the early forties, a mutual friend introduced Ethel and me to a nightclub act called The Revuers. It consisted of Judy Holliday, Betty Comden, Adolph Green, and Alvin Hammer. They had come to Hollywood to appear in a film that had been canceled while they were on the train traveling west. Their agent, however, was able to book them into the Trocadero nightclub for two weeks.

That's where Ethel and I first saw them perform, and we were bowled over. They were superb. They did witty, satirical songs and sketches they wrote themselves. They were the act to see while they were at the Troc. From the moment we met them, we became virtually inseparable—from Judy, Betty, and Adolph, that is. Alvin seemed to be living a life of his own and rarely mixed with the other three socially. But with the rest of us it was as if we had known each other all our lives. We laughed at the same things, liked the same kinds of music, and spent many unforgettable evenings together.

Bernstein, Comden, & Green

We had moved to a house on Orange Grove Avenue in Hollywood built by the movie pioneer Thomas Ince about 1905. Like most Hollywood houses of that period, it was rather large with many rooms. We needed the extra space because Ethel's mother, father, and younger sister were then living with us, having moved from Brooklyn.

We were taking Betty, Adolph, and Judy through the house when we came to a small room off the kitchen. Since we weren't using it, we had left it the way we found it, with a bed and a badly faded unframed picture with curling edges thumbtacked to the wall. It had probably been a picture of a rose, but time had taken its toll so that it was hard to tell exactly what it had been. Adolph took one look and said, "It looks like a disease." He was right. It looked exactly like an illustration in a medical book of a diseased internal organ of some kind. We laughed, and from then on that room became known as the Diseased Room. After a while we referred to it as the Diseased Room without even cracking a smile. We never thought back to how it had gotten its name.

It turned out to be the most useful room in the house. Almost everyone we knew spent a night in it at one time or another. If someone got too drunk to drive after one of our parties, the Diseased Room was available. Gene Kelly slept there whenever he was on leave from the navy. Adolph was a frequent guest because he never wanted to go home. Leonard Bernstein spent an unfortunate night there when he had missed a plane for a Cleveland conducting date, unfortunate because he was allergic to cats, and that was the night that our daughter Judy's kitten had chosen to spend under his bed.

We had met Lenny through Betty and Adolph when the three of them were writing the Broadway musical *On the Town*. Lenny was in Los Angeles to conduct his ballet *Fancy Free* at the Hollywood Bowl. He became another close friend instantly. Lenny had already established a reputation as a wunderkind. Several years earlier, he had won a prize for his First Symphony (the "Jeremiah") and had made his startling conducting debut with the New York Philharmonic as a last-minute substitute for Bruno Walter, who had suddenly fallen ill.

What made the concert a particularly remarkable achievement was that he conducted the program, Walter's choice, without a rehearsal. Shortly thereafter, he composed the brilliantly witty semi-jazz score for Jerome Robbins's ballet *Fancy Free*. He was one of two guest conductors engaged by Ballet Theater to conduct his ballet at the Hollywood Bowl. The other was Igor Stravinsky, who conducted his *Petrouchka*. The Hollywood Bowl Symphony Orchestra at that time was terrible because most of its members were in the service. Musicians who under normal circumstances would not even have been auditioned by the orchestra were now welcomed with open arms. The orchestra consisted of the right number of bodies, but the sound they made was atrocious.

The night Lenny conducted *Fancy Free,* we all sat there with

79

our fingers crossed hoping that the orchestra would hold together. It was touch and go all the way, but they did manage to play the last note at the same time. The ballet was a huge success. The next night, Lenny, Adolph Green, and I watched from backstage at the Bowl while Stravinsky conducted *Petrouchka*. He wasn't as lucky. The music sounded as if it had been commissioned to display the ineptness of the musicians. It was a shambles. There were missed entrances, wrong notes galore, out-of-tune playing—it was frightening. And this time they didn't finish together, just petered out at the end. A desperate, defeated Stravinsky walked off the stage and passed by where we were standing. He was holding his head with both hands, muttering to himself, over and over, "Scan*dal,* scan*dal*"—in French (accent on the second syllable).

On the Town was a spin-off of *Fancy Free,* both about three sailors and three girls. The ballet takes place in a bar during one evening, and *On the Town* is set all over New York City during twenty-four hours. Lenny wrote the music, and Betty and Adolph wrote the book and lyrics. Since we were together almost every night around a piano, we heard all the new material as soon as it was written. We loved every note and every word.

They wrote many more songs than needed, but with Lenny nothing ever went to waste. One of the main themes in his Second Symphony ("Age of Anxiety") was originally written as a song for *On the Town,* "Ain't Got No Tears Left." He was very impressed with Judy, our daughter, and he wrote a song for her called "Who Am I?" He used it later in his 1950 version of *Peter Pan.*

We were having dinner in our Orange Grove Avenue house when Lenny asked me, "Do you know what you want to do with your career?"

I replied, "Yes. I would like to be in a position someday where I can afford to work only on projects I like. And have more control over what I do."

"You're very lucky."

"Why?"

"Because I don't know what I want to do. Should I concentrate on conducting or being a concert pianist? And should I write serious music or just music for the theater?"

To me, that was no problem. "Why not continue doing all of them?"

"I can't live that way—going off in so many directions."

He spent his life doing all of them. He had another extraordinary talent: He was probably the best music teacher there ever was. On his TV programs, he managed to make some of the dullest material not merely interesting but fascinating, an aptitude we should have recognized when we first knew him.

He had obtained one of the first scores of Benjamin Britten's opera *Peter Grimes*. It contains a difficult three-part round. He not only taught us our parts but sang a part himself as he played the piano accompaniment, which was totally different from the singing parts. He also corrected us whenever we went wrong.

He was conversant with every new fad in music. I heard the Beatles for the first time at his country house. He was one of their earliest fans. I attended a concert he conducted with the New York Philharmonic where he included a modern electronic piece on an otherwise conventional program. The orchestra included not only all kinds of electronic hardware but two small radios that were turned on at random. It seemed at random to me. After about five minutes, the audience began booing at the cacophony and didn't let up until the piece ended ten minutes later. He had included similar pieces on three preceding programs, always with the same result.

I later asked him why he insisted on subjecting himself to such scorn from the audience. His answer: "It's not important that they like it. It's only important that they hear it. Electronic music is highly regarded in some quarters and is being played all over the world. My audiences are cosmopolitan New Yorkers, and it's my responsibility to make them aware of every important new kind of music."

Only one facet of music eluded him. He always wanted to play jazz piano, and he couldn't. He even studied for a time with the legendary Teddy Wilson, but it didn't help. It's comforting to know that there was something connected with music that he couldn't do.

On the Town was a smash and got unanimous raves from the critics. Ethel and I wanted nothing more than to see it, but at that particular time there was no way I could afford three round-trip train fares (we wouldn't go without Judy) and hotel expenses in New York. We had to content ourselves with talking to Betty and Adolph by phone. They reported how enormously successful the show was, and that made us all the more anxious to see it. Then one day three round-trip tickets, along with the address of a New York apartment we could use, arrived in the mail from—who else?—Betty and Adolph. It was a touching and generous gesture. I arranged for a two-week vacation from Columbia, and off we went. (Incidentally, I reimbursed them for the tickets within six months.)

Seeing *On the Town* for the first time was one of the major thrills of my life. Ethel and I tingled through the whole performance while Lenny sat next to us *kvelling* (bursting with pride). Betty and Adolph were in the show and were even better than they had been as Revuers. When it was over, we ran backstage, and there was a lot of hugging, kissing, laughing, and some crying with joy. After an hour, we continued our celebration at Al and Dick's Steak House across the street. We ate and drank and repeated the whole show, relishing every line, every song and dance, and reliving each thrilling moment.

Then the check came, and I went for it. Lenny stopped me. "No, you don't. Not after all those dinners I've had at your house. Also, the show is a hit, and I no longer have to have anyone buy me dinner." There was a pause while he stared at the check. Then he said, "Now, let's see. What did you have?" We paid our own shares.

It was customary during the war for all live entertainment to start with the playing of "The Star-Spangled Banner." Later that year, we took Judy to the ballet. The program started as usual with the national anthem. She said excitedly, "Listen! They're playing that song from *On the Town!*"

Several years later, Lenny was a guest conductor of the Los Angeles Philharmonic. We attended, as always when he conducted, and enjoyed the concert enormously. I know that there was a certain segment of his audience (and critics) who objected to his flamboyant style on the podium. To me, that was invalid criticism. A conductor is there to present his interpretation of a piece of music. Nothing more. If his technique interferes with someone's enjoyment, then that person has chosen the wrong concert. Lenny was always outgoing and gregarious, and it was completely natural that his conducting reflected those qualities. More important, he was always an original thinker, and that's why he was considered one of the world's great conductors.

After the concert, we went back to congratulate him. He sounded as if he had a bad head cold. He told us that he was in the throes of an acute sinus attack and talked about the concert. "My ears are all stuffed from this damned sinus condition, so I had trouble hearing. The Mozart seemed all right, but the Tchaikovsky was much too slow and labored. It lacked energy." Which was another thing about Lenny: He was totally objective about his conducting. It isn't that he didn't welcome other opinions, but in the final analysis he was harsher with himself than any of his listeners.

As we were leaving, he said, "See you up at Kurnitz's." Harry Kurnitz was a renowned wit, raconteur, and successful screenwriter who in his youth had been an amateur violinist and a music critic for a Philadelphia newspaper. He often organized chamber music concerts at his house and frequently hosted parties for visiting celebrities. He gave such a party that night. I was chatting with Lenny when he looked beyond me, his eyes suddenly lighting up. "Look! There's Charlie Chaplin! This is exciting!"

Harry brought Chaplin over to Lenny. "You two know each other, I'm sure."

Chaplin replied, "Unfortunately, no. But I'm an admirer of Mr. Bernstein's."

Lenny returned the compliment. Kurnitz laughed embarrassedly and walked away. He later explained the reason for his reaction to Lenny. "When I asked you whom to invite to your party, you obviously said Solly Chaplin. It sounded to me like Charlie Chaplin. Now, I didn't know Charlie Chaplin—until tonight, that is—but I thought it would be all right to call him. I got him on the phone and invited him. I thought at the time that he seemed a bit surprised to be asked, but I figured that maybe that's how he was about parties. Well, something good came out of it after all. You wanted to meet each other, and now you have." It was a night when I was the right Chaplin and Charlie was the wrong one.

The postscript to the incident was the item that appeared in Leonard Lyons's syndicated column (Lyons was notorious for distorting information): "Harry Kurnitz threw a bash for Lenny Bernstein. He invited Saul Chaplin. Charlie Chaplin was also there."

Chapter 9 ■ The war years in Hollywood were exciting. It was a popular war, if wars can be popular, and everyone we knew was contributing to the war effort. There was the enormously successful Hollywood Canteen, which was star-studded every night. Those who could entertain did. Others danced with the GIs, waited on tables, washed dishes. They mingled with secretaries, propmen, grips—all doing their bit. Even the studio heads got together, each assuming the responsibility for the entertainment one night every week. Naturally, they carried over their normal competitiveness to their efforts on behalf of the Canteen. Word that Warner Bros. had put on a better show than Columbia would drive Harry Cohn crazy. One night I was playing for Phil Silvers on Columbia night. He began his "clarinet bit." The following is not verbatim but close enough. He announced as he picked up the clarinet, "I will now play 'Stardust' in four flats and make the eight ball in the side pocket at the same time." He turned to me. "Give me an A."

Frank Sinatra,

Phil Silvers,

& the USO

I played an A on the piano. He blew on the instrument and let out an ungodly squeal.

"That's close enough." He'd say to the audience, "Would the first three rows mind leaning back? Because when I play, sometimes a fine spray comes out," and then to me, "May I have an introduction, please?"

From there, this is how it was supposed to go: I would play a florid introduction, which would seemingly come to an end. At that point, Phil would put the clarinet to his lips. As he was about to play, I would resume the introduction. After repeating the same action several times, he would turn to the audience and say, "Who do you have to know to play a solo around here?" I would continue the introduction and eventually finish, after which Phil would play, and the bit would go on.

On this particular night, after Phil said the line, I got whacked in the back and heard someone yell, "Let him play!" It was Harry Cohn, showman extraordinaire. How could he not have known that it was a set bit? Phil switched to something else.

Russian War Relief was one of many organizations that worked to help the war effort. Some ten years later, it was branded as a Communist front organization by the U.S. attorney general. I always found that laughable. Of course it was a Communist front organization. Its aim was to aid Russia, a Communist state. But the attorney general's accusation that everyone who worked for it was a Communist sympathizer was too absurd to be laughable. It meant that the entire Los Angeles Philharmonic, plus Jascha Heifetz and Vladimir Horowitz, were Communist sympathizers because they gave a combined concert to raise money for Russian War Relief.

It would also include those of us who did a benefit for the organization at the Mocambo nightclub one night. I was there to play for Phil. At rehearsals that afternoon, Lena Horne appeared on crutches. She explained to the organizer of the benefit: "I broke my leg. I showed up because I thought you might not believe me if I told you over the phone. Also, my piano player has gone off to New York, so I've got no one to play for me."

Phil said, "How about Solly?"

She said, "Fine. Let's try."

After I had run through three of her numbers, for which she had no music, she turned to Phil and said, "He's the blackest white man I've ever heard."

I was very flattered because I admired her greatly. I still do. That night during her first song I could hear that the key we had set that afternoon was going to be too low, so during the seventh and eighth bars, when she wasn't singing, I unobtrusively raised the key to one she would be more comfortable with. I made it sound as if there was supposed to be a key change at that point. I

Top: The beginning; Lou Levy, Saul Chaplin, Sammy Cahn, 1935.

Bottom: The Cotton Club, 1937; Saul Chaplin and Sammy Cahn teaching singers and dancers one of the songs. *(Both photos in the Saul Chaplin Collection)*

Top: *Time Out for Rhythm*; the Three Stooges entertaining "the love-lies" (as they were called then), while I accompany them. *(Photo courtesy of Columbia Pictures; "Time Out for Rhythm" copyright © 1941, renewed 1969, Columbia Pictures Industries, Inc. All rights reserved)*

Bottom: *The Jolson Story*; rehearsing with Al Jolson. *(Photo, by Greg Cormick, courtesy of Columbia Pictures; "The Jolson Story" copyright © 1946, renewed 1973, Columbia Pictures Industries, Inc. All rights reserved)*

Top: USO; receiving our passports, left to right, Phil Silvers, Saul Chaplin, Frank Sinatra (1945). *(Saul Chaplin Collection)*

Bottom: *An American in Paris;* left to right, Saul Chaplin, Adolph Green, Gene Kelly. Adolph Green was Oscar Levant's double during the filming of Gershwin's Piano Concerto in F. *(AN AMERICAN IN PARIS © 1951 Turner Entertainment Co. All rights reserved)*

Near right: *An American in Paris;* Johnny Green and I receive the Academy Award for Best Scoring of a Musical. *(Academy Awards ® stills © 1952 Academy of Motion Picture Arts and Sciences)*

Far right: I was awarded my second Oscar with Adolph Deutsch for Musical Scoring of *Seven Brides for Seven Brothers.* *(Academy Awards ® stills © 1955 Academy of Motion Picture Arts and Sciences)*

Below left: *High Society;* rehearsing "True Love," left to right, Grace Kelly, Bing Crosby, Saul Chaplin. *(HIGH SOCIETY © 1956 Turner Entertainment Co.*

Below right: *High Society;* creating and rehearsing "Now You Has Jazz," left to right, Saul Chaplin, Louis Armstrong, Arvel Shaw, Bing Crosby. *(HIGH SOCIETY © 1956 Turner Entertainment Co.*

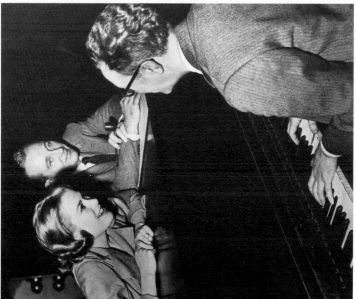

Above: *Can Can;* Saul Chaplin and his daughter, Judy Chaplin Prince. *("CAN CAN" © 1960 Twentieth Century Fox Film Corporation. All rights reserved)*

Facing page, top: *High Society;* rehearsing "Well, Did You Evah?," left to right, Chuck Walters (director), Saul Chaplin, Frank Sinatra, Bing Crosby. *(HIGH SOCIETY © 1956 Turner Entertainment Co. All rights reserved)*

Facing page, bottom: *Merry Andrew;* left to right, Michael Kidd (director, choreographer), Saul Chaplin, Danny Kaye. *("MERRY ANDREW" © 1958 Turner Entertainment Co. All rights reserved)*

Left: *Can Can;* Shirley Mac-Laine, Saul Chaplin, Frank Sinatra. *(Photo by Bob Willoughby; "CAN CAN"* © *1960 Twentieth Century Fox Film Corporation. All rights reserved)*

Below: *West Side Story;* rehearsing "Officer Krupke," left to right, Johnny Green, Jerome Robbins (codirector, choreographer), Saul Chaplin, the Jets. *(Photo by Phil Stern; WEST SIDE STORY* © *1961 United Artists Pictures, Inc. All rights reserved)*

Right: *I Could Go On Singing.* Judy Garland and I went to the London Palladium at 1:00 A.M. so that she could figure out her choreography. I sang her songs to her from the footlights because the piano in the pit was locked. *(I COULD GO ON SINGING © 1963 Miller-Turman Productions, Inc. All rights reserved)*

Below: Bob Wise and I went location scouting for *The Sound of Music* in the snowy Alps of Austria. Six months later, when we began shooting, it was a beautiful verdant green. *("THE SOUND OF MUSIC" © 1965 Twentieth Century Fox Film Corporation. All rights reserved)*

Top: *The Sound of Music;* a first look at some of the children we were considering for the film, along with Julie Andrews's stand-in. In the background, left to right, are Pamela Danova (dialogue coach), Harper McKay, rehearsal pianist, Richard Hayden, Robert Wise, Saul Chaplin, and Mark Breaux (choreographer).

Below: We cheer on the children during the filming of "Do, Re, Mi"; left to right, Saul Chaplin, Mark and Dee Dee Breaux (choreographers), Paul Beeson, camera operator, Robert Wise. *(Both photos from "THE SOUND OF MUSIC"* © *1965 Twentieth Century Fox Film Corporation. All rights reserved)*

Right: *The Sound of Music;* Julie Andrews and I accept Robert Wise's Academy Awards for Best Director and Best Picture. *(Academy Awards ® stills © 1966 Academy of Motion Picture Arts and Sciences)*

Below: Six of the seven children at the twenty-fifth anniversary of the release of *The Sound of Music* (Nicholas Hammond, who played Friedrich, was out of the country). Left to right: Angela Cartwright (Brigitta), Charmian Carr (Liesl), Kim Karath (Gretl), Saul Chaplin, Julie Andrews, Robert Wise, Debbie Turner (Marta), Heather Urich (Louisa), Derayné Chase (Kurt). *("THE SOUND OF MUSIC" © 1965 Twentieth Century Fox Film Corporation. All rights reserved)*

Top: *Star!;* left to right, Saul Chaplin, Julie Andrews, Robert Wise, Michael Kidd (choreographer).

Bottom: *Star!* recording session; left to right, Julie Andrews, Saul Chaplin, Lennie Hayton (musical director). *(Both photos from "STAR!" © 1968 Twentieth Century Fox Film Corporation. All rights reserved)*

Top: At the London command performance of *Star!*, left to right, the Duke of York, Richard Crenna, Penni Crenna, Saul Chaplin, Betty Chaplin. *("STAR!" © 1968 Twentieth Century Fox Film Corporation. All rights reserved)*

Bottom: *Man of La Mancha*; Peter O'Toole and Saul Chaplin. *(MAN OF LA MANCHA © 1972 United Artists Corporation. All rights reserved)*

Top: *Man of La Mancha;* Saul Chaplin and Sophia Loren. *(MAN OF LA MANCHA © 1972 United Artists Corporation. All rights reserved)*

Bottom: *That's Entertainment, Part 2;* Fred Astaire, Saul Chaplin, Gene Kelly. *(THAT'S ENTERTAINMENT PART 2 © 1976 Turner Entertainment Co. All rights reserved)*

Top: *That's Entertainment, Part 2;* Eleanor Powell, Saul Chaplin.

Bottom, left to right, Johnny Weissmuller, Kathryn Grayson, Gene Kelly, Betty Chaplin, Fred Astaire, Saul Chaplin, Marge Champion, Bobby Van, and Cary Grant, about to board the plane for the Cannes Film Festival. *(Both photos from THAT'S ENTERTAINMENT PART 2 © 1976 Turner Entertainment Co. All rights reserved)*

Top: At the Cannes Film Festival, left to right, Cary Grant, Frank Rosenfelt (president of MGM), and Mr. and Mrs. Saul Chaplin. *(THAT'S ENTERTAINMENT PART 2 © 1976 Turner Entertainment Co. All rights reserved)*

Below: Songwriters Hall of Fame; Hal Prince (theatrical producer and director, and my son-in-law) presented me with the document that installed me in the Hall of Fame in 1985. *(Photo by Samuel Teicher; Saul Chaplin Collection)*

thought nothing of it. Lena was knocked out by it. As a result of that evening, we became good friends, and I had the great joy of playing for her many times after that.

When Gene left for the navy, our Orange Grove Avenue house became the center of social activities for our group. The door was always open. When we eventually moved, we had to call in a locksmith to make us a key to return to the landlord. Soon after we moved in, we lost the one he had given us.

It was during this period that we became politically aware. Some years later we all worked for the Henry Wallace presidential campaign. But now our activities were confined to reading leftist material and attending the Actors Lab, a leftist theater. We knew many of the people who worked there. I wrote the music for two of their plays. Of course, I got no fee. They were always operating in debt. It was considered the Hollywood version of New York's Group Theatre, which had turned out so many fine actors, writers, and directors ten years earlier. In fact, some of the Group Theater members were prime movers at the Lab.

Betty, Adolph, or Judy first told us about a musical by Marc Blitzstein called *The Cradle Will Rock*. We acquired the records of several songs and played them until they were worn out. We had never heard anything like it. The music was energetic and abrasive, as it should be; the lyrics used the language of the working class. We sang the songs all day long. Then the exciting day came when we were sent a published copy of the play containing the lyrics and music. I played almost nothing else for months.

On a Saturday afternoon, Ethel and I were at the piano doing a song from it called "Joe Worker." We looked up, and there was Betsy Kelly and an extremely handsome young man standing in the crook of the piano. She stopped us and asked us to start from the beginning. She turned to her friend and said, "You wanna hear something great? Listen to this." The three of us then launched into the song: "Joe Worker gets gypped. For no good reason just gypped," and so on in the same vein. The worker is being exploited by the bosses, and he shouldn't put up with it, and so on.

To say that Betsy's friend was utterly confused would be understating the case. He obviously hadn't the vaguest notion what the song was about and why he was being subjected to it. After we had finished, Betsy turned to him. "Isn't that great? Oh, you haven't met. These are my friends Ethel and Solly Chaplin. This is Louis Jourdan. He just arrived from Paris."

Louis Jourdan had arrived in Los Angeles that very day. He looked up the Kellys and met Betsy, who immediately brought him to our house to meet us. He happened to catch us during our *Cradle Will Rock* period. He must've thought that Americans were peculiar indeed.

It was a marvelously stimulating time. There was very little live theater and few concerts to attend, so we entertained one another in our living rooms. We were all young and, as it turned out, on our way up. We enjoyed one another. We were never concerned whether a particular movie was profitable. In fact, almost all of them were, but it was a subject that didn't interest us.

I also do not understand how I could have afforded to entertain so many people so frequently. True, we didn't serve food, but we did supply booze, soft drinks, and snacks. We finally had to move because the termites had eaten a four-foot-square hole in the living-room floor and it was getting larger daily.

In 1945, after the war had ended in Europe, Frank Sinatra and Phil Silvers planned to do a USO tour through what was known as the North African Theater of Operations. The tour was to include Newfoundland, the Azores, Italy, and North Africa. Neither had been drafted because of physical disabilities. Phil had poor eyesight, and the half-dozen mastoid operations Frank had had earlier in his life had left him with a punctured eardrum.

The general public accepted Phil's 4-F classification but resented Frank's. Why should their husbands, sons, and brothers be risking their lives while Frank was at home making millions? Frank was aware that the GIs felt this way. Their sisters, girlfriends, and wives were swooning over his singing while they were away fighting a war. Frank was determined to contribute in every way he could to the war effort. He did dozens and dozens of USO shows in the States and was now planning a trip overseas. He put together a unit consisting of himself, Faye McKenzie (a musical comedy singer), and Betty Yeaton (a dancer).

While Ethel, Judy, and I were on my annual two-week vacation in New York, Phil phoned me. "Solly, how would you like to come on our USO trip with us?"

"As what?" I asked.

"As a trained seal! As an accompanist—what else?"

"But I'm supposed to be back at the studio at the end of next week."

"Frank'll square it with Harry Cohn. That's if you wanna go."

"I wanna go."

Frank got Cohn's permission. Of course, Cohn made sure that the favor was reciprocated. Later that year, Frank made a track of "All or Nothing at All" for a Columbia film for free. Considering the kind of fees Frank was receiving at that time, the payment far outweighed the value of my services.

At our first rehearsal I went through Faye McKenzie's and Betty Yeaton's music with no difficulties. I didn't have to rehearse Frank's music because I knew it all, having played for him so many times. But Frank and I did have a kind of odd rehearsal that to the unknowing would have looked strange, indeed. We had a "signal" rehearsal—not unlike that of a baseball pitcher and catcher. If Frank crossed his fingers while he was singing, he wanted to sing an extra half chorus. If he made a circle, another full chorus. A horizontal gesture meant an extended ending; a chopping motion, shorten what we had planned and end as soon as possible.

Our signals worked perfectly, but not always. There were occasions when I ignored them. Every once in a while, I would be enjoying his singing so much that even though he would

signal for a half chorus more, I would lead him into a full chorus.
Or he would want me to shorten a song, and I wouldn't.

We gave our first performance at a camp in New Jersey where
among the audience were army censors. It also provided us an
opportunity to see how our show played. With the exception of
a closing number that Sammy, Phil, and I wrote, the remainder
of our two-and-a-half-hour entertainment was put together by
Phil. He came up with the brilliant notion that made us a sensation everywhere we played. Our built-in problem was that Frank
would be facing unfriendly audiences everywhere. To overcome
it, Phil got the inspired idea that Frank should be the butt of
every gag until it came time for him to sing and that he should
not be introduced until then.

Our show started with Phil at the microphone doing a monologue. After five or six minutes—actually the signal was when he
put his hand to his tie—Frank would edge onto the stage from
the wings and stand quietly about four or five feet away from
him. Phil would continue his monologue, suddenly notice Frank,
do a double take, and say, "What the hell is this?" The audience,
who knew full well who it was, howled.

For the next two hours, Frank was the constant underdog and
his audiences got to like him more and more. He wasn't the
brash young wise guy they had been expecting. At the same time,
they didn't dislike Phil because that was his special kind of
magic—a lovable rogue. When the time finally came for Frank
to be introduced, the audience was already on his side.

He was also helped immeasurably by Phil's introductions.
Since he changed them constantly, there's no way to write down
verbatim what he said, but he always included certain elements,
which went something like this: "I want you to meet this skinny
Italian kid who's the star of our show. To the world he's a fine
singer, and to me he's a good friend. But since this tour, I've
really gotten to know him. It would be difficult to tell you what a
kind, thoughtful, generous kid he is. And what a joy it is to travel
with him. I can only tell you that if I were ever lucky enough to

have a kid brother, I would want him to be as much as possible like my pal—Frank Sinatra."

Frank would then sing for from thirty to forty-five minutes, always to a standing ovation at the finish. The only way we could gradually quiet the audience was by going into our finale.

The following evening we left La Guardia Airport for Newfoundland on a C-54. When we finally landed at Stephensville, Newfoundland, I was terribly disappointed. As a kid in Brooklyn, I always imagined Newfoundland as somewhere around the North Pole. I expected to see miles and miles of snow. Instead, we were greeted by a warm, sunny May day. Snow? There were flowers all over the place.

Frank came up with a whole set of suggestions for us to follow. They were more than suggestions. They were orders. First, we should have all our meals with the GI's whenever possible. He knew we would receive a lot of invitations from officers, but he suggested that we accept them only when it was to our advantage. Frank suggested we always perform in civilian clothes rather than our USO uniforms because our audiences had been seeing nothing but olive drab since they entered the service. Also, we were always to look immaculate.

That wasn't as easy as it sounds. We tried our damnedest but never did achieve Frank's standard. He even got himself a shoeshine box and shined not only his own shoes but Phil's and mine. Our USO uniforms were to be used for traveling so our civilian clothes could be kept fresh for appearances. He also suggested that we do as many shows as possible so that we could entertain as many servicemen as possible. As proof that we abided by that suggestion, we played for 575,000 men and women in Italy alone, according to the army's count. That represents a helluva lot of singing, dancing, piano playing, and jokes and bits.

I had always admired Frank's singing, but my admiration for him soared during this trip. We did shows at all times of the day and night under the most difficult circumstances, and if anything, his voice grew stronger and his style more ingratiating. We performed in unbearably hot and stuffy metal Quonset huts where the temperature was well over one hundred degrees, on the backs of trailer trucks in windstorms, in the middle of a rainstorm. It made no difference. Frank sounded fine everywhere. What I didn't appreciate until this tour, however, was what a fine showman he is.

In almost every case, he faced a hostile audience of GIs, who came prepared to throw things at him. I mean that literally because on many occasions soldiers showed us the fruit and vegetables they had brought along as ammunition. But gradually Frank won them over. He answered every request he could. When he didn't know a song they asked for, he came up with the perfect line that made them feel that they had requested the substitute.

Our next stop after Newfoundland was the Azores, where we were to spend two days. After we were through with our activities for the first day, we accepted an invitation from an officer to join him for a nightcap at his billet. We were chatting and sipping our drinks (Coke for me) when we heard a plane overhead. We asked our host about it, and he told us it was an ambulance plane that landed there every night. Its passengers were wounded men who were being returned to the States. It was a stopping-off-place where the patients were carried to a Quonset hut while the plane was cleaned and refueled. The whole process took about an hour. We asked if we could visit the men. He replied that he was sure they would be thrilled to see us.

The sight that greeted us when we entered the Quonset hut was shocking. It was filled with men on cots who had suffered almost every kind of disaster imaginable. We had been to many hospitals before but had never seen anything quite like this. There were arms and legs in splints everywhere. There were amputees, men with bandaged eyes, and some whose entire heads were bandaged. What made it more affecting than a hospital was that there were so many men confined in a relatively small area. Nevertheless, we carried on normally, never showing how upset we were. It wasn't easy.

The men were surprised and thrilled to have Frank and Phil in their midst. Faye and Betty, incidentally, had gone to bed. I found two guys who had been in a jazz band their unit had formed. We talked about music and the relative merits of Artie Shaw and Benny Goodman. Phil and Frank were great. All Phil had to do was grin and say, "Glad ta seeya!" and they laughed.

Frank always found something to talk about, mainly his days with Harry James and Tommy Dorsey. At one point I heard him say, "I'd like to sing for you guys, but there's no piano here. There isn't even an accordion. Anybody got a guitar? Hey, Sol, do you play guitar?"

Before I had a chance to answer, someone yelled, "Sing anyhow."

"Okay. If that's how you want it."

Frank sang half a dozen songs a cappella, moving from bed to bed, and the guys loved it. It was right out of an MGM musical. Then a captain informed him it was time to move the men out. Frank, as usual, came up with the perfect finish for his act: "It's time for you guys to get back on the plane and get some shut-eye. Maybe this'll help." He sang Brahms's "Lullaby" as the men were being carried out. He shook hands with them wherever possible. As they left, the lights were being turned off in the Quonset hut. With Frank singing so beautifully in the fading light, I stood there with a lump in my throat, all teary-eyed. I looked at Phil. He was reacting the same way.

Our next stop was Casablanca. Another disappointment. The only Casablanca I knew was from the movie of the same name, and it looked nothing like that. It was a bustling city with heavy traffic and buses full of people in their native dress. They looked like the cast of a traveling company of *Desert Song*. We were taken to a hotel famous for having been the first meeting place for Roosevelt, Churchill, and Stalin. Our rooms were tastefully and comfortably furnished in soft, muted colors with beautiful heavy satin drapes that hung from the high ceiling to the floor. Our bathrooms had two features we had never seen before: two sinks and a bidet. We knew about the sinks, but what was that other thing that looked like a small toilet bowl? We tried to figure it out for a long time until Phil finally came up with the answer.

"There's desert all around us, right? Well, the guys who work here have to be out there a lot. When they get back, their feet must be hot and tired, so they use this to wash them." It was all so logical. Why hadn't we thought of it before?

Our first show was at 8:00 that night in a theater run by the army. It couldn't be earlier because the electricity wasn't turned on until eight. Actually we couldn't start at eight, even with the lights on, because the piano had to be brought down by elevator. While we waited, I stood in the wings and watched the audience fill the house. Ten minutes later, six Arabs started rolling the piano down the middle aisle from the rear of the theater. That's not the best thing to do to a piano, so I was a little concerned.

Little did I know. They soon reached the pit, which was at floor level, and proceeded to lift the piano onto the stage. They had it more than halfway up when someone who was pushing from the rear must have weakened because the piano went crashing down into the pit. It made an ear-splitting sound, and everyone laughed—except me. But the Arabs didn't give up. They tried again, and this time they succeeded in pushing the piano onto the stage. I indicated where it should be placed, and we were ready for showtime.

Everything went well until I had to play. Then I was struck by such a nightmare that I still shudder when I think of it. Every key I hit stayed down! It couldn't be played again unless I pulled it up. Some of the keys had been knocked out of line by the jolt the piano had received, so on some notes I got two tones instead of one. Between avoiding those keys and pulling up the others, I was frantic and desperate. But what really got me angry was that Frank thought it was funny. While I was trying hopelessly to put together some kind of decent accompaniment for him, he kept looking back at me and laughing. I was furious.

We continued our journey with stops in Oran and Bizerte,

then on to Caserta, Italy, where our trip started in earnest. Everything up to this point was a preamble to what lay ahead. For one thing, our group was enlarged considerably. We were assigned a special services officer—Sergeant Silverstein. We were given our own sound equipment and Private Benson to run it.

Most important, we were assigned a C-46 airplane with a three-man crew to stay with us throughout our travels in Italy. The pilot's orders were "Report to Frank Sinatra USO Unit and proceed as ordered." Frank was shown the itinerary that had been laid out for us. "This is ridiculous. You got us down for only two shows a day. We can do a lot more than that. Especially with our own airplane." The only thing he didn't change was the one day off that had been planned for us in the middle of the trip.

Rome—beautiful Rome—was our next stop. The drive from the airport to the city was exciting. There were constant surprises—like turning a corner and suddenly seeing the Colosseum or the Forum, which I had only known from pictures.

Frank decided that as long as we were in Rome, we should have a private audience with the pope. I still don't know how he pulled it off. He must've known someone who knew Myron Taylor, the American envoy to the Vatican. A private audience was arranged for the five of us. Our biggest decision now was what to wear. Phil, Frank, and I decided to wear our USO uniforms since after all, we represented the United States. Faye and Betty felt their USO uniforms were too mannish, so they agreed to wear the simplest dresses they had brought along and bought lace mantillas to cover their heads.

A visit with the pope is a memorable and mesmerising experience. Upon our arrival at the Vatican, we were taken to a small room where a cardinal briefed us. We were then led through a series of extremely wide corridors—so wide, in fact, that they could easily have passed as ballrooms. We began noticing the treasures that surrounded us. It was an astonishing display of rare religious paintings and sculpture, all lit by rays of bright sunlight that streaked in through the heavily draped windows.

Looking at this awesome exhibition of matchless art transported us into another world. It was a perfect preamble to meeting the holiest of men.

At the end of the last corridor, we were greeted by another cardinal. He told a young man who stood next to him to supply us with the rosary beads we had requested, then led us into a comparatively small room. He told us that when the pope entered, we could remain standing or kneel. He asked us to stand in a line and told us that the pope would speak to each of us individually. We put Faye and Betty first, then me, then Phil and Frank. When the pope entered five minutes later, we all kneeled and kissed his ring. I believe that because we had been told so often that we didn't have to do either, we felt it was expected of us.

Pope Pius XII was tall and thin, his face more stern than kind. But there was an aura of great serenity about him. He seemed slightly annoyed with the rituals that were part of our audience. He seemed genuinely interested in the person he was speaking to, which made us try to prolong our conversations. For him, this was no problem. He just kept moving down the line.

He spoke English with a heavy Italian accent. Faye and Betty were so dumbstruck, they answered the pope in whispers. I never heard any part of their conversations. He asked me whether I had a family. I replied that I left my wife and small daughter in New York to come on this trip. He said he had been to New York and recalled that at this time of year, July, it could be very hot and humid. He then wished me a safe and happy journey, blessed me, and moved on to Phil.

Phil mentioned that he had seen the pope years earlier in Chicago. The Pope replied that he had indeed been to Chicago to attend a eucharistic convention when he was papal secretary. Phil had four strands of rosary beads over his arm. He said, "These are for the Bing Crosby family." I don't know whether the pope didn't hear him or didn't know who Bing Crosby was. He simply blessed the beads, as he did all the others.

Phil told quite a different story about his audience. In his version, the pope not only knew who Crosby was but also supplied Phil with two more strands of rosary beads for Bing and Dixie, in addition to ones for their four boys. That never happened in my presence, but it's a lot better story.

Next came Frank:

POPE: I understand you're a singer.
FRANK: Yes, Your Holiness.
POPE: You are quite well known in America?
FRANK: I've been most fortunate, Your Holiness.
POPE: What do you sing? [He meant, tenor, baritone, or bass.]
FRANK: "Old Man River," "Night and Day," "The Song Is You," and other popular songs.

The Pope made no comment. He blessed him. That was the end of our audience.

We next flew to Florence. We took off in the rain. Phil, who was terrified of flying, stretched himself out over several bucket seats because he thought that being in a prone position might ease his anxiety. He had his Mae West within arm's reach as he always did, whether we were flying over land or water.

I was playing gin rummy with Frank. He picked the first card and immediately said, "Gin."

I yelled, "Oh, my God!"

At that precise moment, there was a loud clap of thunder, and a streak of lightning shot through the plane. Phil jumped up as if he had been shot out of a cannon, feverishly putting on his Mae West and shouting, "We're crashing! We're crashing!"

It took a little time, but we finally convinced him that we were in the middle of a thunderstorm. It turned out to be the first of a long succession of rough flights we were to have over the next several weeks.

Our zigzag journey through Italy next took us to Foggia. We spent a hot, sweltering day performing for our troops in the usual places, finally finishing around midnight.

More shows—more plane trips, sometimes bordering on the perilous—more hard barracks cots or soft hotel beds—more meals that ranged from plain and healthy (an army travels on its stomach) to delicious and elegant. The time we had been looking forward to finally arrived. Our day off. With a plane at our disposal, we could spend that day anywhere in Italy. We agreed unanimously on Venice.

By sheer luck, we played our last show the night before our holiday in an army camp only ninety miles from Venice. We decided that instead of spending the night sleeping on army cots and flying to Venice the following morning, we would drive there after our last show. That would give us a restful night's sleep and a full day in Venice. It was just after midnight when we piled our gear into two large army vehicles and started for Venice. It should have been a three-hour trip at most, but we hadn't figured on bombed-out roads that necessitated many detours. We finally got there at about four in the morning.

We were taken to the boat landing for the Lido, the R and R area, but of course, there was no service at that hour in the morning. We went off looking for any kind of seaworthy vessel that would get us across the lagoon.

We walked along the embankment in pitch darkness until we came upon an amphibious craft anchored right off shore. There was a British soldier asleep on deck whom Frank aroused by shouting at him. He listened to our problem, replied with the British equivalent of "Get lost," and went back to sleep. Frank then suggested that we go back to the landing while he continued looking. Sure enough, twenty minutes later there was Frank walking along the embankment with a gondola, complete with a smiling gondolier following him in the water.

We all lined up on shore with our bags and sound equipment, and the gondolier started assigning us seats in his flimsy-looking craft. There were seven of us with seven pieces of luggage and three cases of heavy sound equipment. The gondolier walked up and down in front of us like a royal potentate reviewing his troops. He pointed to me and indicated that I should sit in the prow. I had a perfect vantage point from which to watch the boat being loaded. He did it slowly and methodically, although I must admit his method was never clear to me. All I could see was that the boat kept sinking lower and lower into the water. By the time he finished loading the boat, the water came right up to its rim. It seemed that if all of us breathed at the same time, we would sink.

With a strenuous push on the long pole by the gondolier, the boat lurched forward with a groan. We were finally under way. It was an incredibly beautiful time of day. The sun was rising, the sky cloudless, the Grand Canal smooth as glass, the air pleasantly cool. There wasn't another boat to be seen anywhere. It was like sailing in an enchanted fairyland. Everything was turning out well after all.

Phil looked back at the gondolier and said, "I never heard of being on the canals of Venice without the gondolier singing. C'mon, sing."

Phil began singing "Hatikvah," which is now the Israeli national anthem. He didn't know the words, so he used "da da's."

But one voice joined him, singing the correct Hebrew words. It was the gondolier! All our heads snapped back so sharply that we almost tipped over. What's a guy who's supposed to be singing "O Sole Mio" doing singing "Hatikvah"? He tried to explain to Frank in Italian that he was an Italian Jew who had been in hiding all through the war. When it was over, he scraped together enough money to buy a gondola and resume his original occupation.

We did more shows during the ensuing weeks; then it was time to leave. No performances had been planned for our return trip. We boarded a plane that was to take us to Casablanca, with stops at Bizerte, Oran, and Algiers. We all sat quietly, a little sad that it was all over but satisfied with the results. Our trip had been a success. We had played before an enormous number of people. Frank had made fans of thousands of GIs who had originally felt otherwise, and we had made a solid contribution to the morale of our troops.

During the flight back to the States, I said to Phil, "We see the same people in Hollywood. Now, I know that you're gonna exaggerate some of the things that happened to us on this trip. I don't mind, but if you'll tell me the stories you're gonna tell, I'll swear to them. Just tell me what you're gonna say."

"Me? Exaggerate? Never!"

After our return, I went to many parties where Phil spun yarns about our experiences overseas. They had me fascinated. They weren't true, but he worked them into terrific tales.

Chapter 10 ■ When I returned to Hollywood, I had a meeting with my boss, Morris Stoloff, the head of Columbia's Music Department.

"Saul, what are you busy with?" he asked.

"Let's see," I replied. "I've got a song to write for *Meet Me on Broadway*, two songs and vocal arrangements for *Klondike Kate*, and the background music for an untitled Boston Blackie."

"Well, I'm sure you'll be thrilled to know that I'm handing you another assignment. It's several months off, so you'll have time. The studio is doing a picture on the life of Al Jolson, and I want you on it."

The

"I've always loved Jolson," I said, "but you'll have to get me out of at least one of those other projects."

Jolson

"No problem. We found a woman in Pasadena who's been a lifelong Jolson fan. She has every record he ever made. We've arranged to rent the entire collection from her, and I'm having them delivered to you. Between whatever else you're doing, listen to as many as you can so we'll be prepared to discuss what songs we should use, orchestrations, and so on."

Story

"That sounds like fun. I'd love to do it."

I can tell you I wasn't exactly heartbroken to have to give up the untitled Boston Blackie to do *The Jolson Story*. I spent at least an hour a day listening to those records to familiarize myself with his songs and how he sang them. I believed then, as now, that Jolson was the greatest entertainer the world has ever known, so listening to his records was great fun. There were well over a hundred songs, and he had his name on many of them as one of the music business's early and most notorious "cut-ins." A cut-in is usually a top performer who'll do your song only if you cut him in on the royalties and put his name on the song as one of the writers. Since it usually guaranteed the popularity of the song, it was considered a good deal among some songwriters.

Jolson usually cut in on a song after it was written, but at least once he is supposed to have been responsible for the origin of a hit. He had gone to the Metropolitan Opera to see Puccini's *Tosca.* On his way home, he stopped at Lindy's where he met Vincent Rose, a fairly successful songwriter. Jolson is supposed to have told Rose, "I just saw *Tosca* at the Met. In the last act the tenor sings a tune that would be a sure hit. Next time they do the opera, go see it." Rose must have been delighted to have a song thrown in his lap that way by the hit maker Jolson, so he went to see *Tosca* and adapted the tenor aria Jolson mentioned into a song called "Avalon." Of course, he included Jolson's name as one of the writers. Jolson sang it everywhere, and the song was and still is a hit.

Inevitably, the plagiarism came to the attention of Ricordi, the Italian publisher of *Tosca.* They sued Remick, the American publisher of "Avalon," and won easily. To this day, Ricordi receives a large share of the song's royalties.

When the film was being planned, certain obvious decisions were made. First and most important, Jolson would sing all the vocal tracks but not appear in the picture because there was no way that he could look twenty. Second, an actor would have to be found who could play Jolson from about twenty to fifty. And last, Jolson would have to work with this actor so that he could imitate Jolson as closely as possible.

Well, Jolson agreed with only one of these conditions. He understood that he had to do all the singing. But he saw no necessity for having another actor play him. With the proper makeup, he could easily look twenty, even though he was in his sixties. Only an extreme egotist would suggest that.

When he finally accepted the fact that another actor was to be used, he would accept only James Cagney, who had just won the Academy Award for portraying George M. Cohan in *Yankee Doodle Dandy,* or a star of equal stature. But he agreed to perform two of his numbers on film so that whoever eventually played the part would be able to study his style and gestures. He did two of his biggest songs—"Toot Toot Tootsie" and "My

Mammy." They turned out to be more than just routine rendi-
tions. They were Al Jolson auditioning for the part. He was so
intent on looking younger that he jumped around the stage as if
the floor were made of white hot steel. It was insanely frenetic,
yet I must admit it was stirring because that voice was there—
vibrant, dynamic, intense, louder than I had ever heard it, but
definitely not younger.

The studio would also have preferred having an established
star play the role, but after many exhaustive tests of everyone
available, no one could be found. Some important stars turned it
down. Others couldn't do it. A contract actor who had been
spending his career in the depths of the B-picture unit kept insisting on being tested. More to quiet him than anything else, the
studio finally consented.

His test was marvelous, but of course no one took it seriously.
A star was going to play Jolson. They continued testing other
actors. With each new test, the B-picture actor's test looked
better and better. They couldn't believe it. They made him do
another test. Finally, over Al Jolson's violent objections, they
gave the part to the B actor, Larry Parks.

Jolson hated the choice, but he would have hated any choice
except himself. And it wasn't only his bruised ego that made him
feel that way. He couldn't accept anyone's success but his own—
in any business. If someone opened a successful laundry in his
neighborhood, Jolson was envious.

There were any number of reasons why he objected to Larry
Parks. To begin with, the fact that he was being played by a
B actor and not a star would tend to diminish his importance.
And if Larry turned out not to be good in the part, it would
reflect on Jolson as a performer. On the other hand, if he helped
Larry, he would be contributing to a nobody's success, and Jolson wasn't looking for reflected glory. What he really wanted
was that the picture should be a smash and that he should be
given all the credit. Eventually he almost had it that way. The
picture was a large hit, and Jolson's career started blossoming

again. What he didn't get was what he wanted most of all—the chance to play the part himself.

He established his relationship with Larry from the outset: noncooperation. In their sessions where he was supposed to help Larry, he spent most of the time complaining. He constantly objected to the gestures Larry was using as too broad. He would demonstrate—far broader than Larry. Nor did his complaining stop there. He kept badgering Cohn, Sidney Skolsky (whose original idea it was to do the film), and Sidney Buchman (the actual producer of the film) to replace Parks because he was a bad mistake that could still be corrected. It was that way through the entire film.

He never once to my knowledge helped Larry in any way. Larry had conscientiously studied Jolson's films of his numbers, learning them down to the most minute gesture. I often saw Jolson standing on the set watching a number of Larry's being shot, shaking his head disapprovingly. No one but Larry was responsible for his incredible performance in *The Jolson Story*. We were all there to assist him, but he very rarely called on us.

In the meantime, I was having my own problems with Al. It was suggested that he run over some of the older songs with me to refresh his memory. He considered that an insult. Did we really believe that he didn't remember every note he ever sang? Ridiculous! We all looked forward to his first recording session.

The song was "April Showers," one of his biggest hits. At that time it was customary for a singer to sing in a vocal booth away from the orchestra, so that a separate track could be made of each. In that way, it was possible to change one and not the other if necessary. Jolson immediately objected to using the booth, and it was understandable. If anyone ever needed a live audience, it was Jolson. A microphone was set up that enabled him to sing facing the orchestra.

After a short introduction, he began doing the verse. I got goose bumps instantly and knew I had never heard a more thrilling voice in my life. The rest of it was equally spine tingling, but the second chorus lacked certain elements I remembered from the record. The problem was how to tell him.

When he finished the recording, it was played back. Everyone cheered. Harry Cohn, Morris, Sidney Buchman, the orchestra—everyone except me. Jolson noticed that I wasn't joining the rejoicing. "What the hell's the matter with you? Didn't you like it?"

"I think it's terrific, but you left a couple of things out."

"You know it ain't easy to get up there and sing—especially with only one lung." (He had had a lung operation years earlier during which, he claimed, he had a lung removed. No one would swear to it, though.)

"I know it isn't easy, Al, but in the second chor—"

That's as far as I got. He pulled a huge roll of hundred-dollar bills out of his pocket, shook it in my face angrily, and shouted, "I made this in show business! Show me yours!"

"Go fuck yourself!" was my reply as I stormed off the stage and went back to my office.

The phone rang. Morris, asking me what was wrong. I explained that on the original Jolson recording of "April Showers" he recited the second chorus until the last eight bars, then sang it to the finish. In the recording he had just made, he had omitted the recitation, always the most exciting part of his rendition.

Morris said he understood and hung up. He called again ten minutes later. "We made a new take. Come over and hear it."

I didn't want to go, but this was my friend and boss asking me; so I went. This time Jolson had included the recitation, and it was wonderful, but he hadn't sung the last note the way he used to. He simply sang the word *long* instead of singing it as he had in the past, as though it had three syllables on three descending notes: "lo-ho-hong." I debated whether to say anything about it but finally mentioned it quietly to Morris. They made another recording, which was perfect. The incident was never mentioned again, and my relationship with Al improved a little.

Jolson's orchestrations for the film were copied note for note from his old records. We thought that the sound of the orchestra was an integral part of his unique performances.

He didn't feel that way. He came in one day and said, "I heard Perry Como on the radio last night. He had terrific, modern orchestrations. That's what mine should be. Modern."

On his next recording session, he wanted to do a ballad. A modern, lush string arrangement was made. He couldn't sing against it because it wasn't what he was accustomed to hearing. But of course he never said that. He said, "That's terrible. That's the corniest orchestration I ever heard. I know somebody who can make a real modern orchestration. Morris, get him. His name is Martin Fried."

Martin Fried had been Jolson's most recent accompanist, a plumpish, medium-height man of about forty who played pleasant old-fashioned piano. He was invaluable to us because he knew exactly what Al would consider "modern." He did essentially the same orchestration we had been doing, but where a trumpet had originally played a figure, he had a clarinet playing it.

Jolson beamed. "Now that's what I call modern." Having learned Fried's secret—he never really hid it from us—we were able to satisfy Jolson from then on.

Unfortunately, Fried couldn't confine his connection with Jolson to doing his orchestrations. After the picture was finished, he went on the road with him as his accompanist. I saw him a year later. He was thin and wan, suffering from a serious heart condition. A year with Jolson had turned him into a physical wreck, a predictable consequence of working with a man who never admitted to being wrong and needed a whipping boy to blame when things didn't go as planned. If an audience wasn't as receptive as he expected, it was Martin's lousy arrangements. If his voice wasn't quite what it should have been, it was because he was forced to sing against Martin's "rotten" accompaniment.

Before every performance, Jolson was hysterically nervous. He perspired profusely, paced back and forth, and kept up a constant stream of complaints against everybody. Since Martin was always close by, he bore the brunt. I suppose the most accurate description of Jolson's personality is that he was a Harry Cohn with enormous talent. He was just as big a bully, with a little less profanity. They both abused people the same way, especially those in their employ.

We were on the set watching the filming of a large close-up of Larry doing "You Made Me Love You." I heard Al mutter under his breath, "That son of a bitch. Look at him." I couldn't imagine what he could be carping about. Larry wasn't moving anything but his lips. He wasn't making any gestures.

I asked Al, "What's wrong? It looks good to me."

Al replied impatiently, "Not Larry. My son-of-a-bitch brother Harry. Look at him standing there. He thinks this picture should be made about him."

I couldn't believe my ears. Harry was at least five years older than Al and looked even older than that. He had never done anything in show business to merit making a picture about. In fact, I was once told that originally he and Al did a brother act and that Harry was a better singer than Al. Al couldn't tolerate that and he is supposed to have supported Harry all his life—*not* to sing. I'm sure that it never crossed Harry Jolson's mind that a film should be made about him. The only person whose mind it crossed was Al's. He simply had to have something to complain about, and he couldn't pick on Larry that day.

After badgering Cohn, Skolsky, et al. throughout the filming, Jolson finally got his way. They agreed to allow him to do "Swanee" in the picture. A long shot of him performing in blackface on a runway is in the picture. Even to the casual viewer it's obviously not Larry up there. It's Jolson at his most frenetic. If Larry had ever been that hyperactive, Al would probably have shot him.

The film is as biographically accurate as most films of this nature. There are, however, several incidents that are depicted inaccurately.

There is a sequence in which Ruby Keeler, played by Evelyn Keyes, is doing the Gershwin song "Liza" in a stage musical called *Show Girl*. She begins dancing down a flight of stairs made of wooden disks when she suddenly gets frightened and stops. At that point, Jolson, who is in the audience, stands up and sings the song. This gives Keeler enough courage to resume the number. The incident is essentially true, with two important exceptions: Ruby Keeler was never frightened by the stairs, so she never stopped dancing, and Jolson actually got up from his seat and began singing at the very start of the song. It was something he had planned to do all along. Jolson and Keeler were newly married, and I can only surmise that he couldn't stand not sharing his new wife's glory. The incident created much publicity at the time—mostly for Jolson.

In another sequence, Jolson is shown performing in blackface in a stage musical. He interrupts one of the scenes, turns to the audience, and tells them the show is too long. He then summarizes the plot that is to come and asks them if they wouldn't rather hear him sing. The audience and cast respond enthusiastically. The members of the cast then drape themselves around the set, and Jolson sings, presumably for hours.

It actually happened just that way. I met a member of the cast of a Jolson show who said it was terrible because instead of being through around eleven, they were often kept there until one—or as long as Jolson felt like singing. I asked him why he didn't just leave before the singing started. He said one member of the cast did that and was fired.

Jolson, Stoloff, Sidney Buchman, and I had lunch together one day to discuss a scene where a song was needed, a dinner celebrating his parents' fiftieth wedding anniversary. The song was not intended to be the main element of the scene. Its purpose was to tell the audience, through dialogue between Jolson's mother and wife, that he had stopped singing since he had been married. In the background we were to hear Jolson's father, a cantor, and perhaps Jolson, half singing something.

There was nothing in Jolson's repertoire to fit the situation, so a new song would have to be written. Instead, Jolson suggested an old classical waltz that I knew very well, having played it on the mandolin at my bar mitzvah. It was called "Waves of the Blue Danube" and was written by someone called Ivanovici in the last century. Of course, a lyric would be needed. I said I would write it as I had written so many other background songs for Columbia pictures.

I went back to my office and finished the lyric in an hour. I don't mean to suggest that I always worked that quickly, but in this case the lyric came very fast, and I didn't bother to polish it since it was only background music and no one would ever really hear it. I called Sidney on the phone. "I've got the lyric ready."

"Okay. Fine."

"I want you to hear it."

"I haven't got a piano in my office, and I don't have time to go to yours. I'm sure it's good."

"I'm coming up to your office."

I sat on his desk and sang him the lyric. He approved it, only half listening, and suggested I do it for Al. If he liked it, we should record it. That was the end of the meeting.

Al liked it a lot, and I began teaching it to him. He told me immediately that he was going to leave out a couple of words when he recorded it. I didn't mind because I knew that as background music it didn't matter if he sang double-talk. He then asked me, "Does everything you write have to be published by the Columbia publishing company?"

"Yes," I replied.

"Suppose I can get a better deal somewhere else?"

"You'll have to talk to Morris about that."

I neglected to mention that as usual, of course, his name was on the song as one of the writers. I admit I thought he was crazy when he talked about the song being published. A waltz hadn't been a hit in over fifteen years. Why should this particularly long one break the pattern?

He did a touchingly beautiful recording of the song, to a perfect orchestration by Hugo Freidhofer. When we heard it, I should have guessed what was in store, but I didn't. The song was elevated from background music to feature. It was now my turn to complain. If it was going to be that important, I wanted to redo the lyric.

Buchman's answer was "Don't improve it. You'll spoil it."

And that's how "The Anniversary Song" was included in *The Jolson Story*.

For the record, I would like to set down what I dislike about the lyric. The second line is "We vowed our true love, though a word wasn't said." When sung, the accent falls on "love" instead of "true." Lyrics should be able to be spoken, and no one would say that line accenting "love."

Further along, there's a line that goes, "The night seemed to fade into blossoming dawn." Nights don't "fade," meaning to grow dimmer. And why did it "seem" to blossom into dawn? It happens every day, so why did it "seem" to? Then the first syllable of "blossoming" falls on a long note and is a very ugly sound for a singer.

The last line is "We'd find that our love is unaltered by time." In order to sing "unaltered" correctly, the rhythm of the tune must be changed, because the way it is, it is virtually impossible to sing the third syllable of "unaltered" so that it is clear.

What will never cease nagging me is that I was never given the chance to fix the offending lyrics or improve some of the other lines in the song. Buchman's argument that improving it might spoil it was not valid. I think he was so unexpectedly thrilled by Al's recording that he didn't want to touch it. He was afraid that Al couldn't duplicate his performance. The truth is, he was never in better voice than he was during that period. It had become richer and mellower as he grew older.

In light of the ageless popularity of the song, there is little to be said for my argument. However, if I had been permitted to improve the lyrics, the song would be just as popular, and I wouldn't be embarrassed every time I hear it. I learned one important lesson from the experience: Nothing is a throwaway. Everything one creates must be approached as though it were going to be embedded in a time capsule.

After negotiating with every publisher in Tin Pan Alley, Al advised me that Mood Music Co., Columbia's publisher, had met the best offer he could get elsewhere and he was giving them the song. When he told me the deal, I stared at him in disbelief. It was for twice the royalties I had received on any other song. But then I thought, Why shouldn't they be generous? Nothing was going to happen with this long waltz anyhow. They were simply building up some goodwill with Jolson.

At the height of the song's popularity, I received a call from Mood Music. Would I agree to reduce my royalty deal since they were spending so much money plugging the song? I knew that not to be true, because for such a wildfire hit, all they had to do was open the door to their shipping department and make sure there were enough stamps on the material they were sending out. Nevertheless, I agreed to the reduction if Al did, knowing full well that he never would. The reduced deal still left me with more royalties than I had been receiving from other songs.

I was told Al had already agreed. I didn't believe them, so I checked with him. To my consternation, he said it was true and that we shouldn't be selfish and should allow the publisher to make a little money too. A *little* money? It wasn't until after Jolson's death, when some renegotiating had to be done on the song, that I learned that Al had lied to me. He had not agreed to the reduction. He just made sure I did. Nice fella.

At Christmastime Jolson came on the set followed by a short man carrying a valise. It contained the gifts Al was giving to the important people on the picture—actors, director, cameraman, and so on. He then came up to me and asked me if I had a wife. When I said I did, he asked his assistant to open the valise, and he took out two very thin packages. They turned out to contain— hold on—two pairs of nylon stockings! He said, "I was trying to figure out what to get you—a record player or something like that, but I knew you must already have one, so I thought you'd like giving these to your wife. They're hard to get, you know."

Just what I wanted.

It was around this time that he told me about driving back from Palm Springs and passing a place where they had all types of medical equipment. How you happen to pass such a place and notice it I don't know. He stopped the car, went in, and saw this beautiful (his exact word) respirator. On the spur of the moment, he bought it and donated it to the City of Hope. He said it was important to him that no one know about it because then he might be accused of doing it for publicity purposes. I assured him I wouldn't breathe it to a soul.

I didn't have to. A few days later, Louella Parsons's column carried the headline *Jolson Contributes $30,000 Respirator to the City of Hope.* I approved of his donation—but why the secrecy? I'm convinced that were it not for the publicity, he would never have made the contribution. I'm also sure that he knew someone who got it for him at a price less than $30,000.

One can use only superlatives in describing him as a performer. On a night when the Friars Club was staging a huge benefit, he accomplished a feat that no one else could have. Every important star and performer who was alive and well in Los Angeles was on the bill. As a closing act, they chose Jolson. It was generally acknowledged that no act could follow him. Under ordinary circumstances, he would go on at about eleven or eleven-thirty. But something happened that no one could have anticipated. Almost every act stopped the show and did an encore. Among those who performed that night were Judy Garland, Bing Crosby, Kay Thompson and the Williams Brothers, Danny Kaye, and a half dozen others. At about eleven, Jolson started serious pacing, perspiring, and swearing backstage. He cursed every act that did an encore and threatened to leave, which of course everyone knew he would never do. He finally got on at one in the morning.

From the moment he started singing, he had that audience in the palm of his hand. They had been sitting there for five hours, and he made it seem as if the show were just starting. Every act before him was forgotten. At a quarter to three, he had to beg off because he was worn out physically. I believe that the audience would have remained in their seats until nine the next morning if he had chosen to sing that long. There is not now, nor has there ever been, a performer who could have accomplished that.

The Jolson Story was an enormous hit. It won the Academy Award for Best Scoring of a Musical, which really meant it was the best musical of the year. Morris, who received the award, made the following acceptance speech, "The only person I would like to thank is Saul Chaplin."

At the time I was flattered, but now I'm annoyed. If my contribution was that important, and it was, then I should have received the award along with Morris. I never investigated it at the time, but I'm sure Cohn would never have stood for that. He might have had to raise my salary.

The last picture I worked on at Columbia was *Jolson Sings Again*. Before our first recording sessions, Morris and I were summoned to Cohn's office. He gave us rather ghoulish instructions. "I'm gonna spend a lot of money on this picture, and Jolson isn't getting any younger. He could croak on us any time. Go down and record every song he knows just in case we want to make a third picture."

We did just that. We recorded every song he could remember on the pretense that we didn't know precisely which songs we would need for *Jolson Sings Again*. The ones we knew were going to be in the film we recorded with orchestra. For the others, I accompanied him on the piano.

The picture was good, but like almost every sequel, it never recaptured the excitement of the original. After working on that film, I left Columbia and never saw Jolson again. Which was fine with me.

Shortly before I left, on New Year's Eve, Cohn called me. "I'd like you and your wife to come to my house tonight."

"Thanks, but we can't. We're busy."

"What the hell can you be busy with?"

"We're having a New Year's Eve party."

"You—having a party?" Only Cohn would find that hard to believe. "How many people?"

"About twenty."

"Call it off and come to my house."

"I can't do that, but we'll be glad to come any other night."

"Any other night I can't use you."

Chalk one up for his side. I've wondered ever since whether he got a piano player for that night.

My contract at Columbia had expired. I'm sure Harry Cohn never thought I would leave. He figured I would just cool my heels as I had in the past until he got around to negotiating with me. This time, however, he miscalculated. The day after my deal with Columbia ended I went to work at MGM.

I was there for about two weeks when the phone rang. Cohn. "What the hell are you doing there?"

"I work here."

"No you don't. Get your ass right back here."

"I can't—I've got a contract here."

"Don't give me that shit. You belong here."

At last, my big chance to get even: "I guess you can use me now, Harry, can't you."

I'd like to report that it was a victory for me. It wasn't. He hadn't the vaguest notion what I was talking about. He just slammed the phone down.

Harry Cohn died in 1958. There's a story about his funeral that may be apocryphal. The funeral attracted an inordinately large crowd. One of the people attending asked the person standing next to him, "Why do you suppose there are so many people here?"

"Just give people what they want, and they'll always turn out."

I don't know of anyone in Hollywood who was hated by more people than Harry Cohn. There may have been other executives who were as evil as he, but I doubt that any of them was as petty. I concede him his talent for making good, sometimes innovative, and almost always commercial pictures, but that in no way compensates for his cruelty to the people who helped him make those films.

What is probably most deplorable is that he reveled in his unsavory reputation. He knew how he affected people. He is supposed to have remarked that he didn't want his son named Harry Cohn, Jr. because he didn't want him to have to go through life with the burdens of his father's reputation.

There are many atrocities attributed to Cohn, but I can't comment on them because I don't know them to be true. From my own experience with him and his machinations, I earnestly feel that were it not for the fact that he made it possible for some fine films to be made, the world would have been a helluva lot better off without him.

Chapter 11 ■ In February 1949, on the recommendation of Gene Kelly, Betty Comden, Adolph Green, and Roger Edens, the associate producer, I was hired by MGM as vocal arranger for *On the Town*. Ordinarily, accepting such a position would have represented a step backward in my career, but leaving Columbia and working at MGM far outweighed all other considerations. It was also tacitly understood that I would adapt all the dance music for the film. By the time it was finished, I was in fact co-musical director, but my screen credit remained *Vocal Arrangements by Saul Chaplin.*

On the Town
& MGM

After nine years at Columbia, working at MGM was like a special kind of heaven. To begin with, I had only one picture to look after. Only one picture! That hadn't happened to me during my entire tenure at Columbia. And the atmosphere at MGM was relaxed. The studio itself was so much roomier and spread out than the crowded little Columbia lot. The Music Department was housed in cottages, each with two good-sized rooms and baby grand piano. Between these rooms was a small reception room.

There was a kind of camaraderie in the MGM Music Department that couldn't have existed at Columbia. We were always too busy. In the MGM commissary there was a Music Department table. If a nonmusician overheard the conversation during lunch, he would probably think he was listening to a foreign language.

I spent most of my time on the rehearsal stages with Gene because *On the Town* had more than the average number of dance sequences. I would watch him choreograph a section while his rehearsal pianist just played a vamp for rhythm. I would then go back to my office, adapt the Bernstein music, and bring it back to Gene. He would dance to the new music, after which I made whatever changes were necessary. Along with that, I taught the songs to the members of the cast.

Working with Gene Kelly, Frank Sinatra, Jules Munshin, Betty Garrett, Ann Miller, and Vera-Ellen—the cast of *On the Town* —was terrific. Except that Frank didn't always show up for rehearsals on time—or at all. It really didn't matter with the songs because he learned them so quickly. But when his absences affected shooting, it definitely did matter. On several occasions, Gene and Stanley Donen, his codirector, decided to rehearse after the day's shooting was finished. Frank would say he would be there, but he almost never was, having left right after his last shot.

His attitude toward rehearsals is well known. He wants his performances to appear spontaneous and is therefore wary of "overrehearsing." And yet, to my knowledge, Frank has never given a performance on screen or in person where he seemed ill prepared. In fact, I am of the strong opinion that Frank can charm any audience, anywhere, anytime, in good voice or bad, when he chooses to. Unfortunately, he sometimes doesn't choose to.

Ann Miller's featured number in the picture was "Prehistoric Man." The setting was a museum that displayed prehistoric creatures. The other five principals, in addition to doing some small bits, worked behind her. Frank objected to being what he called a chorus boy. Rehearsals went on without him until the matter could be settled.

It finally was when Arthur Freed, the producer of the film, promised Frank that he could sing "Lonely Town" in the picture. It's a beautiful song that was in the stage show but had been dropped when the screenplay was written. Frank then joined the "Prehistoric Man" group, and he and I began rehearsing "Lonely Town." He sang it superbly. Unfortunately, I was the only person who ever heard him do it at that time because Freed didn't keep his promise. The song was never recorded or shot for the film.

Lenny Bernstein was very upset that only three of the songs he had written for the stage version were being used in the film. The remainder of the score was written by Comden, Green, and Edens. Lenny became fearful of how the music of his that was being used would be handled. He sent a wire to Freed, part of which read, "Only Saul Chaplin is authorized to adapt the music I wrote for the stage version of 'On The Town.'" Since that included all the ballet music and most of the background score of the film, I found myself quite busy.

Lennie Hayton, the musical director of the picture, wasn't available to conduct the postscoring session because of a sudden death in his family that required him to fly East. Johnny Green, the head of the Music Department, stepped in and conducted in his place.

Months later, at Academy Award time, Johnny called me into his office. "I phoned Arthur [Freed] and asked him whose name I should submit to the Academy in connection with the music for *On the Town.* He said Lennie Hayton and Roger Edens. I told him that from conducting the score, I knew from the conductor parts that you had done at least half of it and asked whether your name shouldn't also be included. He said he would check with Roger. He called back to say he had talked to Roger and that the names should remain as is—Hayton and Edens. Now, I want you to know that you can sue, and most likely win, because it would be a simple matter to calculate the number of minutes of scoring you did for the picture. But it would most certainly jeopardize your relationship with the Freed unit."

I didn't sue and never said a word about it, but I was deeply hurt that Roger, whom I admired enormously, could be so unfair. The music did win the Academy Award, and once again I was excluded. The only mild satisfaction I got was from Lennie Hayton, who said as I congratulated him, "It really belongs to you." Nevertheless, I didn't get it. Columbia revisited.

In October 1949, Ethel and I were divorced. Ethel and I hadn't been getting along for several years but stayed together because of Judy. She was bright, with a lovely outgoing personality, and was extremely talented in several directions, particularly music and dancing. We were concerned—wrongly, of course—that our separation would affect her adversely. Actually, it was much worse for her to be part of an unhappy household. When we told her that I would no longer be living with them, she was relieved—not because I was leaving but that she was at last being told why we had been behaving so strangely for so long.

I didn't have a lawyer for our divorce. I saw no necessity for one. I wasn't contesting the divorce, and I knew I wasn't about to be cheated. We had only one meeting at her lawyer's office. The terms were agreed upon very quickly: a specified sum for alimony, another sum for child support, our assets to be divided equally, and no special visitation rights. When we first separated, I usually joined Ethel and Judy for dinner once or twice a week. I also had Judy to myself weekends. Several months before Ethel remarried—her new husband was a mutual friend, George (Buddy) Tyne, then only an actor, but today a well-known TV director—she called and told me not to send alimony payments any longer.

Ethel and I remain close friends to this day. But at the time, even under ideal conditions, there was no way of avoiding a feeling of rejection and displacement. My entire lifestyle was changed abruptly. I was suddenly on my own. I rented a furnished one-room apartment, which I loathed. It was a fair-sized room, all white. It was like living inside a piece of chalk. I was constantly lonely, which had nothing to do with being among people. My friends kept me as busy as they could, but it never really helped much.

I was having a very rough time. When I split with Sammy, I had Ethel to turn to. Now I had no one. In fact, Ethel had really run our lives. She took care of our financial matters, our social life, our household—everything. Now I had to face all kinds of decisions I never had to cope with before. As simple a thing as my laundry became a problem. And dinner.

After several years of analysis, I adjusted to a life of single blessedness. One thing I was sure of—I would never marry again. Under no circumstances would I again put myself in a position where my life could be shattered by divorce. Besides, if I couldn't make it with Ethel, with whom I had so much in common, how could I possibly have a successful marriage with anyone else? When I moved out of my white cell and into a house, I gradually began enjoying the advantages of being single. I could live my life at my own pace. I had as active a social life as I chose. I never lacked for female company when I wanted it. I had several married friends whom I called when I didn't want to have dinner alone. I had a succession of excellent housekeepers, who looked after my every need. I had it made.

While I was working on *On the Town,* I signed a contract with MGM and became a member of their Music Department. It was the usual studio contract: They owned everything I did, awake or asleep, except perhaps my breath. The truth is that I would have signed it even if it had included breathing. It was a wonderfully stimulating place to work. Shortly after my deal was made, Johnny Green was appointed head of the Music Department. He instituted a meeting of the entire department every Thursday morning. At these meetings, rehearsal and recording schedules were set, and all musical problems were handled. If an arranger couldn't finish an arrangement on time, he would bring it up at the meeting, and someone would be assigned to help him.

But Johnny's most notable achievement was the department he put together. During one of our meetings, I idly looked around and was overwhelmed at the powerhouse of musical talent assembled in that room. In addition to Johnny, there were Lennie Hayton, Adolph Deutsch, Georgie Stoll, Andre Previn, Miklos Rosza, Bronislaw Kaper, Irving Aaronson, Conrad Salinger, Sandy Courage, Bobby Tucker, Jeff Alexander, David Rose, and Skip Martin.

It is generally conceded that the best film musicals of all time were made at MGM during the fifties. They were produced by Arthur Freed, Jack Cummings, and Joe Pasternak. Each made his own kind of musical, and they were equally successful. With a minimum of watching, it was easy to tell who made what picture.

Arthur's films were slick, stylish, and "now"-looking. His

films were the most innovative. He and Roger Edens were instrumental in bringing a great many new musical talents to the studio, in front of and behind the camera. Among Freed's most famous productions were *Babes in Arms, The Wizard of Oz, For Me and My Gal, Meet Me in St. Louis, The Harvey Girls, The Barkleys of Broadway, Easter Parade, Annie Get Your Gun, On the Town, An American in Paris, Gigi, Show Boat, Royal Wedding,* and perhaps the greatest musical of all time, *Singin' in the Rain.* There were at least a dozen others. In addition, Freed was a highly successful lyricist with many hit songs to his credit: "Singin' in the Rain," "You Are My Lucky Star," "You Were Meant for Me," and dozens more.

He was easy to work for. You were given the widest latitude to be creative, without his interference. At the same time, if he approved of an idea you had that required clearance from the front office because of budgetary or other problems, he fought for it and usually won. He had several maddening idiosyncrasies. While he was being shown a newly choreographed number, he would jingle the coins in his pocket and pay scant attention to what he was there to see.

He was a "selective" name-dropper. He constantly said things like "I spoke to Oscar." That meant Oscar Hammerstein. Or, "Irving called this morning." Irving Berlin. He dropped only the names of executives or songwriters, never movie stars.

One Saturday afternoon, he wandered into Oscar Levant's house while we were watching the Notre Dame–USC football game on television. Arthur asked, "What are you watching?"

Oscar replied, "The Notre Dame–USC football game."

Arthur said, "Oh yeah. L. B. [Mayer] ran it for me last night."

His fingernails were usually filthy. We attributed it to the fact that he was an avid and highly successful grower of orchid plants. One day his nails were surprisingly clean. Oscar had an explanation: "Arthur is so rich that he doesn't get manicures like ordinary mortals. He eats his breakfast with one hand and sticks the other hand out the window. There's a manicurist out there who cleans up that hand. When the other hand has to be done, the whole house is picked up and turned around so that Arthur doesn't have to move. He just changes his eating hand and sticks the other one out the window."

Jack Cummings differed from Freed and Pasternak in that besides musicals he also produced straight dramatic films. Among these were *Romance of Rosy Ridge, The Monte Stratton Story, The Last Time I Saw Paris* (a dramatic film despite its title), and *Teahouse of the August Moon.* He was extremely musical, and many a recording session was called off because he didn't like the orchestration. After a while, we found a way to get around his objections. He always stood alongside the cello section, and if he liked what they were playing, even though it was rarely the tune, he approved of the orchestration. Needless to say, from then on, we paid a good deal of attention to the cellos. In most cases, however, he allowed the creative people to function freely.

Cummings's musicals were not as slick as Freed's, but they were often quite innovative and always entertaining. His most important musicals included *Born to Dance, Broadway Melody of 1939, Bathing Beauty* (Esther Williams's first film), *It Happened in Brooklyn, Fiesta* (Ricardo Montalban's first American feature), *Three Little Words, Kiss Me Kate, Lovely to Look At, Can Can, Interrupted Melody,* and his best musical, *Seven Brides for Seven Brothers.* He made many others.

Someone once said (I think it was Dore Schary, the head of production at MGM), "There's a separate country within MGM called Pasternakia where they make sweet, sentimental, schmaltzy pictures that critics never get very excited about but audiences flock to see." Joe Pasternak's films were at the other end of the spectrum from Arthur Freed's. For the most part—there were important exceptions—they were wholesome and dealt with family relationships. His taste leaned toward operetta, and many of his films featured concert performances by Jose Iturbi, Lauritz Melchior, and Mario Lanza. Among his musicals were *One Hundred Men and a Girl, Anchors Aweigh, That Midnight Kiss*

(Lanza's first picture), *Summer Stock, The Great Caruso, The Merry Widow, The Student Prince, Hit the Deck,* and perhaps his best film, atypical Pasternak, *Love Me or Leave Me.*

Joe Pasternak was a sweet man with a Louis Armstrong speaking voice and a thick Hungarian accent. George Jessel once said about Spyros Skouras, who spoke with an incomprehensible Greek accent, "He's been in this country over thirty years, but when he speaks, he sounds like he's gonna arrive next Wednesday." The same could be said of Joe. Samuel Goldwyn was famous for his Goldwynisms, but Pasternak's speech was sprinkled with as many malaprops as Goldwyn's. I heard him say the following sentence in describing a scene that took place in a barn: "When the girls are in the hay loaf [hayloft], they wear their gunga dins [blue jeans]; then in the evening they change into their carolines [crinolines], but the problem is that the scene needs a better transaction [transition] from the last one." And that was just one sentence.

The one quality that Freed, Pasternak, and Cummings shared was enthusiasm. Every film was approached like a new, exciting adventure. There was an unmentioned rivalry among them but never an out-and-out conflict. Several times two of them wanted a particular actor at the same time, but the problem was always resolved quietly and peacefully. For one thing, accepting a substitute never diminished the quality of the film. A prime example is *Easter Parade,* originally intended for Gene Kelly, Judy Garland, and Cyd Charisse. Gene broke his ankle in a skiing accident and was replaced by Fred Astaire. Cyd Charisse became pregnant, and Ann Miller did the part. The picture was wonderful.

Whether it was by design or accident, I don't know, but L. B. Mayer gradually built up a mind-boggling roster of performing talent. During my tenure at MGM, I worked with Fred Astaire, Gene Kelly, Judy Garland, Frank Sinatra, Jules Munshin, Cyd Charisse, Marge and Gower Champion, Vera-Ellen, Ann Miller, Esther Williams, Debbie Reynolds, Red Skelton, Leslie Caron, Howard Keel, Kathryn Grayson, Jane Powell, Mario Lanza, Ann Blyth, Bob Fosse, Betty Garrett, Gloria de Haven, Carleton Carpenter, Ricardo Montalban, Fernando Lamas, and many others who were not under term contract. They all had one thing in common: They knew how to entertain audiences.

It goes without saying that the same level of talent and expertise prevailed in every other department: choreography, direction, costume and set designing. It was a marvelously stimulating time, and we all knew it and enjoyed it. The result was an incredible body of work—the MGM musicals of the fifties.

Chapter 12 ■ My first assignment under my new MGM contract was *Summer Stock*, a landmark film for me because I was no longer given screen credit as a vocal arranger but as the co–musical director with Johnny Green. Through his recognition I finally achieved screen credit for a function I had been performing for years without credit.

The picture starred Judy Garland, Gene Kelly, and Phil Silvers. It was not an outstanding script, but it was a film that Judy simply had to do. She had recently been replaced in *Annie Get Your Gun* because of severe emotional problems. She hadn't worked in months and had become very heavy. There was a distinct possibility that the MGM executives would never cast her in anything again, so when *Summer Stock* came along, she had to accept the role. She had to prove that she could function through the grueling shooting schedule of an entire musical.

Judy Garland

Gene wasn't wild about the project. He did it for Judy because she was a good friend and because she had helped him enormously during the shooting of his first film, *For Me and My Gal,* in which they costarred. This was an opportunity for him to show his gratitude. As it turned out, he was really put to the test. His patience and indulgence were amazing. Judy obviously could not cope with the daily demands of shooting a film. Her absences became more frequent and of longer duration. Gene, who was forced to endure all kinds of inconveniences, never said a word.

The studio sent for Judy's psychiatrist, who came to the studio with her every day. They both disappeared into her dressing room. After many days when she remained there all day and never came out on the set to shoot, the studio finally decided to close down the picture.

Harry Warren and Mack Gordon wrote the songs for *Summer Stock*. At one point, late in the shooting schedule, it was decided that three additional songs were needed. Because of the many delays, only Warren was available, Mack Gordon having gone on to another assignment. Harry, Jack Brooks, and I wrote "You Wonderful You." Then Harry had to leave. I wrote the other two songs myself. "Heavenly Music" was done by Gene and Phil, a hillbilly-type song in which Gene and Phil, with teeth blacked out, red undershirts, and oversized rubber feet, made barnyard noises while a dozen mangy-looking dogs barked at them. In contrast, the other song, "All for You," was done by Gene and Judy, he in white tie and tails and she in an elegant long black evening gown.

At the time I wrote "All for You," Andre Previn was occupying the other room in my bungalow. When I finished the song, I played it for him. He liked it, and we spent the morning playing it four-hands. That night I went to a crowded, smoky, Hollywood-type cocktail party. I was about to leave when I thought I heard someone whistling the opening phrase of "All for You." I looked around to see who it was, but there was such a mob that it was impossible to tell. I decided I had only imagined it. I was saying good night to my host when I heard it again. After at least an hour of hearing it sporadically, I finally caught the culprit. It was Arthur Jacobs, a casual acquaintance. I grabbed him firmly by the arm and shouted at him, "What are you whistling?"

"I don't know. I whistle all the time."

"Just now you were whistling a certain song. Can you do it again?"

"Oh, you mean—" and he indeed whistled the entire first phrase of "All for You."

"Where did you hear it?" I asked irritably.

"I don't know. It must be a pop tune I heard on the radio."

"Are you sure?" I asked.

"Well, *I* sure as hell didn't write it."

"Yeah—well, I sure as hell thought *I* did," I moaned.

I spent a sleepless night trying to devise ways of changing the melody and retaining the lyric. Nothing sounded right. I got to my office very early the next morning and spent two hours experimenting with changes until I eventually faced the inevitable truth: I had to write a new song. At some point during my struggle, I heard Andre arrive and go into his office.

I was in the midst of writing my new song when he came into my office. "What are you doing?" he asked. I told him of the events of the preceding evening. He burst out laughing.

I was furious. "What the hell is so funny!"

Between bursts of laughter, he explained: "You've been framed, but I never dreamed it would work this well. Arthur Jacobs is a good friend of mine. I knew you were both going to the same cocktail party. I spent most of yesterday afternoon at his office teaching him 'All for You.' He couldn't learn the lyrics, so we decided that he would whistle it. He's such a lousy whistler that I didn't think you'd recognize the tune. But you did, and I think it's hilarious." He dissolved into gales of laughter.

I was so relieved I didn't even get angry. In the cool light of day, I think if I had killed them both, it would have been justifiable homicide.

When *Summer Stock* was finally cut together, it obviously lacked a number by Judy during the finale section. By some miracle, she suddenly reappeared a month and a half after the picture had been shut down. She had shed over fifteen pounds and was in marvelous shape. Her old exuberance was back, and she seemed healthier than ever. When she was told that the studio wanted her to do another number for *Summer Stock,* she was delighted. Rather than have a new song written, she suggested that she do a Ted Koehler–Harold Arlen song that she had always wanted to sing, "Get Happy." I made a three-chorus arrangement for her that ranged over four ascending keys.

Working with Judy was a rare experience. She learned music instantly, as if by magic, and she always got more out of a song than you expected. At the same time, if she made a suggestion that you didn't respond to, she abandoned it immediately. Unfortunately, that is not the case with all singers. Very often, more time is spent discussing than rehearsing. Judy trusted the people she worked with implicitly. She, or whoever was advising her, was very selective about who those people were.

We never did rehearse "Get Happy." When I finished the arrangement, we called her, only to find out that she was ill. She wanted to hear the arrangement anyhow. Chuck Walters (the director of *Summer Stock* and choreographer of "Get Happy") and I went to her house to do it for her. She was lying on a sofa. She loved the arrangement. She kind of mouthed it when I went through it again but didn't sing because she wasn't feeling well enough. I did it a third time, and we left.

That happened on a Friday. The recording session was set for the following Thursday. We suggested that we postpone it, but she wouldn't hear of it. She arrived at the recording session looking pale and tired. With nothing but a lyric sheet in front of her (she couldn't read music), she made a perfect take the third time she sang it. That is a most incredible feat that one has no right to expect from mere mortals. But then, Judy was never "mere" anything.

Luckily, the stage set on which the other finale numbers for the picture had been shot was still standing. The original choreographer, Nick Castle, was gone, so Chuck, who started his career as a dancer-choreographer, staged the number. Judy learned dance routines as quickly as she learned music. "Get Happy" was put together in a comparatively short time. The number, in which Judy wore a black fedora she pushed down over her eyes, was shot in two days and turned out to be the most outstanding in the film. Unfortunately, it was also the last film shot by Judy Garland at MGM after a career that had started in 1936 in a short called *Every Sunday.*

During the shooting, an end-of-the-picture party was held, although the picture was far from finished. It was just that most of the company were being let go. It seemed a logical time for a party. I was sitting quietly when Judy suddenly threw herself into my lap, dug her head into my shoulder, and began weeping uncontrollably about how ugly and untalented she was. That she felt that way was no surprise to me, but that she would have picked me to bare her soul to was unexpected.

I was a good friend of hers, but not a close one. I wasn't willing to meet the demands she expected from her close friends. They had to be at her beck and call at all times. That included long middle-of-the-night telephone conversations when she couldn't sleep or was lonely. They had to be available always to sympathize, cajole, praise, and celebrate her triumphs with her. It was something you had to devote part of your life to, and I wasn't ready for that.

Judy's next film was to be *Royal Wedding* with Fred Astaire. Arthur Freed was the producer, and I was again assigned to work with her. By the time the rehearsal period started, she was once again in the midst of emotional upheavals and rarely showed up. On the few occasions she did, we spent most of the time discussing her problems with the MGM executives. They were watching her closely, and I was told to report to them when she missed rehearsals or was late. I never did.

The time finally came when I was asked point-blank whether she had been to a particular rehearsal. I said she had, but they checked and found out I wasn't being truthful. Missing that one rehearsal, in combination with all the other problems, led the studio to the conclusion that the situation was hopeless. They finally let her go.

Much has been written about Judy's emotional difficulties and her many disastrous marriages, but not enough can be written about her towering talent. She was one of the two greatest performers of all time. The other was Al Jolson. She was an excellent dancer, a beautiful actress, and a most affecting singer— affecting because her vulnerability was evident in everything she sang. And she made you believe every lyric.

Even toward the end of her life, when her voice had lost a

certain amount of quality and her vibrato had become uncontrollable, her audience found her exciting and moving. It's easy to predict that there will never be anyone like her. She was an original, and like all artists of that caliber, they come around only once.

Chapter 13 ■ Arthur Freed activated an idea he had nurtured for a long time: a film based on the George Gershwin orchestral piece *An American in Paris*. The main character and setting were right there in the title, but it obviously needed more than that. As usual, Freed hired an unknown (to films), but extremely talented writer to do the screenplay: Alan Jay Lerner, who had written the Broadway hit musical *Brigadoon*.

Several other facets of the film were clear in Arthur's mind from the very beginning. The songs would be by George and Ira

An American

Gershwin, and a ballet would be created, based on George's *An American in Paris*. He also visualized Gene Kelly as the American.

in Paris

I was assigned to the picture as co-musical director with Johnny Green again.

At a meeting in Freed's office, Alan Lerner related the story he had written for the film to Vincente Minnelli, Gene Kelly, Johnny Green, and me. Minnelli was another Freed import. A highly regarded scenic designer for many Broadway shows, he left his position as art director and producer of the stage shows at the Radio City Music Hall to come to Hollywood, where he became a highly regarded director. Out of the ensuing discussion came several very exciting ideas: a search would be made to find a French dancer to play opposite Gene; the score would consist of known, unknown, published, and unpublished Gershwin songs; the *American in Paris* ballet would be choreographed by Gene; Oscar Levant, the Gershwins' close friend, would play the concert pianist; and Gene, Vincente, and I would have sessions at Ira Gershwin's house to go through the entire Gershwin catalog from which we would assemble the score.

Gene and Vincente were concerned with more than just the music, so I had many sessions with Ira alone. Every ten days or so we would all meet at Ira's, and I would play the songs we thought should be considered for various spots in the picture. By an odd coincidence, we all picked the same love song before we ever even met with Ira: "Love Is Here to Stay," the last song that George wrote. There were several others that simply had to be used: "I Got Rhythm," "Embraceable You," "S'Wonderful," and Vincente's favorite, "I'll Build a Stairway to Paradise."

I met with Ira at least three times a week and always had a marvelous time. Going through the lesser-known and unpublished works of the Gershwins was like walking into a hitherto undiscovered gold mine. I would play an obscure song and say, "We have to use this." Then I'd play another and say, "This song just has to be in the picture." By this process, I wound up with a score of about twenty-five songs—more than three times the usual number—in addition to the standards that had to be included. We used a hitherto unknown song called "Tra La La" and one that was relatively unknown, "By Strauss," from a show called *The Show Is On,* which had been directed on the stage in 1936 by Vincente Minnelli.

Before rehearsals could get under way, a leading lady had to be found. Gene went off to Paris and looked up an eighteen-year-old gamin named Leslie Caron he had seen dance several years earlier. She was a featured dancer in the Ballet des Champs Elysée. Gene immediately knew he had found his leading lady and made an extensive test of her. When it was shown at the studio, the reaction was unanimous: She was not only ideal for the picture; she was obviously a "find." She was sent for and put under long-term contact. MGM had done it again—another outstanding musical artist added to its illustrious roster.

On a bright, sunny Sunday afternoon, Leslie Caron and her mother made their first appearance in Hollywood—in Gene's backyard. Her mother, an American, was attractive and stylishly dressed, which was not true of Leslie. For some unfathomable reason, she decided she should look older. She wore one of her mother's dresses and had on much too much makeup. She looked like a young girl playing dress-up.

But what came through in spite of that was her charming face and her appealing manner. She was a bit shy and bewildered at what had happened to her so suddenly: from a dancer in a French ballet company to the lead in a large MGM musical in a few short weeks. But there was no question that she was the perfect Lise to Gene's Jerry Mulligan in *American in Paris*.

Rehearsals went smoothly until Gene began choreographing "By Strauss." It featured Gene, George Guetary (a French musical comedy star), and Oscar Levant. Since Oscar was at the piano during the entire number, he played it like a true Viennese waltz with all its hesitations and accents. Gene objected. It didn't fit what he had in mind. What started as a normal discussion soon turned into a shouting match, with Gene threatening to hit Oscar, who threatened to sue Gene if he did. Now it seems quite laughable, but not then. It was a confrontation between Gene's Irish temper and Oscar's resistance to having his expertise questioned. Oscar finally stormed out of the rehearsal hall.

He returned the next day as though nothing had happened. What is surprising is that neither of them won or lost the argument. They both really wanted the same thing but could not admit it the day before. From then on, they were friends, and the incident was never mentioned again.

Oscar was exceptionally intelligent, knowledgeable, witty, clever, talented, eccentric, neurotic, moody, unpredictable, provoking—the most stimulating person I've ever known. I would rather spend a few hours with Oscar when he was in a proper mood than a whole day with the brightest person I know. But he was strange. It was a strangeness you learned to expect and eventually ignore.

On occasion, for example, he drove me home from the studio. But he would never drop me in front of my door, even though it was not out of his way. It was just that I lived on Olympic Boulevard, a taboo street to him. That meant that he had once had an unpleasant experience on that street and would never drive on it again. Many streets and houses fell into that category.

One afternoon during the shooting of the film Oscar found he had some time off. He called and asked me to have coffee with him. Incidentally, he was never without a cigarette and a cup of coffee. I went to the set to pick him up. As we were leaving, the assistant director said, "Oscar, you have about two hours off, but don't come back to this stage. We're moving to Stage twenty-seven, so go there."

I said, "Okay. No matter where we go, we'll end up on twenty-seven."

As we were walking toward the commissary, Oscar asked, "What did you tell the assistant?"

"You were there. I said that no matter where we went, we would go to Stage twenty-seven in two hours."

"That's not what you said. I want you to repeat it exactly."

I, of course, knew what he objected to. I had used the words "end up." To him that meant death, with which he was constantly preoccupied. I was determined not to give in. I adamantly refused to say it again. We spent a miserable hour together during which he never stopped badgering me to repeat exactly what I had said.

A solution suddenly hit me. "I know what I must have said. 'No matter where we go, we'll wind up on twenty-seven.'" After forcing me to swear that that was what I said, he accepted it as the truth. "Wind up" was not quite as final as "end up" in Oscar's mind.

He was a world-class hypochondriac who practiced his craft continuously. Hardly an hour passed that he wasn't complaining of some ailment, real or imagined. He took his pulse whenever he thought of it, and he thought of it often. If it was faster than he expected, he immediately sat down and assumed his "I'm dying" position.

Every morning he described in lurid detail his bouts of the night before with his wife, June. I'm sure many of them were imagined and all exaggerated. He claimed one time that she had thrown a knife at him that hit him in the leg. He limped that day, but whatever wound had been inflicted had miraculously healed by the following morning.

He was constantly popping the newest mind-altering pills before they were put on the market. One could never sympathize with him because it would preclude all other conversation. I'm not sure he ever expected sympathy.

Besides playing Gershwin expertly, he was an excellent concert pianist. One night Adolph Green and I went to his house and walked into his darkened living room where the only light was on Oscar at the piano. He was playing Brahms. He didn't know we were there, so we just stood in the dark while he played. I have never heard those pieces played more beautifully. They were full of a sensitivity and gentleness that belied the personality Oscar projected to the world. Yet several of his fingers were always covered with Band-Aids. He had cut them playing his piano in his music room. Many of the ivories that cover the keys on that piano were off, and striking the rough surfaces underneath had a tendency to cut the fingers. He obviously took out his aggressions on that piano.

Oscar's quick wit has been widely recognized. He got off some of his funniest lines at the most unexpected times. After the last recording session of *On the Town*, Lennie Hayton, Roger Edens, Connie Salinger, the arranger, and I decided to celebrate by having lunch at Romanoff's, the most expensive restaurant in town. To make it even more festive, we each ordered a drink. Well, Connie had a lot of drinks. In fact, he got plastered. Oscar appeared from nowhere and sat down next to Connie, who draped himself all over Oscar and in a thick drunken mumble said, "Oscar, whadaya say we get drunk?" Oscar shot back, "Connie, you're living in a flashback."

Oscar's contributions to *American in Paris* were considerable. One of Arthur Freed's ideas was to have him play a medley of Gershwin tunes. Oscar would have played them marvelously, but the idea was not very original. Oscar then came up with the wonderfully innovative notion of playing the *Concerto in F,* where he played all the instruments in the orchestra, conducted, and was in the audience applauding himself. It was shot in a yellow, misty haze—Vincente's idea and one of the high points of the film.

Oscar's performance in the picture is excellent, partially due to his inventiveness. There is a scene where he is sitting between Gene and George Guetary at a small café table. They are singing "S'Wonderful" to express their deep love for their sweethearts. What Oscar knows and they don't is that they are singing about the same girl. To hide his nervousness, he smokes a cigarette and drinks a cup of coffee at the same time. His fumbling with the cup and the cigarette and trying to appear nonchalant at the same time is comparable to some of the best silent-screen comedy. It is unfortunate that his only serious scene, with Nina Foch, was cut. In it he displayed what a sensitive actor he could be.

It would be unfair to write about Levant without mentioning his interests besides music and himself. He was a voracious reader, knowledgeable about art, and an avid sports fan. In fact, he never ceased to amaze me by coming up with things like Ty Cobb's lifetime batting average or Red Grange's longest run. He was a most attentive father, extremely proud of his three daughters. Despite the evidence to the contrary, I believe he felt a great affection for June. That's only conjecture because it was a side of him he never displayed in public. It must be assumed that she was willing to endure his obsessive neuroses and weird behavior because they were married for many years until Oscar died.

The *American in Paris* ballet was a risky venture, even for MGM. It was budgeted for $500,000. No musical sequence that was pure dance had ever cost anywhere near that amount. Never before had an audience been asked to watch a seventeen-and-a-half-minute ballet at the end of a film. I am not suggesting that the studio made the decision to do the ballet without a lot of corporate soul-searching. There was formidable opposition to its cost and length from the New York executives, but in the end the talents of Arthur Freed, Vincente Minnelli, and Gene Kelly prevailed. By coincidence, a film called *Red Shoes,* which also had a seventeen-minute ballet, was released at that time, and it was doing well at the box office, so the anxiety about our ballet subsided somewhat.

The backgrounds for the ballet were to be different sections of Paris, as represented by French painters. But how? That took many meetings with Vincente, Gene, and Irene Sharaff, an extremely gifted costume designer. They finally decided that it should reprise Gene's relationship with Leslie throughout the picture. The backgrounds were to be done in the styles of Dufy, Utrillo, Renoir, Rousseau, Van Gogh, and Toulouse-Lautrec. When that was settled, everything started in earnest. Sets were planned, costume sketches drawn, budgets for the various elements made, and we began dealing with the music.

During the shooting of the film proper, I made myself thoroughly familiar with every note and nuance of Gershwin's *An American in Paris*. In addition to playing and studying the music and the score, I played every record of it I could find. Gene was doing the same thing, but obviously on a much smaller scale. Then came the nightly meetings during which Gene, his assistants Jeanne Coyne (later to become Gene's wife) and Carol Haney, and I began to match the sections of the music with the painters who had been selected.

At our very first session we faced our first problem. The painters were to be represented one at a time, so that if we chose a musical theme for Dufy, we should not use it again during the section when the background was by Van Gogh. But Gershwin's music intermingled the themes constantly. Also, Gene wanted the Toulouse-Lautrec section, which would employ jazz, to come toward the finish. In the original piece it comes very early. What it all meant was that more adapting would be necessary than I had anticipated.

I had great trepidations about repositioning and adapting Gershwin's themes. I regard his serious music with the same respect I feel for the music of any other important classical composer. I identify with him even more, because his roots are in jazz, which I was brought up with and understand. In fact, he was the first composer who made American jazz an acceptable art form, to be played in concert halls all over the world. I felt his music should be played the way he wrote it. And yet there was I, about to tamper with it. Every time I made a change, I was haunted: Would Gershwin approve?

I established my headquarters on Gene's rehearsal stage again (two were used) and proceeded to work on the ballet. We used two pianos so that Gene would be able to hear every note that would be in the orchestration. Every time I moved a theme or motif from one place in the music to another or repeated it, a new transition was needed to connect one with the other. I tried to make these transitions sound as though Gershwin had originally written them that way. Whether it all succeeds as music, I'm in no position to judge, but I do know that it serves the ballet well.

Of all the seventeen-and-a-half minutes of music I adapted, there was one small section of only sixteen bars that I was proudest of. In it I was sure I had captured exactly what Gershwin would have done. It was a variation on the blues theme that I felt he could have written. Gene choreographed a sensuous dance to fit it. But the inevitable happened. Of the entire seventeen-and-a-half minutes of music, that was the only section cut. It was the kind of frustrating experience that every composer who works in films has to learn to endure. Occasionally his best efforts are left on the cutting-room floor.

The background music for the film obviously had to be based on the Gershwin songs that were in the picture, and his orchestral suite *An American in Paris* had to be used for the ballet. I used the walking theme from *American in Paris* for the main title but added a simple, unobtrusive piano figure to the original orchestration because Gershwin was always closely associated with the piano.

When I walked on the recording stage amid the cacophony of the orchestra tuning up, I could hear the piano figure being practiced over and over again. I couldn't understand why something so simple had to be practiced. I went over to Jacob Gimpel, a fine concert pianist, and asked him if there was a problem.

"There sure is!" he said. "It's unplayable! Did you write this?"

"Yes."

"Then let me see you play it."

He got up. I sat down and played it.

Now he was really annoyed. "What kind of fingering is that? You don't finger it, you just move your hands! I can't play like that!"

"Okay," I said, "I'll change it."

"Never mind. I'll figure out something."

I don't know what he did, but he played it. I never thought my unorthodox fingering, the result of being a self-taught pianist, would haunt me after so many years.

The first sneak of the film was at the Crown Theatre in Pasadena. It was a disaster. There was something wrong with the theater's sound system. The dialogue was totally incomprehensible, and the music sounded as if it were coming from an early twenties radio, static and all. To this day, I don't know why the picture wasn't turned off, unless it was because we all unconsciously hoped that the problem would correct itself. Of course, it never did. We all just sat there, numb.

We went back to Ira Gershwin's house after the preview, dismally depressed. We were so high on the picture and found it difficult to believe what we had just gone through. There was no audience response to anything. They neither applauded nor booed. We tried to console ourselves with the knowledge that the film had been shown under impossible conditions, but it didn't help much. It was decided to hold another preview as soon as possible in another theater.

It was shown again within a week, and this time the audience went wild. They applauded almost every number and had a marvelous time. We were euphoric. The only place they did not applaud was after the ballet, but we knew why. It ends with the camera fading down to a single rose that Gene holds in his hand. I matched this quiet ending by writing a quiet ending to the music. The audience wanted to applaud but didn't know where because the music never spelled out "The End." We rescored the finish by using Gershwin's original ending of his symphonic suite. Audiences have never failed to applaud the ballet ever since.

At Academy Award time, it was nominated in seven categories and won all but one. Vincente Minnelli did not win for his direction, which was bitterly disappointing. How could anyone vote for it as Best Picture of the Year and not recognize Vincente's obvious contribution? George Stevens won for *A Place in the Sun*. That night, Arthur Freed received the Thalberg Award, and Gene was given a special award "for his brilliant achievement in the art of choreography on film." It was a triumphant evening.

Johnny and I had been nominated in the Best Scoring of a Musical category, but our competition was fierce. We were competing against our own colleagues, who had done two very impressive musicals at MGM that year—*The Great Caruso* and *Showboat*. Both were enormously popular. I sat there with sweaty palms waiting for the seemingly endless show to wind down to our category. Then I thought that on the off chance that we might win, I'd better prepare something to say. I decided on "There are many people responsible for our winning this award, but I would like to confine my thanks to the two men without whom this picture could never even have been planned—George and Ira Gershwin."

I kept repeating the speech over and over to myself. I was in a kind of haze when I heard Donald O'Connor announce that Johnny and I were the winners. I ran up to the edge of the stage and waited for Johnny to leave the pit (he had been conducting the show that night) to join me. When we both got to the microphone, Johnny motioned for me to speak first.

As I was about to say my piece, Donald handed me the Oscar— my first, finally! I was so surprised at how heavy it was that I almost fell over. Gone was my composure, along with my speech. After ten seconds of silence, I managed to mumble, "Thank you very much."

I was glad to get that much out. I was told that Johnny said something very complimentary about me, but I never heard it.

Chapter 14 ■ After *An American in Paris,* I helped out on two other films: *Two Weeks with Love* and *Three Little Words.* *Two Weeks* had a score that consisted of already published material. The producer was looking for a novelty song for Debbie Reynolds and Carleton Carpenter.

Three Little Words, Lovely to Look At, Kiss Me Kate, & Seven Brides for Seven Brothers

I remembered a vaudevillian I had seen many years before who did a song I liked, "Aba Daba Honeymoon." I had always thought it was special material that had been written for him. In rummaging through some old sheet music in the MGM music library, I was surprised to find a published copy of it. I suggested it for Debbie and Carleton. The producer liked it, and I made an arrangement and taught it to them. It was used in the film and was later released as a record that turned out to be a big hit.

Three Little Words was based on the lives of Bert Kalmar and Harry Ruby, the successful songwriter-librettists for many Broadway shows and later for films. The picture starred Fred Astaire as Kalmar and Red Skelton as Ruby.

At my very first rehearsal with Red, he was hardly in the door of my office when he asked, "What time is it?"

"I've got ten-thirty, but don't count on it," I replied. "My watch doesn't run right, and I haven't had time to get it fixed."

"Here," he said as he handed me an oblong leather case.

I opened it, and there was an elegant gold wristwatch. "It's beautiful," I said as I started handing it back to him.

"No, it's for you," he said as he pushed it back to me. "I always meant to get you a present for what you and Sammy did for me in the old days at Vitaphone." Sammy and I had been responsible for getting Red a series of shorts.

I was flabbergasted. I had never gotten anything but an end-of-the-picture gift from an actor before. It was a rare expression of gratitude, and I was very touched.

Rehearsals with Red and Fred were hilarious. Fred was rather proper. Not only did he never use off-color language, but he was embarrassed by it. That was all the ammunition Red needed. His speech was an endless outpouring of profanity from then on. He would even insert it in the middle of ordinary English words. The word *sensational* became *sen-fucking-sational*. Fred simply laughed uncomfortably. After a while he got used to Red's language, and it didn't phase him. So Red stopped. The only times Red became dead serious was when he and Fred rehearsed their songs.

One of the riches I acquired from working on *Three Little Words* was my friendship with the legendary Harry Ruby. He was talented and intelligent, a fascinating storyteller with a wry, offbeat sense of humor. He was once described by George S. Kaufman as looking like a dishonest Abe Lincoln. He was tall and thin, and had an angular, Lincolnesque face, without the chin whiskers. His manner was gentle, and in the years I knew him I never heard him say an unkind word about anyone.

Ruby was as famous for his idiosyncrasies as he was for his accomplishments. He never learned to drive a car. When he wanted to go someplace, he would stand on the corner of the block where he lived. Invariably someone he knew would drive by, pick him up, and take him to where he wanted to go. He always looked down at the sidewalk when he walked, searching for lost coins. He said he had been doing that since childhood, having come from a very poor family. He claimed to have found money every day. I was with him once when he found a nickel. He looked at me. "See?"

One night we were at a large party. He motioned to me from across the room that he wanted to talk to me. I made my way through the crowd to where he was standing, surrounded by people. He excused himself, took me by the arm, and walked me to a corner of the room.

He looked both ways to make certain that no one could overhear him, then whispered in my ear: "Do you think this is a good time for a hit picture?"

A group of us lunched together every day. Our conversations ranged over every subject imaginable. One day we were talking about suicide. Harry's contribution: "During my twenties I constantly thought of committing suicide."

"So why didn't you?"

"Well, I was out of town so much."

He was away from the studio for several weeks, during which time one of the MGM executives had been discharged.

"How did they do it?" Harry asked. "Just tell him he was fired?"

"Oh no. They paid off his contract to the penny—gave him a million dollars in cash and a five percent interest in the fifty pictures that were made while he was here."

"That'll teach the son of a bitch!" said Harry.

Harry was on the set almost daily. Every time Red saw him, he asked, "How do I feel today?"

Gene Kelly and I had just begun to go through the catalog of songs by Arthur Freed and Nacio Herb Brown to put together the score for *Singin' in the Rain* when I was made assistant-associate to Jack Cummings. He had complained to Dore Schary, the head of production, that Freed had Roger Edens, that Pasternak had an able assistant (Irving Aaronson), but that he had no one. He requested that I be assigned to him as an assistant-associate on a permanent basis, and Schary agreed.

I had ambivalent feelings about the promotion. It meant leaving the Freed unit, where we all knew each other so well and enjoyed working together. At the same time it represented a promotion and a little more authority. I never yearned for power, to hire and fire people, but I always wanted authority so that there were fewer critics above me who could tamper with my work. However, there was never any question of my accepting the new assignment. I knew Jack, liked him, and felt sure we would get along well.

My first film under this new arrangement was *Lovely to Look At*. The cast consisted of Howard Keel, Kathryn Grayson, Marge and Gower Champion, Red Skelton, Ann Miller, and Zsa Zsa Gabor in her first American film. It's interesting to note that with the exception of Zsa Zsa, every member of the cast was under long-term contract to the studio. It was a remake of *Roberta*, a film that had been done almost twenty years earlier. The magnificent score had music by Jerome Kern and lyrics by Otto Harbach and Dorothy Fields. Harry Ruby was a cowriter of the screenplay.

Jack Cummings was married to Jerome Kern's daughter, Betty, who had divorced Artie Shaw. Cummings had more than the usual interest in the film, particularly the music. I got into trouble at our very first recording: Kathryn Grayson, singing "Smoke Gets in Your Eyes." Jack came to an early rehearsal and hated the orchestration. What's more, he was right. Kern had written certain musical figures that were part of the song and were not used in our version. When we first laid out the number, I had raised some objections to changing these figures but acceded to the arranger's more modern version because I didn't want to appear too authoritative or dictatorial. None of that altered the fact that it was clearly my fault for allowing it. The recording date was called off, and the song was rerecorded the following week with a proper orchestration. It was not an auspicious beginning for me.

Things ran smoothly from then on with no unanticipated problems. We knew that there was no comedy song in the score for Red and that he would perform one of his own. I knew that

Kathryn Grayson often slid into high notes and that these slides would have to be cut out of her sound tracks. We knew that Ann Miller, with whom I had worked at Columbia, would always ask to do everything "just one more time" and that after she reached a certain point, she never improved. But most important, Jack got a brilliant notion that helped us avoid a potential difficulty— the picture's fashion-show finale, which was as important to *Lovely to Look At* as the ballet was to *An American in Paris.* Jack felt that Mervyn LeRoy, who was the director of the movie, was not the ideal person to do the fashion show. He wanted Vincente Minnelli to direct it and Tony Duquette to do the decor. He knew that they would come up with a fresh concept and give the sequence the kind of style and chic it required. Minnelli and Duquette were both available and agreeable.

Jack had to clear it with the studio, Mervyn LeRoy, and the Art Department, since a studio art director had done the rest of the picture. Eventually he got the studio to OK the added expense. Mervyn recognized Vincente's unique talent for this particular kind of sequence, and our art director worked along with Tony Duquette. I don't know whether it was by agreement, but on the screen the credit is *Fashion Show by Tony Duquette.* There is no mention of Vincente.

After *Lovely to Look At,* I was assigned to the film of Cole Porter's smash Broadway musical *Kiss Me Kate.* Andre Previn and I were co–musical directors. *Kiss Me Kate* was the only full-length musical to be filmed in 3-D. By the time the film was ready for release, the 3-D fad was over, so the film was never released that way.

Cole Porter's score for *Kiss Me Kate* is one of his best. Years later, he told me that only twice in his career did the theater critics unanimously praise a score of his. One of those was for *Kiss Me Kate,* the other for *Anything Goes.* Yet the hit song that emerged from the film was not originally from *Kiss Me Kate* but from a flop Porter musical, *Out of This World.* I had interpolated the song, "From This Moment On," because there was nothing in the *Kiss Me Kate* score to accommodate a number we wanted to do with three dancing couples.

One of the couples was Carol Haney and Bob Fosse. Their two-minute section, choreographed by Fosse, was very exciting. Bob's unique style, even this early in his career, was easily recognizable: economical movement, intensely rhythmic, sharp and sexy. It was by far the best dancing in the film, the rest of which was choreographed by Hermes Pan.

When *Kiss Me Kate* was released, Robert Griffith and Harold Prince were planning to produce their first Broadway show, *Pajama Game*. They asked Jerry Robbins to do the choreography, but he turned it down. He suggested they hire Bob Fosse. He went even further: If Griffith and Prince didn't like Fosse's work, Robbins would take over. Fosse's two-minute number in *Kiss Me Kate* convinced Robbins that Fosse was the right man for the show. Robbins's advice proved right because Fosse went on to win the Tony Award that season for his choreography of *Pajama Game*.

One of the first things Bob did when he got to New York to work on *Pajama Game* was send for Carol Haney. He cast her in the show, and she was a smash. One night she sprained her ankle on stage and couldn't perform the next night. Her understudy replaced her. As fate would have it, Hal Wallis, a very important Hollywood executive and producer at Warner Bros., was in the audience. He was so impressed by the understudy that he immediately arranged for her to be placed under term contract to the studio. The understudy was Shirley MacLaine.

Shirley, of course, has enjoyed a highly successful career in the theater, movies, and nightclubs, and as an author. Bob Fosse went on to direct or choreograph such shows as *Damn Yankees*, *Bells Are Ringing*, and *Pippin*, and films like *Sweet Charity*, *Lenny*, and *All That Jazz*. It's amazing that Carol Haney, Bob Fosse, and Shirley got their start from a two-minute sequence in a film that ran 109 minutes.

In a sense, *Kiss Me Kate* was the end of an era for me. It was the last of fourteen Ann Miller films I was associated with. Ann was at Columbia for eight of the nine years I was there and moved to MGM a year before I did. Of all the Ann Miller films, the only title worth remembering is *On the Town* at MGM. At Columbia, I worked on such Ann Miller efforts as *Reveille with Beverly* and *Eve Knew Her Apples*.

Ann Miller's lightning-fast tap routines lit up many a dull movie musical. I always thought she was a true original until I met Eleanor Powell, the legendary MGM tap-dancing star of the 1930s and 1940s. She told me that everything Ann Miller did was stolen from her.

At Academy Award time, Andre Previn and I were nominated in the Best Scoring of a Musical category for *Kiss Me Kate*.

In the meantime it was rough living in Hollywood during the early fifties because of the Communist witch-hunts. It was dangerous to be anything but an archconservative Republican. The group I ran with and I were all liberal Democrats. We had worked for liberal causes and belonged to left-wing organizations. Several of my friends might even have been Communists, but I wasn't aware of it, and nothing could have been less important. We were all working for social changes we felt would benefit our country.

Then suddenly just admitting that could easily result in your being hauled up before a congressional committee who sat like supergods controlling your future. It was living in fear of being persecuted for having committed no crime.

Although I was never called up before one of the committees, I had a small sample of the aftermath. Sol Kaplan, a fine composer of movie scores and a good friend of mine, did appear, and he was an unfriendly witness. The next day one of the Los Angeles newspapers described him as "the tall, blond musical director at MGM." Sol and I looked nothing alike. He was about three inches shorter than I, weighed about twenty pounds more, and had dark brown hair. Obviously the reporter hadn't attended the hearings but knew that Sol Kaplan, composer, was testifying and assumed it was I. For several days thereafter, my friends at the studio acted peculiarly toward me. When I approached groups of people, their conversations stopped. I was stared at no matter where I went. I had to go to each person separately and explain the error. For some reason, I felt that by having to explain it, I was letting Sol down in some way. It was, at best, degrading.

During this unpleasant period, MGM bought a short story called "Sobbin' Women" by Stephen Vincent Benét for $1,500. It was such perfect picture material that several producers, including Freed and Cummings, went after it to do as a musical. Jack must have been very persuasive because he succeeded in having the studio assign it to him. He gathered together the creative people who would work on the film: Frances Goodrich, Albert Hackett, and Dorothy Kingsley to write it; Stanley Donen to direct; Johnny Mercer and Gene De Paul to write the score; and Michael Kidd to choreograph. I assisted Jack and was co–musical director with Adolph Deutsch.

The story, which takes place in the nineteenth century, deals with seven brothers who are backwoodsmen in Oregon and are lonesome for female company. They kidnap six girls from the closest town to make them their brides. The seventh (Jane Powell) goes willingly. This naturally angers the townspeople, who try to rescue them.

It was decided to cast the picture with the best dancers that could be found anywhere. The studio okayed the idea, with two conditions: first, Jane Powell and Howard Keel had to star in the film, which was fine with us; second, we had to use actors who were under contract to the studio but not working, which was not so fine with us. There were quite a few young actors and actresses under contract. But we got lucky. The only two who weren't working at the time were Jeff Richards and Russ Tamblyn.

Having seen Jeff Richards in other films, we knew he couldn't dance, but we knew nothing of Russ Tamblyn. We asked him to come in so we could find out what he could do. He caught up with us while we were in the office of the Make-up Department.

It was a cold day, and he was dressed warmly: heavy boots, overcoat, and muffler.

"Can you dance?" asked Michael Kidd.

"Na-a-a. But I can do a few tricks," he replied.

"Like what?"

"Let's see. A back flip."

"We might be able to use a back flip."

Before Michael finished his sentence, Russ slowly pulled himself up from the couch he was slouching in and did a perfect back flip, his overcoat, muffler, and boots flying.

We howled with laughter, and he didn't understand why. "You asked for a back flip, so I did a back flip. I can do other things too, like a back somersault—"

Michael yelled, "Not now! Please!"

It turned out that he had been a champion gymnast in school. He learned to dance for the picture.

Four male dancers had to be cast to join Howard Keel, Jeff Richards, and Russ Tamblyn. That was relatively easy because Michael and Stanley knew the best male dancers available: Tommy Rall, Matt Mattox, Mark Platt, and Jacques D'Amboise, who arranged to get a leave of absence from the New York City Ballet Company. Auditions were held to cast the dancers who played townspeople.

We needed six girl dancers who along with Jane Powell would be our seven brides. After several auditions, five were hired: Virginia Gibson, Nancy Kilgus, Betty Carr, Ruta Kilmonis (now Ruta Lee), and Norma Doggett, who left a New York show to do the picture. For the sixth girl, Michael wanted someone tall; since they were all unknowns, there was a danger that they might look alike to audiences. More auditions were held, with unfruitful results. Either they couldn't dance well enough, or they weren't attractive.

This search for dancers was taking place during the summer when my daughter, Judy, who was living in New York with Ethel and her husband, Buddy Tyne, was staying with me. Judy was an excellent ballet dancer and always looked forward to coming to Los Angeles so that she could take classes with her original ballet teacher, Carmelita Maracci.

At dinner one night, I happened to mention that we were looking for a tall, beautiful dancer. She said there was just such a girl in her ballet class. I ignored her. What would a fourteen-year-old know about tall, beautiful dancers? Over the next few days, she mentioned it several times until finally, to mollify her, I told her to ask the girl to get in touch with Michael at the studio. A few days later Michael called me. Judy was right! The girl was perfect. Tall, beautiful, terrific figure, and a very good dancer. Her name was Julie Newmeyer—now Julie Newmar.

After the casting was completed, another problem had to be dealt with. How would an audience distinguish between the brothers and the townspeople? Someone—I think it was Stanley—suggested that the seven brothers be redheads. It was a brilliant idea, except to the brothers. They had to have their hair dyed every few weeks, and apparently there was some pain connected with it. They never stopped complaining. Especially Russ.

All rehearsals, of anything, go through the same progression. Everything is interesting and exciting in the beginning, but the endless repetition becomes a crashing bore. Except for *Seven Brides for Seven Brothers*. Watching so many extraordinarily talented dancers never became dull.

When they weren't rehearsing, they were challenging each other. Tommy Rall refused to recognize the fact that Russ could do more improbable things with his body than he could. Every few days Russ would come in with some new impossible stunt to show Tommy, who couldn't rest until he had mastered it, which he always did. We stood on the sidelines, watching apprehensively. We were convinced that it was only a matter of time before one or the other would do serious injury to himself and be lost to the picture. All that happened was a few minor sprains, which neither Russ nor Tommy admitted to.

The sneak preview of *Seven Brides* happened to occur when

the New York executives of MGM were visiting Hollywood, and they all attended. They were overwhelmed at how well the picture played. They had expected the usual Howard Keel–Jane Powell picture and had made a release schedule to accommodate such a film. Now they had to rethink their entire plan. The picture opened at Radio City Music Hall, where most MGM musicals played, and broke all records to that time for number of weeks played and grosses.

At Academy Award time, Adolph Deutsch and I were nominated for Best Scoring of a Musical. The competition was stiff because the other four nominated musicals were also extremely popular: *A Star Is Born, Carmen Jones, There's No Business Like Show Business,* and *The Glenn Miller Story.*

MGM had been nominated in fourteen different categories that year. The music awards are always toward the end of the presentation. I sat there as winner after winner ran up to the stage to accept an Oscar. Not a single one was for an MGM film. I was now sure we weren't going to win. I relaxed. Then Donald O'Connor announced, "The winners are Saul Chaplin and Adolph Deutsch for *Seven Brides for Seven Brothers.*" I still didn't move, until Adolph, who was sitting behind me, nudged me. Then I suddenly realized that we had won. We each said "Thank you" and proceeded backstage to the press area where we were interviewed and had our pictures taken.

In the crowd I spotted Sammy Cahn, Oscar in hand, waiting to be photographed. He and Jule Styne had won in the Best Song category for "Three Coins in a Fountain." We hadn't seen each other for a very long time, and it was nice to meet again under such happy circumstances. We congratulated each other warmly and went our separate ways.

Chapter 15 ■ Sol C. Siegal had been a successful producer before he brought his independent production company to MGM. He had contracted to make a number of films for them, the first of which was to be *High Society*, a musical remake of Phillip Barrie's play *The Philadelphia Story*. I was being loaned out to Siegal to work on *High Society*. Sol was a pleasant, affable, dignified-looking man who would be perfectly cast as the president of U.S. Steel. With his ever-present cigar and imposing manner, he was about as executive-looking as you can get.

High Society

When he told me my first assignment, I immediately wanted out. He said as he handed me a script, "This is a first draft. You'll find indications of where the songs are supposed to go, but we don't have any yet. Cole Porter is writing the score. He's been at it for several months, and we've yet to receive anything from him. That's where you come in. I'd like you to go to New York and find out what's holding him up. Maybe you can help him."

Help him! He'd done pretty well without me for all those years. Why would he suddenly need me now? Besides, he is one of my idols, and you don't tell your idol how and what to write. That's chutzpah to the nth degree. I hoped against hope as I asked Sol, "Does he approve of my coming?"

"He doesn't know it yet, but I'll call him and let him know."

"Maybe he won't go for it."

"Cole? He'll welcome you with open arms."

I arrived in New York, checked in at the Plaza Hotel, and called Miss Smith, Cole Porter's secretary. She said Mr. Porter was expecting my call and would like to see me at three the following afternoon. I spent that entire morning reading and re-reading the script, and came to an important decision regarding my attitude toward the songs: I was going to approve everything Porter played for me because I probably would like whatever he had written, and if I didn't, I didn't have the guts to tell him. I certainly valued his opinions over my own when it came to songs. But what if he really hadn't written any? I knew I couldn't handle that. All I could do was hope that that wasn't the case.

I got to his thirty-third-floor apartment at the Waldorf Towers promptly at three. The door was open, and his man, Paul, was there to greet me. He ushered me into a spacious, elegant living room and said Mr. Porter would join me momentarily. I hardly had a chance to admire the beautiful brocaded walls and the exquisite objets d'art on the end tables when he appeared.

He walked toward me, his hand extended, smiling warmly. I was surprised at how slight he was and that he limped so badly despite the fact that he was using a cane. We sat down on a sofa and chatted about goings-on at the studio: *Kiss Me Kate* (which he knew I had worked on), pop tunes, and other matters of mutual interest. His friendly manner relaxed me. It was like catching up on what's new with an old friend.

He then moved to one of his two grand pianos and played a song for me that he had written for a particular scene in *High Society*. His method of demonstrating was interesting. He first played two choruses of the music alone. The third time he sang the lyrics. He maintained that it was unreasonable to expect anyone to listen to a new song and assimilate the words and music at the same time, so he first familiarized his listener with the tune, then sang the words.

The song he played was lovely, as I knew it would be, but I didn't feel it was quite right for the situation in the picture. I wasn't about to tell him that, and I confined my reaction to telling him what a beautiful song it was.

He played it again. I feigned even more enthusiasm than before. At that point he asked me to join him on the sofa. "I can tell from your reaction that you have certain reservations about the song." I started to protest, but he interrupted. "Oh, I don't doubt that you like it, but not completely. Now if we're to work together, you must give me your honest criticism. If I think you're right, I'll either change the song or write a new one. If I don't agree, we'll use the song as I wrote it. Now, what do you really think?"

I was ecstatic. Never before—or since, for that matter—had a songwriter offered such flexibility. Usually they go to the mat fighting for what they wrote. There are, of course, exceptions. I understand Jule Styne writes an entirely new song with very little protest rather than make changes in one he has already written. I explained that we—Siegal, Chuck Walters, the director, and I—felt that a song that sounded old-fashioned would be effective in that particular scene and that while the song he had just played was beautiful, it was a bit more sophisticated than what we had hoped for. We then read the scene where the song was to be used, and he agreed that a simple song would be more appropriate.

At our next session, three days later, he played his new song, "True Love," the hit of the picture. And of course it was perfect for the scene.

That same afternoon he asked me whether I would like to go to the theater with him the following week. I said an embarrassingly quick yes. He asked me what show I would like to see, and I told him I was having difficulty getting tickets for the new Lawrence and Lee play, *Inherit the Wind.* He said he was sure that that would be no problem and arranged for us to go the following Tuesday evening. I was to come to his apartment at seven—"We'll dine first." I don't know whether it was coincidence, but every time I went to the theater with Cole, it was on a Tuesday night.

As we rode down the elevator, I noticed that he had a hat but no overcoat, although the weather was bitterly cold. When I asked him about it, he said he wouldn't need one. When we got to the street, I understood why. There at the curb was his limousine with the chauffeur holding the door open. It was no more than three or four steps from the building to the warm, comfortable limo. The chauffeur had apparently been told of our plans because he drove us directly to the Chambord restaurant without instruction from Cole.

We were led to a table near the front. This was obviously arranged so that Cole wouldn't have too far to walk. I later learned that he had a similar table at every restaurant he frequented.

I shall never forget our conversation at that first dinner. We talked about songwriters. He was extraordinarily generous about his colleagues. I told him that I had been impressed by a story Johnny Mercer had told me. When Johnny had his very first hit, a song called "Here Come the British with a Bang Bang," he received a most complimentary note from Cole, whom he had never met. Cole couldn't understand why I was impressed by his congratulating a fellow songwriter. When I pointed out that no other songwriter alive would have done it, he didn't believe me.

We spoke of everyone and eventually got around to Irving Berlin. I related a ritual I had seen Berlin go through many times when I first started as a songwriter. At that time, Sammy and I virtually lived in a music store on Forty-sixth Street and Broadway. At least once a week, Berlin would come in, rub his fingers over the sheet music of his songs in the rack, and leave. The manager of the store explained to us that he was checking on which of his songs were selling and which weren't. If there was dust on the outside copy, nobody was buying that song, and he would immediately lambaste the manager of his publishing firm.

At that point, Cole admitted that he occasionally found Berlin slightly annoying because every time they met, Berlin would ask him, "What's the name of that lo-o-o-o-ong song of yours?" When the question was first asked, Cole would answer, "'Begin the Beguine.'" But after the first four or five times, he simply responded by smiling.

Our car drove up to the front of the theater—in the red zone—and parked. I was about to get out when Cole motioned for me to wait. We sat in the cozy warmth of the car until the crowd that had been milling about in front of the theater went in. Cole then said, "Now." I got out and held his arm as he did. He put his hand lightly on my shoulder, and we walked to our seats, which were in the third row on the aisle. As the curtain came down at the end of the first act, we proceeded up the aisle ahead of the rest of the audience and went back to the limo, still parked in front. We spent the intermission there chatting about the play. We repeated this procedure between the second and third acts—a civilized way to attend the theater.

Inherit the Wind was about the famous Scopes trial in which Clarence Darrow was pitted against William Jennings Bryan, arguing the right of a teacher to teach the theory of evolution as opposed to the Bible's explanation of the origin of mankind. It was one of the most famous trials in the history of jurisprudence, but Cole had never heard of it. There's every chance that during the time of the trial, he was living in his villa in Venice or château outside Paris. But he had such an insatiable intellectual curiosity about everything that I found it surprising that he didn't know of the trial.

When we discussed the content of songs to be written for *High Society*, we met in his library. Like all the other rooms in the apartment, it was elegant, beautifully appointed, and comfortable. On one wall there were silver (or could they have been chrome?) bookshelves from the floor to the ceiling containing reference books. Opposite it was his specially built sofa. The seat was extended so that he could stretch his legs straight out without bending his knees. That took all pressure off them. At his left, within easy reach, were a radio, cigarette box, ashtray, pads and pencils, phones with buzzer and intercom. On his right, laid out neatly, were all the daily newspapers, current issues of *Life, Time, Look,* and so on, and whatever books or articles he was interested in at the moment.

At the session after we had attended *Inherit the Wind,* I noted that along with the usual newspapers and magazines were two books on the Scopes trial, another on Darwin, and at least a dozen clippings from newspapers of the time reporting the trial. He said he was sure that the play only scratched the surface of the events that must have taken place and wanted to know more about the entire subject. He probably did almost as much research as Jerry Lawrence and Bob Lee had in writing the play.

I stayed in New York for about three weeks, during which time my working relationship with Cole became easy and enjoyable.

At one session he played eight bars of a new song he was writing and asked me whether I thought it was good enough for him to finish. Unfortunately, he could no longer play well enough for me to tell what it was like. I asked him whether he had the eight bars written down. He produced a manuscript with the most neatly written music I have ever seen. It was as carefully and meticulously done as his songs. I played the eight bars through twice, then said enthusiastically, "Finish it! Finish it! It's marvelous! I can't wait to see what you do with it!" It became a song called "I Love You, Samantha," sung by Bing Crosby, and although it wasn't a hit, it is my favorite from the score of *High Society*.

What was most fascinating about Cole was that despite his urbanity, he was hopelessly addicted to several radio soap operas, and he never missed $64,000 Question on TV. On one occasion he insisted that we stop working to watch it.

I had the most elegant lunches and dinners with Cole at his Waldorf Towers apartment and his luxurious home in Brentwood, California. There was always a fancy handwritten menu at each place. I never had to look at it because as soon as we sat down, Cole recited what was on it. He would say something like "We're having a little soup—then some lamb—a small salad—dessert—a little cheese and coffee." I found it odd that despite the fact that there were just two of us, the table was always set for four. When I first noticed it, I thought it was impolite for us to start before his other guests arrived. I soon learned there were no other guests. I could never determine why the extra place settings were there, unless Cole disliked looking at a partially bare tablecloth.

By the time I left New York, Cole had finished all the songs for the film except one, a comedy duet to be sung by Bing Crosby and Frank Sinatra. Cole made several tries at it, but none of them was right. One of the reasons he was having difficulty was that the scene indicated for the song made no story point; it was inserted so that Bing and Frank could do a number together. The scene had them both at an elegant Newport society party where they happen to wander into a room containing a bar. There's nothing particularly funny about that. Yet a song for Bing and Frank was a must.

Sol Siegal and Chuck Walters were delighted with the songs I brought back from New York, but we were still concerned about the elusive comedy song. I had a published copy of Cole Porter's lyrics on my desk for several weeks but had never opened it. I thought that maybe if I looked at some of his old lyrics, an idea for the elusive song would come to me. I was just about to look at it when I was called to a story conference in Siegal's office. Without thinking, I took the book with me.

When I got to Sol's office, he had someone with him, and I had to wait. As I sat outside his office, I idly opened the book somewhere around the middle. When I looked at the lyric in front of me, I couldn't believe it. There on page 44 was a song called "Well, Did You Evah?" ("What a Swell Party This Is"). It satirized the insipid small talk that high society indulged in at parties and how they nonchalantly ignored everything from the least important events to horrendous disasters.

I burst into Siegal's office, yelling, "I found it! I found it!" forgetting completely that he had a visitor. He was just leaving. I'm sure he thought I was out of my mind. I think I was. I tried to apologize, but Sol laughed and introduced me to his stockbroker. After he left, I showed Sol the lyrics: "I don't know what the tune is like, but I don't care if it sounds like a prehistoric fertility dance. It's perfect!"

I asked the Music Department to locate a copy of the song, which they did immediately simply by going to their files. It was from a Cole Porter show called *Du Barry Was a Lady*, which MGM had made as a movie twelve years earlier. A more incredible coincidence is that it was introduced by Chuck Walters, the director of *High Society*. He later recalled dancing to it with Betty Grable in the show but never remembered singing it.

I called Cole and gave him the triumphant news. He was as

relieved as we were. I asked him whether it would be even better if he wrote some new lyrics for part of the first chorus that would pertain directly to our characters. He replied that yes, it would be better, and why didn't I write them and send him a copy of what I wrote.

The prospect of writing lyrics for Cole Porter was frightening in the extreme. I didn't know of any professional lyricist who could write as he did, and I knew that I most certainly couldn't. But he kept insisting that it would at least give him an exact idea of what the new lyrics should be like. I agreed. I agonized over each syllable for days, then sent him an example of the kind of lyrics I thought we needed, along with a covering letter of apology for everything but my very existence. I got the reply I should have expected, knowing Cole. My lyrics were fine. He suggested one minor change, but if I preferred my version, it was OK with him.

In the film we did a reprise of the song, for which we needed added lyrics. Once again, I contacted Cole with exactly the same results, but this time he didn't even suggest any changes.

I hasten to add that I don't for one instant believe I can write lyrics like Cole Porter's; nor do I believe that the parts I wrote wouldn't have been better if he had written them. He was aware, however, that I knew exactly what was required and if changes had to be made, I was right there to make them.

To be able to cast Frank Sinatra and Bing Crosby in the same picture was something of a coup at that time. It would never have happened if Frank had not pulled a Sinatraism (a *Sinatraism* can be loosely defined as something "only Frank Sinatra would do"). In this case he had been cast to play the lead in the film version of Rodgers and Hammerstein's *Carousel.* Everything was fine until he arrived on location where the film was to be shot. I was told that he didn't like the place and simply left. I could just imagine him looking around the place and saying, "Oh, brother." His objection had nothing to do with whether the location was right for the film, more with his lifestyle. He couldn't see himself spending several months in what I understand was a rather bucolic environment.

He found himself back in Hollywood without a film to do and with further proof of his already tarnished reputation as difficult to work with. At that most propitious moment, Sol Siegal offered him *High Society*. That has to be counted as one of the luckier breaks in Sinatra's undulating career. Not only did it reestablish him as employable, but the picture he was being offered was much better for him than the one he had walked away from. He would be working with Bing Crosby (his idol), Celeste Holm, and Grace Kelly in a funny movie with songs by Cole Porter. What singer could ask for more? And to make it even more attractive, the entire film was to be shot at the studio.

Several weeks before rehearsals started, Cole gave a luncheon at his Brentwood, California, home for Sol Siegal, Chuck Walters, Frank Sinatra, Bing Crosby, and me at which Cole and I demonstrated the score at his twin grand pianos. It was received with great enthusiasm, but what disturbed me was that Frank addressed Cole as "Coley" all afternoon. That seemed too familiar, considering that they had just met. I remained behind after the others had left and asked Cole, "Did you mind Frank's calling you 'Coley'?"

"No. In fact, I rather enjoyed it."

"Why?"

"It reminded me of Linda. Whenever I did something she didn't approve of, she called me 'Coley.'"

Linda was his wife, who had died some years earlier. The only painting hanging in his Waldorf Towers apartment was a large, beautiful portrait of the elegant Linda. That was the closest he ever came to reminiscing. He spoke either of the present or future, never the past.

It amazes me to this day that not once during the many times I was with Cole did he complain about the constant pain he was suffering from the emaciated leg that was almost useless to him. It had to be massaged every day since the horseback-riding accident some twenty years earlier. As part of his therapy, he also swam in his pool every day when he was in California. To keep friends from dropping in during these periods, he devised a system. He installed a flagpole near his pool and hoisted a flag when he was swimming. Friends knew that he wasn't available while the flag was flying.

For anyone else, having a single flag to fly every day would have sufficed, but not for Cole. He acquired the flags of every state in the Union and most of the countries of the world. He would fly the flag of a particular state on the date it was admitted to the Union. He applied a similar principle to the flags of foreign countries. For example, on July 14, Bastille Day, the French flag would be run up; on July 4, the American flag. When he couldn't find a meaningful event, he flew the California flag or one from an obscure country that had somehow come into his possession.

Of all the films I've been associated with, *High Society* was the most pleasant. What else could it be when it involved working with Crosby, Sinatra, Louis Armstrong, Celeste Holm, and Grace Kelly? The respect and admiration they had for one another was something to behold. Even Frank changed. He still came late to rehearsals, but he occasionally felt guilty about it, especially when it involved the number he was doing with Bing, who was always prepared. Frank would pull me aside during a break, and we would go to a piano elsewhere so I could teach him what he had to learn to catch up. Heretofore, such behavior by Frank was unheard of.

In most cases in the past, I had made vocal arrangements before the rehearsal period started. In *High Society,* two of the arrangements were put together on the rehearsal stage. I made a complete vocal arrangement for "Well, Did You Evah?" but Bing and Frank decided to indulge in some light banter between the lines. They were both so good at it that to this day I'm not sure we chose their best lines for the final version.

The other arrangement manufactured at rehearsals was "Now

You Has Jazz." Cole, aware that he knew very little about the subject, prevailed upon his friend Fred Astaire to take him to a couple of jazz clubs. He became familiar enough with musicians' jargon to learn that a piano was called a "box," a trombone a "bone," drums "skins," and so on. He wrote a clever song using this language, demonstrating how a jazz band is formed. It was fine as far as it went but needed a lot more musical material to make it a complete number. It was to be done by Bing and Louis Armstrong and his band.

We held two-hour rehearsal sessions every afternoon for a week. They were the equivalent of jam sessions based on the tune. Whenever Johnny Green, co–musical director, could free himself, he would join the group. Among us, we put the number together. Bing, Louis, and I ad-libbed extra lyrics—with Cole's permission, of course. He even ok'd a word Louis said that doesn't exist in any language. I tried to get Louis to say the Italian *arriverderci,* but what came out was "averaduci." Coming from him, it sounded right.

Princess Grace of Monaco is the only monarch ever to have recorded a million-copy seller. The song was "True Love," which she sang with Bing. In the beginning it was assumed that her voice would be dubbed by a professional singer. But when I rehearsed with her, I realized that while she could never carve out a career as a singer, her voice had a sweet, innocent quality that would blend perfectly with Bing's. I devised the arrangement so that she never had to carry the tune by herself. Either she sang in unison with Bing or did a harmony part. The track that resulted had a pleasant, relaxed feeling that had great appeal and made it a hit record.

I was determined to keep Cole apprised of everything that went on during the rehearsals and filming so that when he finally saw the picture, there would be no "surprises." I kept up a steady correspondence with him in which I detailed the changes being made. He in turn wrote me his reactions. In one, he wrote that he was worried about "the great waves of enthusiasm" that I was expressing for the entire project. It had been his experience that this often led to disaster. *High Society* was the exception.

Most of his letters concerned minor lyric changes, but there was one letter that I shall cherish forever. I received it after I had sent him sound-track records of the entire score. I know that quoting it is immodest, but in this case my pride takes precedence, so here it is:

Feb. 1, 1956

Dear Saul,

The recordings arrived last night. They are dreams of beauty, and throughout every number I feel your infinite care. Also, as I wrote to Johnny Green, they are *not* over-orchestrated. Even Louis Armstrong's diction is good. I don't see how you did it all.

My congratulations and gratitude.

Your pal,
Cole

Apparently the Academy membership agreed with him because they nominated Johnny and me for our work on *High Society.*

Chapter 16 ■ About a year later I was back in New York working with Cole on the score of the film *Les Girls*. As a result of the success of *High Society* and at the suggestion of Sol Siegal, I was elevated to associate producer of the picture. That meant that in addition to my involvement with music, I was now also concerned with such things as sets, costumes, shooting schedules, and costs. I therefore had less time to spend with Cole.

I was distressed to find Cole frailer than he had been on my last visit. He wasn't walking as well and occasionally had to use two canes to get around. We had our usual lunches and dinners, but not as frequently, and I was alarmed at how little he ate. He just picked at the minuscule portions that were set before him. Often it seemed he was just there to keep me company.

Les Girls

& Can Can

His mind, however, was not frailer. He was as alert, articulate, and witty as ever. Since I was not a member of his jet set and knew none of his friends, our areas of conversation were limited, as usual, to studio gossip, the theater, and songs and songwriters. He hadn't been going out as often as in the past, and he asked me in detail about the shows I had seen. I described a musical I had attended the previous evening that I thought had a bad score. Cole would have none of it. He said he knew of the writer's earlier work and was sure that I was being too harsh. I also knew of the writer's earlier work, which I considered terrible, but there was no way of convincing Cole, so I just dropped it.

Les Girls was about a dance act that consisted of a man and three girls. It starred Gene Kelly, Mitzi Gaynor, Taina Elg, and Kay Kendall, the only nondancer among them. Yet such was her magnetism—today it's called charisma—that when the three girls danced together, all eyes were riveted on her. Kay, who later married Rex Harrison, was tall, not overly pretty, but very stylish. She was a wonderful light comedienne who had never been in a musical. She loved doing it, but because of her insecurity as a dancer, she often complained that she had been miscast. Of course, there was no way that she would give up the role. Actually, Jack Cole and Gene, who choreographed the picture, never gave her anything to do she couldn't handle.

She was one of those rare people who make you feel you're old friends from the moment you meet them. She was a delight to be around. Occasionally she displayed a surprisingly violent temper, but only with Gene, an old friend from the year and half he had spent working in London. They would disappear into one of their dressing rooms and scream at each other, using the foulest language imaginable. I never knew what prompted the arguments, but I'm quite certain they had nothing to do with the film. Just when we thought that there would be no more shooting that day, they would emerge arm-in-arm, laughing and joking as though what they had just indulged in was normal behavior. For them, it was.

Every once in a while she would appear for rehearsal and say she couldn't dance because her legs ached and were swollen. Since we could never see the swelling, we put it down to her nervousness about dancing. Or perhaps she had a muscle strain because she wasn't accustomed to this kind of physical activity. The fact is, she was having early symptoms of leukemia, which took her life two years later when she was thirty-three.

The last Cole Porter film for which I was associate producer and music supervisor was *Can Can,* several years later. It was made at Twentieth Century–Fox and marked my reunion with Jack Cummings. It starred Frank Sinatra, Shirley MacLaine, Maurice Chevalier, and Louis Jourdan. There was another part for a female dancer, which was originally to be played by Barrie Chase, who was under contract to Fox. However, she had attained a certain fame from having been Fred Astaire's dancing partner on TV and wanted her part made larger or she wouldn't do the film. The studio refused to accommodate her, and a replacement had to be found. Hermes Pan, the choreographer of the movie, suggested a girl from South Africa he had recently worked with in Europe. Her pictures were sent for, and after the decision makers saw them, she was hired. Hermes had made an excellent choice, because she's a marvelous performer—Juliet Prowse.

She had only one scene of consequence in the film, but what a fateful scene it was. It included Frank Sinatra singing "It's All Right with Me" to her. Earlier in the week he had recorded it at one of those magical sessions that happened only with him. He walked onto the scoring stage and asked Nelson Riddle to run down the orchestral accompaniment. After hearing it, he stood with his hands in his pockets, his hat tilted back, and sang it into the mike. Before it was even played back, he said, "That's it" and left the stage. He was right. In his single rendition he had not only sung the song flawlessly but had also captured the emotion required by the scene. The wonder is that he knew it without having to hear it played back.

The scene called for Sinatra to be drowning his sorrow in drink at a bar in an empty cabaret because he had just broken up with his girl. One of the dancers who works at the club, Juliet Prowse, appears and tries to console him. He sings the song to her, which says in essence, "You're not the girl I'd prefer to be with, but you do have a pretty face, and maybe spending some time with you can help me forget her, so it's all right with me." From the moment he first saw Juliet descending the wide staircase in the cabaret set, he must have felt something, because we could all see him turn on the charm. And when Sinatra turns on the charm, he is irresistible to everybody and everything.

What followed were several years of stormy romance. As for Juliet, through Frank she met everyone in the business, and I'm sure it quickened her success considerably. There's no doubt that she would have been successful without Frank because of her startling figure and enormous talent as a dancer, but having her name linked with his made her an instant celebrity people wanted to see.

Not everything went smoothly with Frank on the film. One day I received a call that he wanted to see me in his dressing room. Cummings was out of town, or he would have received the call. Frank had the script open and pointed to one of the pages as he said, "I don't like this scene."

"What's wrong with it?"

"The speeches are too long."

I looked at the scene. The speeches didn't seem inordinately long, but I knew I'd get nowhere if I said that. I opted for "I suppose Charlie wanted them that way."

"Well, I won't say them. I'll get the sense of the scene without saying all those words."

I called Charles Lederer, the screenplay writer, and asked him to get to the studio as quickly as possible because we were holding up shooting until this matter was settled. In less than ten minutes, Charlie appeared at Frank's dressing room, dressed in pajamas, bedroom slippers, and a brown felt hat. He asked, "Is this quick enough?" I explained the problem. Charlie, Frank, and I worked on the scene, making the speeches shorter.

Yet when it was shot, Frank ignored the changes and did it his way. The scene worked, but it would have been funnier if he had used the rewritten version. Lederer is a better writer than Sinatra.

Several Cole Porter songs that hadn't been written for *Can Can* were used in the film. Among these was "Let's Do It." It was decided, however, that the original lyrics were too well known and that new ones should be written. I wrote to Cole, and within a week I received a letter from Miss Smith. Cole wasn't well and suggested as usual that I do the rewrite and let him see it when I was through.

No force on earth could have induced me to attempt to match Cole's wit. But I knew one lyricist who could: Ira Gershwin. I called and asked him if he would be interested. "Okay," he replied. "Come over tonight about ten o'clock."

"No," I said. "First, I want to call your agent, Irving Lazar, and make a deal for you to write the new lyrics."

"You don't have to call Irving. I'm doing it for you, not for anyone else."

"But, Ira, this is not *my* picture. It's Fox, and you should be paid."

"I'm not doing it for Fox. I'm doing it for you."

I continued insisting that he had to be paid, and he kept refusing until he finally said, "Look. Why don't you come over tonight, and we'll work something out."

I arrived at Ira's just as he, his wife, Lee, and several of their dinner guests were finishing their coffee. He excused himself and led me upstairs to his study. For the next hour and a half, I watched him work with words, phrases, and ideas as if they were playthings until he had put together two choruses of delightfully charming and witty lyrics. What was most marvelous about what he had done was that they sounded like Cole. I was thrilled and once more brought up the subject of his fee. He said we would discuss it some other time because he had guests waiting downstairs. It was then clear that he would never accept any kind of payment.

I was excited when I went to the rehearsal stage the next day. I was about to tell Frank about Ira's lyrics when he handed me two pages and said, "Here are the new lyrics for 'Let's Do It.' Sammy wrote them." Again I tried to tell him about Ira's lyrics, but he interrupted with "Read them. They're very funny. They're perfect for Shirley and me."

I knew then that it was hopeless. Having asked Sammy Cahn to write new lyrics, Frank could not very well go back and tell him they weren't being used because someone else had written better ones. I was sure Sammy would not object because I knew he admired Ira's work, but Frank would never put himself in a position where he asked for a favor that was granted and then turned it down.

I was now in the unhappy position of having asked Ira to write lyrics—which he did, free—and not only not using them but using someone else's. I didn't know how to tell him, and I didn't until many years later. I did buy him an elegant, expensive gift. I couldn't have the studio pay for it, because if he had found out, it would have upset him. Besides, he did it for me, not the studio.

One of the stipulations in Frank's contract was that he had to work only from one in the afternoon to seven in the evening. Our starting time was eleven in the morning, and between then and one, scenes that didn't include him were filmed. We were shooting on the large cabaret set with about two hundred extras one day. It was almost one, and Frank still hadn't arrived. It happened to be a memorable day for the city of Los Angeles. For the first time in its history, its baseball team, the Los Angeles Dodgers, was playing a World Series game at the Los Angeles Coliseum against the Chicago White Sox.

There was such excitement about it that a TV set was installed on the set so that everyone could watch the game between shots. At the start of the telecast, the announcer described the festive atmosphere at the Coliseum. He also mentioned that only in Los Angeles would so many motion-picture stars attend a baseball game. The camera showed the stars in the crowd, and there, big as life, was Frank Sinatra. His manager later said that Frank hadn't gone to the studio because he disapproved of the scene he was scheduled to shoot. That seemed unlikely. When it was shot with him the next day, not a word of the scene had been changed.

The film was shot during the late summer while my daughter, Judy, was staying with me. In discussing the picture with her one night at dinner, I mentioned that Hermes Pan was having trouble finding dancers who would be able to do the can-can as he had planned. It finished with the girls jumping in the air and landing in a split. I knew Judy could do it, but since she had never danced professionally, I didn't know whether she'd be interested. She said she would like to audition for it.

I knew she would get no special consideration, but to make sure, I went to Hermes and told him that her audition was to be the same as all the other girls'. If he hired her, he could not later come to me and say he'd made a mistake. Until the day and time of the audition arrived, Judy and I were nervous wrecks. When it was over, Hermes called me. "I'm glad to have her. She's as good as most of the dancers I've hired and better than some. She'll be fine."

She fell in with the other dancers as if they'd known each other for years. They sometimes made her uncomfortable, however, because they brought her all their complaints in hopes that her father, the associate producer, would take care of them. Their most constant gripe was the classic one: The costumes were too heavy to dance in.

I courageously transmitted the complaint to Irene Sharaff, the costume designer. She told me off in no uncertain terms: All dancers are children who have no regard for anything except their own comfort. They don't give a damn about how the costumes look. They're overpaid for what they do. I never approached her again, although Judy made me hold up the can-can costume once. It was so heavy, I don't know how they even walked in them, much less danced.

Can Can will be best remembered as the film that was visited by Nikita Khrushchev. The "Can Can" number, which had already been shot, was restaged for him as an example of a flashy American production number. For security reasons, he was seated on a small balcony overlooking the stage. Part of the number had the dancers lying on their backs kicking up their legs. It was shot for the film from floor level so that all that could be seen was legs kicking into the air. From Khrushchev's overhead view, however, he looked down on two lines of underwear. He was understandably offended. Newspapers and magazines all over the world reported his assessment of what he had witnessed: "tasteless and obscene."

Nor did the gala luncheon given for him in the Fox commissary improve matters. In attendance were all the important executives and movie stars in Hollywood. After the coffee was served, the speeches began. Spyros Skouras, the head of Twentieth Century–Fox, made a ten-minute speech of greeting that was almost completely unintelligible because of his thick Greek accent. He was followed by several other industry leaders, a representative of the actors, and George Jessel. I don't know why George was included—perhaps to add humor to the occasion, which it sadly lacked.

Finally Khrushchev was introduced. He spoke for a very short time and confined his remarks to thanking his hosts. If the celebration had ended there, it would have been fine, but Skouras then went back to the mike and said, "Mr. Chairman. What a wonderful country this is. I came here as a poor boy of eleven from Greece, and today I am the head of this whole studio."

Khrushchev followed him to the mike and replied, "I am the son of a poor miner, and today I am the head of a whole country." It was not a banner day for Twentieth Century–Fox, or for Hollywood.

Every time I was in New York in succeeding years, I called Cole, and he almost always invited me to dinner. We spent marvelous evenings together, except for the final one. Since I had last seen him, he had had his right leg amputated and had undergone surgery for ulcers. Nevertheless, I wasn't prepared for the kind of evening that awaited me.

I was greeted at the door by his man, Paul, as usual. But this time, before he ushered me in to see Cole, he whispered that when he announced dinner, I was to busy myself looking at the bookshelves and not come to the table until he came for me. It seemed a rather odd request, but of course I would obey it. He then led me to Cole.

He was obviously ill. His face was ashen, and he was frighteningly thin. He had a drink in one hand and a cigarette in the other. He forced a smile, although it was easy to see that he was in pain. After our usual small talk, he suddenly launched into a detailed description of the misfortunes that had befallen him. It was the first and only time that he had even remotely spoken of his health to me, and I found it unsettling.

He had a half smile on his face and spoke in a quiet, uncomplaining voice, which made what he was telling me even sadder. He said he was having terrible pains in the part of his leg that had been amputated. The knowledge that it was common among amputees and was known as "phantom pain" didn't help. Nor did the pain pills he was taking. Also, he had been fitted for an artificial limb that he simply couldn't learn to use. He had been told it would require practice, but he doubted that practice would do any good. I sat there stunned and saddened by what he was telling me. His speech was rather thick, and he had difficulty pronouncing certain words. Was it from the drugs he was taking or the alcohol? I don't know. I was full of compassion and close to tears when Paul appeared and announced dinner.

I dutifully walked to the bookshelves and looked at the books without seeing them. I waited an interminable time, then slowly turned my head and peeked at what was going on. I saw Paul carrying Cole to the dinner table and seating him in a chair—a sight that Cole never intended for me to see. I felt as if I were betraying a trust. In fact, I'm sorry I saw it because it has lingered with me for all these years and never fails to depress me. I snapped my head back just as Paul asked me to join Cole.

Dinner started as usual with Cole reciting the menu. It was just as well, because I was in such a state, I could think of nothing to say. It was a most difficult dinner because he kept closing his eyes and apparently falling asleep. I didn't know whether to leave or continue talking. I did the latter. It was the right choice because every time he opened his eyes, he seemed to know what I had been talking about. That night I ate almost as little as he did. The dinner finally over, I left his apartment with a heavy heart. I had a premonition that it was the last time I would see him.

The next morning I received a call from Cole's secretary, Miss Smith. She asked me how it had gone the previous night. I described the evening in detail. She asked whether Cole smoked or drank. When I told her that he had done both, she wasn't pleased. He wasn't supposed to. She was pleased, however, when I said I didn't leave until eleven-thirty. It was the latest he'd been up in months. Until our dinner, he hadn't entertained for a long time, and she hoped that maybe after last night he would resume a more normal life. She added that Cole must have enjoyed the evening to have allowed me to stay so late. I hoped she was right.

Cole Porter died on October 15, 1964. The world lost a genius, and I lost a treasured friend. His genius as a songwriter needs no corroboration from me, but as a friend and idol, he is irreplaceable—stimulating as a companion and gracious and generous as a collaborator. I shall always be grateful that my career led me to him, and to this day I still miss him. I'm sure I always will.

Chapter 17 ■ The last film I worked on at MGM was *Merry Andrew.* That was in 1958, more than nine years after I had started there on *On the Town.* I was back with Sol Siegal. The director and choreographer was my close friend Michael Kidd. It starred Danny Kaye and Pier Angeli. I was the associate producer and I also wrote the songs with Johnny Mercer.

Collaborating with Johnny was a revelation. He was acknowledged to be one of the most innovative lyricists—"Come Rain or Come Shine," "Blues in the Night," "Accentuate the Positive"—

My Last
Picture
at MGM

and working with him confirmed it. He never chose the obvious idea to write about, and having chosen his subject matter, never wrote it in an obvious way.

Danny Kaye played an English college professor who among other subjects taught mathematics. Only Johnny would have thought of writing a song called "The Square of the Hypotenuse of a Right Triangle Is Equal to the Sum of the Squares of the Two Adjacent Sides." (For the uninitiated, that is the Pythagorean theorem.) Incidentally, I consider setting that title to music one of the major achievements of my songwriting career.

Johnny had one maddening idiosyncrasy. Often when we were working together he would lean his head back, close his eyes, and seem to be asleep. I would play the tune for which he was writing the lyrics several times, and when I'd get no reaction, I'd stop. Sometimes he remained motionless for as long as fifteen minutes. Then he would suddenly open his eyes and reel off a half-chorus of brilliant lyrics. For one song, he wrote the entire lyric in that position.

I related the experience to Harry Warren, a longtime collaborator of Johnny Mercer's. He said that was nothing compared to what happened to him. He and Johnny were writing a song for a score at Warner Brothers. At one point, Johnny leaned his head back and closed his eyes. Harry, to find out whether he was asleep, asked him, "How's Ginger?" (Ginger was Johnny's wife.) Johnny didn't answer. Harry looked at his watch. It was lunchtime, so he went to the commissary. He returned in an hour. Johnny hadn't moved. As Harry sat down at the piano, Johnny, without opening his eyes, said matter-of-factly, "She's fine."

Although I had known Danny Kaye socially for many years, I had never worked with him. I was impressed. It seemed there was nothing he couldn't do. And do well, because he was a perfectionist, like every other great performer I had worked with. The script called for him to join a circus, and as part of his act he had to juggle. He learned very quickly. There was a chimpanzee in the picture whom Danny immediately befriended. Danny spoke the most authentic-sounding Italian double-talk ever heard. He was amazing.

During the shooting of *Merry Andrew,* the bottom dropped out of musicals once again. Their popularity had always run in cycles, and we were suddenly in the middle of another downturn. Ours was the only musical shooting at the studio, and orders were given to finish it as quickly and inexpensively as possible. Mercer and I were in the process of writing two more numbers, one of which we had finished. They were canceled.

Michael Kidd was told to wind up shooting within two weeks. That meant cutting the remaining schedule in half. It was the first picture he had ever directed, and he was doing wonderfully until he was hit with this horrendous obstacle. It took considerable ingenuity to determine the proper scenes to shoot during the allotted time so that the picture could be cut together and make sense. It was a rotten break for Michael, and the film is nowhere near as good as he could have made it.

When I finished working on *Merry Andrew,* the last of many contracts I had signed with the studio through the years came to an end. When the realization struck me that I was finally leaving, I became depressed. It had been—and for that matter still is—the most stimulating and creatively fulfilling period in my career. I had been given the rare opportunity of working with extraordinarily talented people from the moment I arrived nine and a half years earlier. I learned from them. In fact, my entire tenure at MGM was like taking postgraduate work at a university.

Actually, the atmosphere was not unlike that of a college. The executives were our equivalent of college professors. And we told jokes about them in the same way that college students do about their professors. For instance, Benny Thau, an important executive, was a nice man, but he always looked sad and depressed. Keenan Wynn said, "I told Benny Thau a joke. He laughed, and dust came out of his mouth."

There was another executive with the unlikely name O. O. "Bunny" Dull. Try as we might, we could never figure out what he did. Herman Mankiewicz, the cowriter of *Citizen Kane,* solved the mystery: "Dull's job is to stand on the roof of the Administration Building, and when he sees a glacier coming, he has to run down and warn everybody."

The era of the great MGM musicals of the fifties had come to an end. Actually, the period ended triumphantly with Freed and Minnelli's *Gigi.* These musicals were the culmination of those made during the thirties and forties.

Busby Berkeley really led the way. He did enormous numbers that were innovative, inventive, and astounding. During the fifties, it was no longer feasible to do Berkeley-type numbers. No studio could afford to hire several hundred dancers and keep them there around the clock until the number was shot.

In place of size, the innovation stemmed mainly from advanced cinema techniques: Gene Kelly's cartoon number in *Anchor's Aweigh,* Fred Astaire's revolving-room number in *Royal Wedding.* Songs were more frequently integrated into the plots of films than they had been. Wide-screen, Cinemascope, and stereo sound were uniquely suited to the enhancement of musicals.

But most of all, what made the MGM musicals so outstanding was the unsurpassed personnel behind and in front of the camera. It was the best of all places and times to be involved with musicals, and I was fortunate enough to have been part of it.

Chapter 18 ■ Bob Wise, the director, phoned and asked me to have lunch with him. He was a casual friend I knew at MGM where he had directed such pictures as *Executive Suite* and *Somebody up There Likes Me*. He wanted to talk to me about the movie version of *West Side Story,* which he had just signed to produce and codirect with Jerome Robbins.

The original idea for *West Side Story*—a modern musical version of Shakespeare's *Romeo and Juliet*—came from Robbins. Leonard Bernstein and Stephen Sondheim wrote an excellent score, and the show ran for over seven hundred

West

performances. It has always been considered a landmark musical and was now about to be made into a movie. Ernest Lehman, who had

Side

been offered the assignment to do the screenplay and was a mutual friend, had suggested to Bob that he ask me to acquaint him with the

Story

special problems he faced in doing a musical, his first.

When I enumerated what was involved in making a movie musical and he began asking questions, it was the first time I realized how much more complicated and different musicals were than other films. All they have in common is a script. But a musical is concerned with dance rehearsals, prerecordings, playbacks—when to use them and when not to; dubbing voices, postsynching footsteps, temporary music tracks—when to use them and when not to, style of performance; and much more.

The lunch lasted for three hours. At the end of that time, Bob asked me to work on the picture with him as associate producer. I told him I would think about it and let him know.

I then got in touch with Ernie and described my talk with Bob in detail. He asked, "Are you going to do it?"

"I don't know. Are you?"

"I'm not sure."

"I loved the show. I saw it five times," I said.

"Yeah, but it'll be a tough picture to make."

"Well, what's easy?"

"Look," he said, "I'll do it if you do it."

"I'll do it if you do it" was my reply. We circled each other that way verbally for a while, then decided that we would both do it.

Ernie started immediately. Among other changes, he repositioned several of the songs. He had also chosen new locales for some of them, and at our meetings we finalized the rest. The brilliantly sardonic song "Officer Krupke" was placed much earlier than it had been in the show and was to be performed outside the candy store instead of inside. "Cool" was positioned much later and was to take place in a pressure-cooker garage, where it was infinitely more dramatic than it had been on stage. "I Feel Pretty" was placed earlier so that it didn't stop the dramatic action as it had in the show. The rest of the numbers were retained as indicated in the playscript, although in some cases where they were done in limbo (no setting) in the show ("Something's Coming," "The Prologue"), real settings were used in the film.

I don't mean to suggest that all the above decisions came easily. Some of our meetings on the script were more like confrontations than conferences. We were good friends and felt free to say anything that was on our minds. In the final analysis, however, it doesn't matter how close you are to someone. If he rejects one of your pet ideas, you find it unsettling.

Our script discussions sometimes became so heated that when I phoned Ernie one night, he said, "I'm glad you called. After this afternoon I wasn't sure you would ever talk to me again." Ultimately, our difficulties didn't matter because the two projects on which we collaborated—*West Side Story* and *The Sound of Music*—turned out well and we're still good friends.

Casting the film proved next to impossible. A decision was made very early that stars were not going to be sought because the project would be a large enough attraction to audiences. Screen tests were made of the leads in the New York and London companies of the show. In every case except one they looked too old. The exception was George Chakiris, who played Riff in the London company but was cast as Bernardo in the movie.

When the news that we were looking for unknowns hit Hollywood, it was like loosing the bulls in Pamploma. Aspiring candidates came from everywhere. Eight-by-ten glossies with résumés attached arrived by the dozens daily; agents brought in every teenage actor they could find; every young member of the Screen Actors Guild, and many that weren't members, appeared from nowhere; and some attention had to be paid to each of them. They did fulfill one of the requirements: They were all unknown. But there were several other conditions that most of them could not meet.

A vast majority looked too old and knew it, but figured they had nothing to lose by trying. Others weren't gang-member types. But there was an added prerequisite peculiar to this project. The score required the female lead, Maria, to be a soprano and the male lead, Tony, to be a tenor. I was perfectly prepared to use voice doubles for the two leads, but their speaking voices had to be in a range that would make that sound plausible. There was one actress, Ina Balin, who read for the part beautifully but had such a low speaking voice that it would have been ludicrous to hear her sing in a soprano voice. The same problem existed with the male lead.

There was so much to do that Bob and I evolved a method of working. While I was busy organizing a music department, Bob read with the actors. The ones he thought worthy of serious consideration were sent to me. I tested their speaking voices and their musicality. Even though they might not have to record the songs themselves, they had to look as if they had. I had learned years earlier that that requires a certain degree of musicality. I would then go over my reactions with Bob, and we decided which ones were to be screen-tested. Parenthetically, George Segal recently told me that he had tried out for the lead. He passed Bob's test, but I turned him down. He has managed rather well in spite of it.

We began by making screen tests of members of the New York cast. Several members of the London company—the show was still running at the time—were tested there. Then every actor with even the vaguest potential was tested, about forty in all.

When the Mirisch Company first acquired the motion-picture rights to *West Side Story*, they had intended casting it completely with stars. Everyone from Marlon Brando to Elvis Presley was mentioned. Natalie Wood was suggested—she was Ernie's choice—but when it was decided to go with unknowns, she was eliminated. After testing many young actresses, our tentative choice for the part of Maria was Barbara Luna. She was not only tested by herself; she also played the part of Maria several times when we were testing young actors as Tony. Then, for reasons I no longer recall, Natalie Wood was tested. It was immediately apparent that our search was over. She was perfect for Maria, as she subsequently proved. But it was one of those rare situations when being a star name almost lost an actress a part.

Casting the part of Tony was even more difficult because the only male teenage stars were rock singers. Among the many actors tested was Keir Dullea. He might have been chosen if he had agreed to have his headful of wavy blond hair cut so that he would look like a gang member. He refused. Then Richard Beymer was tested. He was as impressive for Tony as Natalie Wood had been for Maria. He looked as if he could have been the leader of the Jets, whom he had outgrown, and was enough of a dreamer to know that there must be a better life out there that excluded gangs and rumbles. He was far and away the best actor we tested for the role.

That brings me to something that has been bothering me ever since the film was released. What is it that impels friends to say "I saw *West Side Story*. I loved it, but I *must* tell you I thought Richard Beymer was terrible"? Why *must* they tell me? Could I redo the picture and choose a different actor for the part? (I wouldn't, incidentally, because I think they're wrong.) Is there anything I can do about their objection now that the film is playing in the theaters? What reaction do they expect from me? Most of all, why can't they just say they liked the picture and keep their reservations to themselves? I eventually learned to stop them by asking "Who would you like to have seen in the part?" They never had an answer.

I don't mean to limit my objections to *West Side Story*. It's an ongoing syndrome in Hollywood, where it almost becomes a cult to knock a particular phase of an otherwise excellent film. It is proper for paying audiences to respond any way they choose, but when a filmmaker is accosted by a friend that way, it is an act of sheer hostility, and often envy.

This was the first time I was working on a nonstudio film, where I had to put together my own music department. I made a list of the personnel I thought would be ideal: Bobby Tucker as vocal coach—I had worked with him extensively at MGM; Sid Ramin and Irwin Kostal as orchestrators—they had done the orchestrations for the show, and we were going to use expanded versions of them; Richard Carruth as music editor—by reputation, the best there was; and Johnny Green as conductor—it was a difficult score, and I knew Johnny would handle it brilliantly.

I went to Bob's office with my list and was about to tell him about it when he said, "You're in charge of the music. Pick anyone you want except one guy—Johnny Green."

I couldn't believe it. "Why?" I asked.

"When I was at Metro and had appointments with him, he kept me waiting in his outer office for hours. He never stops yapping and telling dialect jokes and wasting a lot of time. I don't ever want to work with him again."

I left his office dejected. Of all the people I had chosen, Johnny was the one I considered irreplaceable. I knew it would be a tough music job, made even more difficult because we had to please a hard taskmaster, Jerry Robbins, who was to be the choreographer as well as the codirector. Johnny had infinite patience, and I knew he could cope with any demands Jerry might make of him and still smile.

Yet Bob wasn't wrong. I too had spent endless hours in Johnny's outer office waiting to see him. But I always put it down to the fact that the job he was trying to do was too much for one man. His resolve to supervise every note that went into every MGM picture made it impossible for him to stick to a rigid schedule. Bob's other complaint was also valid. Johnny *was* long-winded and did tell lots of dialect jokes, but I had always found them funny, so I never minded.

I spent the better part of a week trying to think of another conductor who had the technical skill, temperament, and talent to do this particular picture and concluded that there wasn't anyone as qualified as Johnny. There was only one thing to do. I went back to Bob and tried a different approach. "I've just about completed our musical staff. A couple of them had conflicting commitments, but they're going to make themselves available because they're all anxious to do the picture. There's just one spot I still have to fill. I want to hire Johnny."

I could see him getting upset. "You mean there's nobody else in Hollywood who could do it?"

I told him there wasn't, went through the names of some other conductors, and pointed out why Johnny was preferable. "Suppose I go to Johnny and lay it all out for him. I'll tell him about your objections. If he wants the job, he has to stop with the dialect jokes and the long-winded speeches. Bob, you know I wouldn't be putting myself through all of this if I didn't think he was the best guy for the picture."

"What about the demands he makes—offices, private secretary, a dressing room on the scoring stage? It's ridiculous!"

"Okay. I'll tell him he can't have any of that either. He can only come in to watch rehearsals and then conduct."

After a momentary silence, he said, "All right. But keep him away from me." I said I would and called Johnny to arrange a meeting with him.

As I look back at it now, I can't believe that I went through that session with Johnny. It would have been so much easier if we hadn't been good friends. He greeted me in his best Yiddish dialect, but when he saw my grim face, he immediately dropped it. I related down to the minutest detail how I became involved with *West Side Story*.

Suddenly I realized that I was stalling to keep from telling him the real reason I was there. As a result, instead of breaking it to him gradually, I blurted out the whole thing in practically one breath. "Goddammit, Johnny! I want you to conduct the picture, but Bob Wise is against it—he says you're always talking in dialect and you're too damned long-winded and you want offices and secretaries and dressing rooms and God knows what else and I'm having the fight of my life trying to get him to okay you for the picture!"

He couldn't have been more stunned if he had been hit in the head with a brick. He said softly, "Solly, I don't know what you're talking about, but whatever it is—Please tell it to me again—slowly."

Having gotten it all out, I was relieved. I began again from the beginning and enumerated Bob's complaints, one by one. It was all depressing, and we were both close to tears. We didn't have the kind of relationship that could withstand this kind of emotional confrontation.

He said, almost in a whisper, "Why hasn't anyone ever told me this before?"

"I suppose because most people don't mind," I replied, not at all sure I was right. At the end of the long afternoon, he agreed to Bob's terms but said he would like to have an office even if it were no larger than a broom closet. I told him I was sure I could arrange it.

I drove back to the studio a happy man. There was a message

waiting for me from Harold Mirisch, the president of the Mirisch Company. He wanted to see me.

"I hear you want to hire someone that Bobby Wise doesn't want," he said.

"That's not completely true. I just came from a meeting with Johnny, and I'm about to see Bobby. If he still wants someone else after what I tell him, then I'll look for someone else. But it'll be a mistake, because Johnny is the best man for this picture."

I spoke to Bob, who reluctantly consented to hiring Johnny and to his having an office.

The story has a happy ending. Bob watched two recording sessions conducted by Johnny and was so impressed with the results that he ordered a dressing room brought to the stage for him. Eventually his dialects even reappeared occasionally, and Bob never objected. In fact, several times I caught him laughing. By the time the film was over, Bob, Johnny, and Harold Mirisch were good friends.

Jerry Robbins, who as I mentioned before was to choreograph and codirect with Bob Wise, didn't arrive on the scene until we were halfway through our script sessions. He came fresh from the success on Broadway of *Gypsy,* a musical he had choreographed and directed. From the very onset, there were problems. Jerry wanted everything in the play to be retained in the movie exactly as it was on stage. Whenever we arrived at a scene where we had changed the order of the songs, he objected strenuously. Nor did he approve of the new settings for several.

There is a musical sequence in *West Side Story* called the "Quintet" that occurs before the "Rumble." It is performed by the Sharks, Jets, Tony, Maria, and Anita, the girlfriend of Bernardo, the leader of the Sharks. In the theatrical version it is done in limbo, and as each element joins in the singing, it is hit with a spotlight. At the end, they all sing, the stage is flooded with five spotlights, and it's very exciting.

For the movie, we obviously had to use real settings. Ernie

typed up each section of the number on a file card and tacked them all up on a bulletin board next to his desk. For example, "SHARKS moving towards RUMBLE area," followed by the lyrics the Sharks would sing in that shot. Another card had "MARIA on the fire escape," followed by the lyrics she would sing during that shot, and so on. There must have been about a dozen cards in all.

Ernie and I returned from lunch one day to find that Jerry had written his comments on each of the cards while we were out. To quote several: "Jerry thinks this stinks," "Jerry vomits," "Jerry leaves town." The sequence was shot exactly as indicated on the cards and proved to be one of the high spots of the picture.

The principal difficulty that had to be surmounted in transferring *West Side Story* from the stage to the screen was one of style. How do you get movie audiences to accept gang members not only dancing but dancing in the street? On the stage it's simple. The program mentions that the setting is a street, and audiences accept it, even though there is no street setting. In fact, in the stage version, the entire opening was done against a black backdrop.

The screen is a more literal medium. Jerry took about ten dancers and shot endless feet of film with them in a parking lot, a studio street, and other real locations. All this footage was then treated optically in various ways to determine whether a mixture of real and unreal would work. The results were fascinating but unconvincing. It was clear, however, that the only way to solve the problem was for the dancing to start unobtrusively and gradually out of natural movement. Eventually, it evolved out of a shot of the Jets walking menacingly down the street.

Jerry Robbins gathered the dancers from the New York, London, and touring companies of the show, and rehearsals began in earnest. He started with the "Prologue" because that was to be shot first and was to undergo the most drastic changes from the stage version. For one thing, it was to be almost twice as long because several new elements were to be added. It was to be filmed on West Sixty-eighth Street and East 110th Street in New York, and sections of those locations were chalked out on the floor of the rehearsal stage.

I attended rehearsals, as usual, and was both amazed and appalled by what I witnessed. Jerry was by far the most exciting choreographer I had ever watched. He seemed to have an endless stream of exciting ideas. He would try one, then replace it with another, then substitute something else, and occasionally throw out everything and start over. He would then come up with something that was even more thrilling. He had the most facile, quicksilver mind I had ever seen at work.

At the same time, he was such an insane perfectionist that it was impossible for any of the dancers to achieve the standards he demanded immediately. To make matters worse, he had a very low tolerance point. When he was displeased, he heaped such verbal abuse on the dancers that the place took on the atmosphere of a concentration camp. They didn't dance out of joy, they danced out of fear. His reputation for being difficult had preceded him, but this was much worse than I had expected. I wondered how he ever got anyone to work for him until I asked one of the dancers. The reply was "How else would I ever get a chance to dance like that?" I didn't invent the notion, but it's further proof that being a successful dancer requires a certain degree of masochism.

In the meantime, I wasn't finding Jerry easy to work with either. As mentioned earlier, I was accustomed to attending dance rehearsals and finding out what new music or changes the choreographer required. I would then go off and adapt the music to fit his needs and bring it back. Not with Jerry. By the time I got back, he had not only thrown out the entire idea but had his rehearsal pianist adapt the new music he needed.

With the "Prologue," it really didn't matter because I knew that the music they were going to dance to in New York would be just a temporary track and that the actual music would be scored after the number was shot and cut together. But it was still disturbing. I had never been in a situation where I was responsible for the music yet wasn't consulted about it. Jerry had created his own clique, and I was being treated like an outsider. I didn't like it. I was aware during the entire time that in the final analysis I would make the decision about which music went where, but it didn't help. I was miserable.

Nor was he particularly considerate of his own staff. His rehearsal pianist was a lovely, talented lady we had brought out from New York. She was invited to join some friends who were going away for a weekend if she could get off Friday before 5:00 P.M. She asked Jerry about it on Monday, at which time he said he didn't know. For the next few days he said nothing, so she asked him again on Thursday morning. Again he said he wasn't sure. She told her friends not to include her in their plans.

Jerry worked late every night that week, except on Friday when he quit at a quarter to five. By then it was too late for the pianist to join her friends. It would have been so easy for Jerry to have arranged to quit early on Friday and to have told her. And what was perhaps worse, he had her so brainwashed that she wasn't as upset as she should have been.

There was one recording session that will live forever in my memory. It started at one in the afternoon, and we were using our largest orchestra, seventy-two pieces. Johnny took about an hour and a half to rehearse with the orchestra alone before we called Jerry to join us. Ten days earlier, we had had a long session with Jerry on his rehearsal stage. He defined for us exactly what he wanted to hear in this number. He was very articulate musically and had no problem making himself clear. In any event, it was an orchestration that came right out of the show, with minor alterations, so we were sure the recording session would be a breeze.

Jerry listened to Johnny run the number down with the orchestra and said it was fine, but he would like to hear a particular section played by woodwinds instead of brass. That meant reorchestrating, which took time, but it was done. He heard it and decided it was better the original way. But in another section he thought it might sound better without strings. That was tried. He picked at the orchestration in that way for about two hours. Then he found fault with the various tempi. Some parts were being played too loud, others too soft.

A certain amount of this is to be expected, but in this case it was exasperating. There seemed to be no way to satisfy him. And this was an orchestration he had been listening to in the show for several years. After five hours, Johnny somehow managed to comply with every one of his suggestions.

Jerry then uttered a line that I had never heard before, one that will be forever engraved in my memory: "Now that you've given me everything I asked for, let's see if I want it." In fact, eventually Jerry didn't. It was too slow, and we had to rerecord the entire number. Incidentally, the least perturbed person through the whole grueling afternoon was Johnny Green.

Our West Sixty-eighth Street setting in New York was like shooting on the back lot of a studio. It was one of several streets that had been reclaimed by the city and was being leveled to make way for Lincoln Center. The buildings were uninhabited and, except for some broken windowpanes, were intact. We had police at either end of the street to keep sightseers away, but we experienced danger from an unprotected source.

Several times rocks were thrown at us from the roofs of nearby buildings. None of us was hit, but that was purely a matter of luck, and there were some very close calls. The street was allocated to us for a specified number of days, but for various reasons we fell behind schedule. Our last two days were a race against time. While we were shooting on one end of the street, the city was tearing down the buildings on the other end. By the time we finished, the only structures left standing were the ones we were using as background.

Our 110th Street location was a schoolyard. It was August, so the school was closed, It was surrounded on all sides by jam-packed rundown tenements. We were in the middle of a poverty-stricken Puerto Rican neighborhood where the prevailing language was Spanish and the only laws were those enforced by street gangs. We had police protection, which was largely ineffectual. Our New York production manager had searched out and hired the gang that controlled the turf we were using, and they made it possible for us to shoot with minimum interference.

On one occasion, a short feisty old woman carrying a bagful of groceries began walking through our shot. The policeman stationed there tried to stop her, but she screamed and kicked at him as she tried to get out of his grasp. At that point, a gang member who was working for us took her gently by the arm, said something to her in Spanish, and led her away. She went quietly. The explanation is simple. She knew the policeman could do nothing to her except throw her in jail. That didn't scare her. But she wasn't so sure what the gang member might do. And that frightened her.

The kids we hired didn't know what to make of the Jets and Sharks. They surely weren't "gangs," yet that's what they were supposed to be. And what was all that jumping around? Dancing? Gangs don't dance like that. When they saw the Jets playing basketball (part of the number), *that* they understood. They offered to put together a team to play them. They were turned down, most diplomatically.

We never got to know any of them well, but they upheld their end of the bargain to the letter. They were always there when we needed them and handled matters quietly and efficiently. We could not have filmed in that schoolyard without them. I've often wondered whether any of them ever saw the movie. Their comments would have been interesting.

Jerry Robbins's contract stipulated that he was in charge of shooting all the musical numbers and the scenes that led into them. The latter condition proved impractical since almost every scene led into a musical number. In essence, Jerry would have been directing the entire film, and that was never intended. So

Bob and Jerry struck a compromise: Jerry would do all the musical sequences and Bob the scenes, but he would consult with Jerry when they led directly into a number.

One of Bob's major strengths is his enormous talent as a film editor. He had edited such films as *Citizen Kane* and *The Magnificent Ambersons* before he turned to directing. As he watched Jerry shooting the "Prologue," he saw him shoot several angles he knew could never be used. Bob didn't say anything until we had fallen way behind schedule because of rain and the time it took to set up some of Jerry's unusable shots.

Bob finally told Jerry as politely as possible that the scene he was about to shoot could never fit into the "Prologue." Jerry, just as politely, said that it shouldn't be rejected just because it had never been done before. Bob, still politely, replied that he had taken that into consideration, but the scene still couldn't possibly work. The conversation continued for several minutes, after which Jerry shot the scene anyhow. It ultimately turned out that he shot quite a few scenes that couldn't be used. But he was in charge of the musical sequences, and he always did what he wanted.

In truth, most of the film that Jerry shot for the "Prologue" was wonderfully inventive. He knew how to get the most out of his choreography. He got all the drama, humor, and tension of the number on film. He had a great camera-eye for single shots but not for the whole.

While we were still shooting in New York, Johnny Green had a party at his Beverly Hills home and invited Lenny Bernstein, who happened to be in town. The high point of the evening was to be Lenny's first hearing of the tracks we had made for the film. It's a party I'm glad I missed. It was a disaster. Lenny hated almost everything he heard. When I got back to California, there was a long telegram from him waiting for me. He was about to take off for Europe and couldn't call, but he pleaded with me to rerecord four of the pieces he had heard because they were all "abysmally slow."

I told Jerry about it, and he immediately agreed with Lenny, conveniently forgetting that he had picked the tempi of all the numbers in the film, and if they were too slow, it was because he wanted them that way. On several occasions, I mentioned to him that our tempi were slower than the show album, but he replied that that didn't matter. I wrote to Lenny about the discrepancies in tempi, and we then rerecorded the four numbers.

Our schedule had been planned so that upon our return from New York, we were to shoot three numbers in a row at the studio. Jerry was again in charge, and he continued at the same pace he had established while shooting the "Prologue." He slipped further and further behind. He was cautioned about it many times by our production manager and various executives, but he was intent on doing this his own way and made no attempt to make up the lost time. Finally, United Artists, who was financing the film, determined that we were $300,000 over budget, and less than one-third of the film had been shot. They demanded that the Mirisch Company do something about it.

A meeting was held at which the decision was made to fire Jerry. His only champion at the meeting was the last person one would have expected to fight for him—Bob Wise. I thought he had gone mad. Jerry and Bob had never had an actual falling out, but many times I saw Bob literally grit his teeth as he watched Jerry make one of his ridiculous shots. And here he was trying to defend him. It was just that Bob had so much respect for Jerry's talent that he didn't like to see this happen to him.

Jerry was let go, his assistants were retained to restage his original choreography for the numbers yet to be filmed. All of the choreography in the film is by Jerry Robbins. The musical numbers he shot were the "Prologue" (more about that later), "America," "Cool," and "Something's Coming." All the other musical sequences were done by Bob.

The announcement to the cast that Jerry was leaving created a minor upheaval, which turned out to be more sound than fury. Quite a few dancers threatened to quit, as did Natalie Wood. She and Jerry had become good friends. It simmered for a few days, but in the end no one quit.

Only one person remained loyal (here we go again)—Bob Wise. He insisted that Jerry be brought back to the studio, all expenses paid, to cut together the "Prologue." Since we were still shooting, it would have been awkward for him to work during the day. He might run into someone on the film, and that would be embarrassing. Our music editor, Dick Carruth, who had some experience cutting film, was assigned to him, and they worked at night.

Dick's descriptions of some of those sessions were startling, to say the least. Jerry would cut sections of the number together one night and pull them apart the next. Every conceivable combination of shots in a sequence was tried. Dick offered suggestions, which were ignored. They were getting nowhere. The night finally came when Jerry broke down completely. He was totally frustrated and began to cry. Over and over he repeated, "I can't do it, I can't do it." When he returned to New York, he left behind several cut sequences. The number was far from complete. Bob eventually untangled the mess and edited the "Prologue."

On a few occasions I have found myself working with someone who is so extraordinarily talented that the word *genius* crossed my mind. But I was never sure. The only person I am sure about is Jerome Robbins. There isn't the slightest doubt that he is a man of genius. His talent as a choreographer goes beyond extraordinary in its scope, originality, and effect on his dancers and audiences. His range is astounding. No other choreographer could have created the ferocity of the "Rumble," the insane fun of "Officer Krupke," and the poignant lyricism of Tony and Maria's dance in the gym. And that's only part of the genius he demonstrated in the film.

In spite of all of that, he proved utterly impractical as a filmmaker, and that's unfortunate. With his incredibly creative mind and keen eye, he unquestionably would have become a major force in the art of the cinema. He proved that in the few sequences he shot for *West Side Story*.

Yet he is the only person I have met in my entire career that I vowed never to work with again. I can't function well in the kind of atmosphere he creates. He destroys personal relationships and is cruel. There are many people who believe the results justify the means. I'm not one of them.

Jerry had been promised that when there was a final cut of the "Prologue," I would fly to New York with it and show it to him. Before that, however, I got a print of the film and adapted Bernstein's music to the long early sections that were shot without playback. I found that despite what I had done, new music would be needed. I suggested that as long as I was going back to New York, I should arrange to meet with Lenny and go through my adaptation with him. Sid Ramin and Irwin Kostal, the orchestrators, and Dick Carruth, the music editor who had edited the "Prologue" with Bob, flew back with me. Arrangements were made for us to meet Lenny in an editing room at three in the afternoon on a Sunday and for me to show the "Prologue" to Jerry in a projection room the following afternoon at two.

We had reservations on a 1:00 P.M. flight to New York on Saturday, the day before we were to meet with Lenny. We arrived at the airport and were told that all flights to New York had been canceled because of a devastating blizzard that was battering the entire East Coast. I was just about to postpone our trip when I suddenly felt a familiar let-down feeling. I was damned if I was going to let it get the better of me. I went up to the American Airlines counter and asked, "How far east can we fly?"

"Chicago. The flight leaves at two o'clock."

"Can you get four of us on it?"

"Just a minute." He picked up a phone and in about ten minutes told me there were four seats available. Without consulting the others, I told him to rewrite our tickets to Chicago and give us credit for the rest of the flight. The writing that went on was interminable, as it always was with airline tickets until they did it by computer.

I hadn't the vaguest notion what we were going to do about

getting to New York when we reached Chicago. All I knew was that we were getting closer and I would deal with that problem when we got to Chicago. I was hoping that by the time we arrived there, the storm on the East Coast would have subsided and we could fly right on.

No such luck. New York was still closed in. I asked about Newark. No. Philadelphia? No. In desperation, I finally asked, "How close to New York can we fly?"

There was much phoning, then the answer: "Washington, DC"

"What time does the plane leave, and can you get four of us on it?"

More phoning. "It leaves at one o'clock in the morning, and there are four seats available."

"Okay. Rewrite our tickets."

We sat in the airport until 1:00 A.M. when we boarded our Chicago-Washington flight. By then, the four of us had been traveling for a long time, and gone were our jokes and one-liners. The others were becoming more and more weary, and I more and more determined. We were not unpleasant with each other, just silent. When we approached Washington, my heart leaped with joy. Not a cloud to be seen anywhere. I was positive the storm was over.

When we landed, I ran up to the American Airlines counter and confidently asked for four reservations on the first flight to New York.

"I can't tell you when that will be," the clerk replied. "New York is closed in."

"Isn't the storm over?" I asked in disbelief.

"Yes, but the runways have about five feet of snow on them, and there is no estimate as to when they'll be in use again."

I finally felt beaten. I was tired, hungry, frustrated—ready to give up. But then I got a brainstorm. Train! We could go to New York by train. I asked the clerk about it. He called the railroad station and found out that the milk train from New York left in about an hour—at 5:00 A.M. He couldn't reserve seats for us but suggested we get to the train station as quickly as possible and try to get on it.

We climbed into a taxi and told the driver to get us to the depot as quickly as possible. On the way we passed the National Theater, where, Sid and Irv pointed out, the stage version of *West Side Story* had had its first public performance. They had had difficulties then too. I ran up to the ticket window at the station only to be told that there were no more seats on the milk train to New York. I pleaded, I cajoled, I offered the clerk any amount of money he wanted.

He thought of a possibility that might work. "When the train comes, get on it. Look for the conductor and tell him you'd like to buy four seats. If you happen to hit a nice guy, he might sell you seats in the club car. Otherwise, you'll have to get off at the next station. It's worth a try."

That was the one thing that went right. I bribed the conductor who let us buy four seats in the club car, where we sat dazed and half dozing while the train made endless stops until it finally reached New York. When we got out at Pennsylvania Station on Thirty-fourth Street, there was no way of getting to the St. Moritz Hotel on Fifty-ninth Street, where rooms had been reserved for us. The streets were piled high with snow, and there wasn't a vehicle of any kind moving. After what we had been through, we considered that a small obstacle. We trudged through the twenty-five blocks of snow to the hotel carrying our luggage.

The room clerk couldn't imagine how we had gotten there, but how could we explain the insanity we had experienced for the past seventeen or eighteen hours? It was then 10:00 A.M., Sunday. We went up to our rooms and left calls to be awakened at 1:30 P.M. I was in bed asleep almost before the door to my room was closed.

At about 2:30 that afternoon, we trudged through the snow to the building where we were to meet Lenny. Naturally it was locked. What else? We banged on the door until a janitor appeared. He said he hadn't been expecting us until much later. He led us through an unlit hall to the elevator. We got off on the fifth floor and groped our way by the light of the janitor's flashlight to the editing room. Someone was obviously working there during the week because there were cans of film everywhere. It had a proper moviola, and that was all we really cared about. Also, wonder of wonders, the janitor turned the lights on.

Lenny arrived at 3:15, having gone through the same ritual with the janitor. Lenny and I hadn't seen each other for a long time, so we had a happy reunion. Then we ran the "Prologue" for him, which he loved. Dick rethreaded it, and we ran it for him again. This time he looked at the piano sketch I had made of the early part as we sang along.

His comment was typically Lenny—to the point and amazingly honest. "I don't like it . . . but wait. I don't know if I really don't like it or I don't like it because I didn't do it. Run it again." This time he not only liked it but said enthusiastically, "It's terrific!"

He immediately saw where new music was needed. Watching him work was wonderful. He explained exactly what the new music should sound like. He then jotted down several ideas, on manuscript paper any one of which would have worked perfectly.

In the midst of our discussion, the janitor reappeared. It was time to close up, and he had to go home. We said we needed just another half hour, but he said he had orders to lock up the editing room and leave. Dick asked about moving the moviola into the hall.

"I guess that's okay if the electric cord will fit under the door. But I have to turn off the elevator, so you'll have to walk down. Just close the front door when you leave. It'll lock by itself."

We finished our work on the "Prologue" in the dark out in the hall. Would anything connected with this picture ever run smoothly?

The following day at 2:00 I showed the "Prologue" to Jerry and Lenny, who decided he wanted to see it again. He then explained to Jerry what the music would be like.

All I can say of Jerry's reaction is that he didn't disapprove. His only comment was "Lenny, whatever happened to the idea we had to make it as a small black-and-white picture?" It was a question that didn't call for an answer, and none was forthcoming.

I returned to the coast, where I immediately launched into the background score for the film. I made piano sketches from which Sid and Irv would do the orchestrations. I also went through all the vocal tracks in the film, replacing some from other takes and redoing several completely. I had never been satisfied with Russ Tamblyn's track of the "Jet Song." By accident, I found that Tucker Smith, who played Ice in the film and did the song "Cool," could sound exactly like Russ, so I had him redo the track. There was a short section in the "Quintet" that was too high for Rita Moreno's voice. After Marni Nixon had resung all of Natalie's songs, I had her do the small section Rita couldn't manage. I was working virtually day and night.

Bob was equally busy—redoing dialogue, checking outtakes to improve several scenes, ordering reprints to improve the color. There was one period when we hadn't seen each other for at least two weeks. We met on the lot one afternoon.

"How're you doing" I asked.

"Chipping away at it."

It was an apt description of our activities. The film was like a large block of granite we were hammering at with a feather.

Despite my darkest thoughts, the day finally came when there was nothing left to do on the film until after the sneak previews. Bob had always screened his films for his friends the night before they were sneaked. A screening was set up at the Directors Guild projection room the evening before we were to take off for Minneapolis and Chicago. Neither Bob nor I allowed ourselves the luxury of wondering whether the film was good or bad. We just hoped it would hold together for its first showing.

About fifty people were present. I don't know how it played because I was too nervous to be aware of audience reactions. All I know is that the film didn't break and the sound didn't suddenly disappear, as it had occasionally during our mixing sessions.

When the lights finally came on, there wasn't a sound in the house, and for the first time I was sure we had a huge flop on our hands. Audiences always applaud after private showings, even if they hate the picture. Here—nothing.

After a few tortured minutes of staring straight ahead, I slowly turned my head and looked around. I then saw why no one had made a sound. There wasn't a dry eye anywhere. A sea of white handkerchiefs. Eyes were being dried hurriedly to hide embarrassment.

Then the congratulations started. I've never heard such praise. Everyone was talking at once and throwing words like "fabulous," "remarkable," "fantastic," and every other superlative they could think of.

Only one person wasn't heard from: Ernie Lehman. He and his wife, Jackie, had driven me to the screening. On the drive home we spoke of everything but the film.

When we finally got to my house, I could stand it no longer. I yelled, "Okay, Ernie. Even if you hated it, you have to tell me. What did you think of the picture?"

Silence. Then he replied, "I was less disappointed in it than in any of the other movies made of my scripts."

Talk about left-handed compliments. I knew that for Ernie, who had written such films as *Sweet Smell of Success* and *North by Northwest*, that was high praise.

Nevertheless, it quashed my enthusiasm considerably. Up to that point, I had been reveling in the reaction of close friends. What made me think that general audiences would respond favorably? I left for Minneapolis worried.

We had sent our head sound man a day earlier to check out the theater technically. He measured the brightness of the screen and balanced the five front speakers so that they responded with the same level of lows, highs, and volume. By the time we arrived, the theater was in perfect shape, and we had a smash preview.

This time I listened to the audience, and they had a great time. When there was no applause at the end, I wasn't concerned. The opinion cards the audience filled out were ecstatic. We flew on to

Chicago the next day, so elated we could have flown there without a plane.

Bob and I went to the theater in Chicago the following evening at a quarter to eight and found our sound man embroiled in a heated argument with a man who turned out to be the manager of the theater. It had been agreed that the manager would empty the theater at six that evening so that it could be checked in the same way the Minneapolis theater had been. He hadn't done it and had continued showing his regular feature.

Our man insisted that it would be unfair to screen the film unless the speakers were balanced. Then Bob became extremely angry and shouted, "Either let him do his job, or I'm pulling the picture!" The manager couldn't have that because the Midwest representatives of United Artists, the distributor, were going to be in the audience. He finally consented to having the speakers checked, but with the audience in the theater. We had no choice, so we accepted his condition. The overall reaction to the film was even more enthusiastic than it had been the night before.

When we returned to the studio, there was very little left to do. A few places needed sound correction, and a few trims were made in the film. At long last, we were through. I had been with the film almost every day, including many Sundays and holidays, for eighteen months. As I have often told friends, it was more like joining a cult than working on a film. "Working on" is not quite accurate. *Struggling with* was often closer to the truth. Yet out of all the chaos came what is generally considered a landmark musical. There's probably a lesson to be learned from all of this, but I haven't the vaguest notion what it could be, unless it's "If you work on anything long enough, there's an excellent chance you'll finish it."

When it was released, *West Side Story* received mixed reviews. Fortunately, it attracted enormous audiences, so reviews were meaningless in this instance. The Hollywood community was mad about it, and it won ten Academy Awards, among them: Best Scoring of a Musical. Johnny Green, Sid Ramin, and Irv

Kostal were there to pick up their Oscars. I was in London working on the Judy Garland film *I Could Go On Singing*. I was awakened at 7:00 A.M. by a call from Ernie, calling from a phone booth to tell me I had won. I would have liked nothing better than to be there, but at this late date why should I have expected anything to have happened normally with this film?

Postscript: Samuel Goldwyn said to Bob Wise, "I love your picture—*West End Avenue*."

After a year and a half of battling *West Side Story*, I decided to take some time off. For the first time in many years I found myself with no future commitments, so I could loaf as long as I could stand it. I got in touch with my daughter, Judy, then living in Paris with Ethel and Buddy, and asked her to come along with me on a journey through Europe and then to New York. She had been studying music at the Marguerite Long Conservatory, but she was able to rearrange her schedule to join me.

My original itinerary included almost every country in Europe, but when it was pointed out to me how impractical that was, I narrowed it down to France, Italy, Greece, and Israel. Judy had lived in France and Italy for a considerable length of time. She spoke French fluently and managed very well with Italian. She and Ethel laid out our itinerary—cities, hotels, lengths of stay—and arranged for our plane tickets. By the time I got to Paris, I had nothing to do but enjoy the ten days I was to spend there before Judy and I left on our trip. It turned out to be a great vacation.

When we got to New York, Judy called the only theatrical producer she knew—Harold Prince, whom she had met at a party in Paris several months earlier. She asked him for a job, but instead he invited her to dinner. She accepted but pointed out that having dinner was not her problem. He continued to take her out but steadfastly avoided discussions about her working.

Chapter 19 ■ Shortly after I returned to Los Angeles from my trip with Judy, Larry Turman called me. He and Stuart Millar were about to produce a film called *The Lonely Stage,* starring Dirk Bogarde and Judy Garland. She was to sing five songs in the film. At Judy's suggestion, they engaged me to choose the songs and supervise the music.

Any chance to work with Judy always appealed to me, but what also attracted me was that it was to be shot at Shepperton Studios in London. I had never worked in Europe and looked forward to it.

I Could Go On Singing

The producers had promised Judy that of the five songs, one would be new. Harold Arlen and Yip Harburg were chosen to write it. They were obviously the perfect choice because they had written Judy's biggest hit, "Over the Rainbow." I was therefore surprised when their new song arrived. Not that it was bad, but it was not the kind of song Judy could sing better than anyone else, and that's what we wanted. It was pleasant enough, but I had a sneaking suspicion that it had come out of their trunk, had originally been written for some other project.

I phoned them, and after diplomatically complimenting them on the song, I said, "But I have what I think is a good idea. You know what Judy kicks the hell out of in her personal appearances? The Jolson song, 'Rockabye Your Baby.' What do you think of writing that kind of song for her?"

I don't think I fooled them for one second about how I felt about the song they had submitted, but they agreed to do the Jolson-type song, and that's really all that interested me. They came through with an excellent song, "I Could Go On Singing," which became the title of the film.

Among the other songs in the film was one suggested by Judy with a title that always amused me—"Hello, Bluebird." It was obviously the songwriter's answer to "Bye, Bye, Blackbird."

Judy wanted to do the film for more than one reason. She liked the script, which bore a marked resemblance to events in her life. But more important, she wanted to get out of the country because she lived in constant terror that Sid Luft, her estranged husband, would take their children, Lorna and Joey, away from her. Despite her devastating emotional problems, she was a passionately devoted mother. Several times, Sid appeared in London, which caused all kinds of difficulties. It was actually sad because Sid genuinely loved Lorna and Joey.

One night during the time we were shooting, Judy found out that Sid was in town. She hurriedly packed several bags for herself and the kids and fled to the airport in an attempt to leave the country. Everything went well until Immigration asked to see her passport. She searched through her clothes, her bags— everywhere—but it was nowhere to be found. She didn't have it. By a fortuitous stroke of luck, the producers had taken it from her several days before to have her labor permit renewed. Otherwise, she would undoubtedly have left the country with no regard for what would happen to the film.

Judy's home life was a shambles. In addition to Lorna and Joey, Liza (Minnelli), then sixteen, was living with her. In fact, while we were looking for a choreographer, I spotted Liza backstage at the Palladium singing one of Judy's arrangements and inventing choreography for it. She is said to have found Judy unconscious on the bathroom floor at least once after one of her suicide attempts and called a doctor. Judy was drinking quite heavily and Liza was there to look after her.

Yet there were other times when they all had great fun together. But with Judy's apprehensions about Luft in addition to her general emotional instability, she had great difficulty coping with her daily life.

Judy was unbelievably difficult during the filming. I had no problems with her because nothing she did could surprise me. Not even when she appeared for a rehearsal at 7:00 in the evening when it had been called for 11:00 that morning. Mort Lindsey, the musical director, and I just went on doing our day's work and checked every few hours to see if anyone knew when she might be coming. No one did.

Whenever she was late, she made no excuses. She usually had a joke or an unusual incident to relate and made it seem she was really on time. I am obsessively punctual and have very little patience with people who are late. But not with Judy. Maybe it's because I never expected her to show up when she was supposed to.

Unfortunately, her lateness often necessitated working past the usual hour for quitting. The English crew hated her for that because it interfered with their nightly ritual of stopping at the local pub for a "jar of bitters" on their way home. She argued with everyone, including Dirk Bogarde and Ronald Neame, the director, who had started the film adoring her. There was a constant air of tension on the set. I had never seen Judy behave this badly, and it was depressing.

Several times she refused to come to the studio for two- and three-day periods. The first time was caused by a scene that was being shot. It was slightly complicated. Judy entered her apartment carrying several packages, which she had to put down in certain places. Although she did it perfectly every time, Neame kept shooting take after take. (I must interject here that Ronald Neame is not only extremely talented [*The Horse's Mouth, Tunes of Glory,* and many others] but is the gentlest of men. It was always, "Judy, dear" or "Judy, darling.") After four takes, Ronnie asked her to do still another.

Judy blew up. "Why the hell are we doing it again? Was anything wrong?"

The set fell silent. "Please," pleaded Ronnie, "just one more."

"No, dammit," she stormed back, "not until you tell me what's wrong!"

"Judy, dear," Neame said in a conversational voice, "I was hoping not to have to explain this, but you leave me no choice. Every once in a great while a director works with an actor of

such extraordinary talent and invention that he or she unconsciously improves a scene each time it's shot. What is added is
intangible and not on the written page, or in the director's mind.
Each time you did the scene, you added an element to it that
hadn't existed before. You did it unconsciously and spontane-
ously. But now that we've discussed it, both those qualities are
gone, so let's set up for the next shot."

A few seconds of silence. Judy said, "No. Let's do it again."

"It's pointless, Judy darling. Besides, we already have it."

Judy left the set and was gone for three days.

Whenever she took these lengthy breaks, a hurried phone call
was placed to her New York agent, David Begelman, one of the
men who was responsible for Judy's reemergence as a performer
in a series of enormously successful concerts after she had not
been seen for several years. After a few days, Begelman would
report Judy's complaint to the producers. In every case it was
minor, imagined and meaningless.

One time she felt that Bogarde and Neame were mistreating
her. Nothing could have been further from the truth, but to
indulge her, a reconciliation was effected. Another time she objected to a scene that required a minor alteration to satisfy her.
Her most surprising complaint was that she needed a choreographer. She sang every song in the film alone on the stage of the
Palladium in front of an audience. That is exactly what she had
been doing very successfully in theaters for over a year, without
a choreographer. But as it happened, Joe Layton was in town
staging the English version of a Broadway show he had done,
and he was asked to help.

He spent several hours trying, but nothing came of it. Judy
then decided that we—mainly *she*—could do it ourselves. Late
one night, Judy, David Begelman, and I went to the Palladium
after their last show to try to solve the nonproblem. The stage
was empty except for a work light. The piano in the pit was
locked, so I sat in the footlights and sang her songs (unaccom-

panied) as I watched her devise movements for herself. We decided which ones to use. The entire session proved an exercise in futility. When the numbers were eventually shot, she ignored everything we had done that night. The enthusiasm of the Palladium audience dictated her choreography.

Judy was marvelous in *I Could Go On Singing*. Her voice was as full-bodied, vibrant, and exciting as ever. Her acting was sensitive and in several areas intensely moving. In a scene toward the end of the film, she proved what a superb actress she was. She played a famous singer who comes to London to perform at the Palladium and to reclaim her son (whom she had deserted years earlier), who has been living with his father (Dirk Bogarde) for all those years. She is about to do a show when she sprains her ankle. Just as she is about to cancel the performance, Dirk appears. He pleads with her to go on because she owes it to the public. She argues that she owes the public nothing. She has given them half her life, and what has she gotten in return? Misery. At the same time, she pleads for the return of her son and Dirk's love. She accomplishes neither.

Neame had intended to shoot the scene from several angles. But Judy, who had had a couple of drinks before the scene started and was a little high, was so brilliant that Ronnie just let the camera roll, and the entire seven-minute scene was shot in one take. We all watched in wonder as she improvised lines, wept, laughed, and seemed to be baring her soul. We were all feeling the same thing: She wasn't playing a character. She was playing herself.

After it was over, there was a hushed silence. Then Ronnie whispered, "Cut." This was followed by loud cheers and bravos from all of us. We had all had the rare privilege of watching a consummate artist practising her craft.

I Could Go On Singing had its premiere at a royal command performance in London. The audience loved it, and there were unanimous raves from the critics the following day. Judy's performance was called everything from "magical" to "remarkable." The film was hailed as one of the best pictures of the year. The people from United Artists were ecstatic, sure they had another *Jolson Story.*

Despite all that, the film was an abysmal flop. It did absolutely no business. Apparently, Judy had enough of an audience to fill concert halls, but not movie houses.

Several years later, Liza, making her Broadway debut, starred in a show produced by Harold Prince called *Flora, the Red Menace,* for which she received the Tony Award. Judy attended almost every evening performance, and as the final curtain came down, she leaped to her feet, applauded wildly, and shouted, "Bravo! Bravo!" And all over the theater one heard "It's Judy Garland! It's Judy Garland!"

In the meantime, Hal Prince continued taking my daughter everywhere and finally asked her to marry him. I was still occupied with the Garland film, but I flew to New York for the wedding and reception, having promised Millar and Turman, the producers of the movie, that I would return to London the morning after the festivities.

And festive it was. Hal, who is very gregarious, knew everyone in New York theater, and they all appeared at the reception at the St. Regis Hotel. It was the laughingest party I've ever attended, and it will long be remembered by everyone who was there.

They decided to honeymoon in London, where Hal had many friends. They left on the morning after the reception, and by coincidence we were on the same plane. In London there was a constant round of parties for them, and as the father of the bride, I was invited to all of them.

Chapter 20 ■ "Hi. How you doing with the Rat Pack?" It was my agent, Phil Gersh, on the phone. I was working on *Robin and the Seven Hoods* with Frank Sinatra and his friends.

"As a matter of fact, I'm having a helluva lot of fun. But that could be because Frank hasn't shown up yet. You know how he is about rehearsals. I'm just working with Dean, Bing, Sammy, and tone-deaf Peter Falk."

"Where's Frank?"

"Who knows? I guess he's wherever he goes when he doesn't show up for rehearsals."

The

"Listen, the reason I called—can you drop by my office tonight on your way home around six o'clock?"

Sound

"Why? What did I do? Did Jack Warner catch me coming in late?"

of Music

"No. Nothing like that. And besides, it's none of Warner's business when you come in. You're working for Sinatra. No, I want to talk to you about something."

"Okay, Phil, I'll see you at six.

That seemingly innocuous phone call changed my life drastically.

I arrived at Gersh's office to be greeted by him and Bob Wise. I hadn't seen Bob in some time and was glad to have the opportunity to tell him how much I had enjoyed his last film, *The Haunting.* There was more small talk, then Phil launched into the reason for the meeting.

"As you know, Fox is looking for a director for *The Sound of Music.* Dick Zanuck has offered it to Bob three times, and he's turned it down because he doesn't feel it's his kind of material. Now it's being offered to him again. So we decided we'd ask you to read Ernie Lehman's screenplay. If you think it's right for Bob, he might reconsider."

If ever there was a chore I didn't want to fulfill, this was it. I also knew that there was no way I could turn down the request because Bob and I had been through so much together. "All right," I said halfheartedly, "I'll read it."

"Solly," Bob said, "just see if you think I would enjoy doing this kind of show. In fact, you don't even have to read the whole script. Just enough to make a decision."

"Oh no," I said. "It's Ernie's, so I'll read it all tonight."

It was a heavy responsibility. I was not unfamiliar with *The Sound of Music*. I had seen it on the stage in New York and hadn't liked it. I thought it had a first-rate score, but the story was a bit too sweet for me. Several months later, Ernie Lehman saw the show and called me as soon as he got back to his hotel. He was all excited by what a wonderful movie he thought it would make. I told him about my reservations, but he said they could be taken care of in the screenplay. I didn't believe him.

Ernie found out that Twentieth Century–Fox owned the movie rights, and when he returned to Hollywood, he signed to do the screenplay. It was during a period when Fox was in a state of upheaval and executives were coming and going like through a revolving door. There was no producer or director assigned to the film, and Ernie was having an exasperating time trying to get a decision when and if the picture was going to be made. At long last, Richard Zanuck took over as the studio's head of production. Sanity was restored, and they began their search for a producer and director.

I was now being asked to read the screenplay of a show I didn't like, written by a person I'd told the show would not make a good film. Before I began reading, I composed polite ways of expressing my objections: "It's a helluva job, Ernie, but it's still too saccharine." "Bob, it's an improvement over the play, but it's still not for you." And so on.

Then I read it. I was never so happy reading a script in my life. It was wonderful. Ernie had retained the elements that made *Sound of Music* such an enormous hit, but by changes and additions, he had improved it immeasurably. The characters were more clearly defined, it was more charming, and he had invented a truly exciting and suspenseful finish. Also, it read as if it had been written originally for the screen instead of being an adaptation of a stage play.

I called Phil the next day and enthusiastically recommended that Bob direct it. Further, I insisted the project needed Bob. My reasons? First, it was a simple, sweet, and appealing fairy tale with a little too much *schlag,* even though Ernie had toned it down considerably. In the hands of anyone but a realistic director—which Bob is in spades—the sweetness could contaminate the film and make it unbearable. Second, it had one of the best scores Rodgers and Hammerstein had ever written. Third, the film needed pace, a quality that typified most of Bob's films. Less important, this was a perfect project for Bob to demonstrate to the film community that he could handle a romantic love story as well as the dramatic films on which he had built his reputation.

Phil related my opinions to Bob, who finally decided to do it. I was later signed as associate producer. Three years after we had worked on *West Side Story,* Bob, Ernie, and I were reunited on *The Sound of Music.*

Casting the film was not easy because there were so many parts. We were shown some footage from *Mary Poppins,* which had not been released, and we immediately knew that Julie Andrews was perfect for the part of Maria von Trapp. However, she wasn't sure she wanted to do it. She was playing a dramatic role in *The Americanization of Emily,* which was still filming, and she felt she might want to play a nonmusical part again. Everyone from Audrey Hepburn to Anne Bancroft was mentioned for the part. The leading contender to play Captain von Trapp was Bing Crosby. He was the studio's suggestion, which we never really took seriously because we never considered him right for the part.

Then there were the seven children. A conservative guess would be that about two hundred children were interviewed for those seven parts. Of them all, there are only two I remember vividly.

The first, a five-year-old girl, came marching into the room with the self-assurance of a seasoned veteran, a portfolio under her arm that was larger than she was. As she handed it to Bob, she declaimed, "I'm here to interview for the part of the youngest child. I'm perfect for it. I can sing and dance and have had lots of acting experience." She continued on and on in the same vein.

I whispered to Bob, "Get her out of here before she starts climbing the wall." Bob, who had more experience at this sort of thing than I, simply listened with a smile on his face. Later she was signed to play the part because she was far better than anyone else we had seen. It took the kind of brash confidence she displayed to take direction, as opposed to the other five-year-olds we had interviewed, most of whom were too shy.

The most difficult child to cast was the oldest. She was supposed to be sixteen and to sing and dance. It was important that she look that age because the song she had to sing was "I Am Sixteen Going On Seventeen." At one of our early interviews we met a young lady named Charmian Carr. She was so pretty and had such an engaging manner that she was my immediate choice. Bob liked her too but thought she looked too old, so we continued looking.

We would see three or four others and choose one. Before our final choice, however, we had Charmian come in again, and we rejected the other girl. We repeated this procedure several times. Each time Bob said that Charmian looked too old, and I insisted it didn't matter. Actually, I hadn't a clue how old she was. I wanted her in the picture. She was eventually given the part and was wonderful. For the record, it can now be divulged that Bob was right. She was older than sixteen, much older—twenty-one. It goes without saying that had we known, she wouldn't have been considered.

On November 1, 1963, Bob Wise, Boris Leven (the art director, who also did *West Side Story*), Saul Wurtzel (the production manager), and I flew to Austria to scout locations. There was snow everywhere, and we had to know how the locations would look after the snow melted because we were scheduled to shoot in late spring and summer.

Our German production manager took us to a large field that was knee-deep in snow and surrounded by tall, barren stalks also heavily laden with snow. He suggested it as the place to film Maria singing the opening title song. He assured us that at the time we planned to shoot, the field would be a verdant green surrounded by lush foliage and tall trees. I couldn't imagine how that was possible, but it turned out to be true.

We wanted to use the Nonnberg Abbey, where Maria had been a postulate, but we were turned down. It was a very strict religious order where less than a handful of nuns were ever permitted to leave, and then only on rare occasions. The rest spent their entire lives within the abbey walls. We were given permission, however, to shoot at the entrance and right outside the building but most definitely not in it.

We had one further need. There is a scene where the children go to the abbey looking for Maria. They pull a cord that hangs on a wall, which presumably rings a bell inside. Since there was no such cord, we asked for and got permission to install one. When filming was finished, we were about to remove it but were informed that the nuns would like us to leave it. They knew it served no useful purpose, but they liked having it.

While we were in Austria, we got word that Louella Parsons had stated in her column that Julie Andrews had consented to play Maria in *The Sound Of Music*. We checked with the studio, who verified it. We were overjoyed and furious. Why did we have to find out about it through Louella Parsons's column? It was a case of everyone at the studio assuming that someone else was going to let us know. In the meantime, we had wasted hours discussing other actresses who could play the part.

One important piece of casting remained: an actor to play Captain von Trapp. Christopher Plummer had been suggested, and we were interested, especially when we were told that he was very musical. He could sing, and he was a fine pianist. But he kept vacillating about the role. In the meantime, the more we searched, the more attractive Plummer became. He finally consented to do the movie if he could have his part rewritten. He wanted Captain von Trapp to be much lighter and more humorous. He had several sessions with Ernie. Virtually imperceptible alterations were made in the script, but he was satisfied, and that was all that mattered.

His musicality had been exaggerated. The most that could be said for his singing was that he could carry a tune in a moderately pleasant manner. But Captain von Trapp was supposed to be an excellent singer, and there was no way that Plummer could fill that role. He nevertheless insisted on shooting to his own voice, and he recorded all of his songs himself. I later replaced his tracks using a voice double named Bill Lee who was as adept at emulating male voices as Marni Nixon was at female voices.

As for Plummer's skill as a pianist, he would never play when I was within earshot. But one night in Austria when he had had too much to drink (he played only when he was drunk) he didn't know I was in the room, and I heard him play. He had a florid style that used incessant, meaningless arpeggios and scales, so much musical decoration that it was difficult to tell what song he was playing.

His relationship with the other actors left a lot to be desired. He behaved as though he were a distinguished legendary actor who had agreed to grace this small amateur company with his presence. He sometimes wore a cape, which made him look like an escapee from Transylvania. He never mingled with the cast, except for one or two he considered worthy of his occasional attention.

He did lose his haughtiness once. Bob had the film editor run the first hour of footage that had been cut together. Chris was very impressed and for a few days forgot who he thought he was. It must have crossed his mind that doing a musical might not, after all, be beneath him. But after a few days he reverted to haughtiness.

Christopher Plummer is a fine actor. His contribution to the success of *Sound of Music* was considerable. During the shooting he was very professional. He was always on the set when he was needed, always knew his lines, and often made valuable suggestions. But he felt that the film was unworthy of his talent and apologizes for having done it to this day.

In transferring the stage play to the screen, several songs were affected. "My Favorite Things" was given to Maria to sing to the children instead of the Mother Abbess singing it to Maria. "The Lonely Goatherd" was used as the basis for a puppet show. "How Can Love Survive" and "No Way to Stop It" were deleted because we decided that the characters who sang it in the stage version should not sing in the film. "An Ordinary Couple" was replaced because we wanted more of a love song for the film. How the new song came to be written must be told in more detail.

The screenplay included a series of scenes that showed Maria leaving the abbey and after traveling through Salzburg and its environs, arriving at the Trapp villa. Ernie thought that perhaps Maria could sing a song as she went from place to place. If a song didn't work out, it could be a montage showing the beauty of Salzburg and its surroundings. We talked about it and decided that of course she should be singing as she progresses on her journey.

When Bob Wise and I were in New York, we met with Richard Rodgers and explained our needs: a new ballad to replace "An Ordinary Couple" and a new song for Maria's trip from the abbey to the Trapp villa. Rodgers was to write the lyrics as well as the music since his longtime lyricist Oscar Hammerstein had died several years before. I described what Maria's song should be about. She leaves the abbey because she is fearful of facing the outside world alone, yet it is God's will—she must obey. She believes everything in life has a purpose, so perhaps her fears are groundless. Gradually she convinces herself that it will all turn out fine. By the time she reaches the villa, she is looking forward to this new challenge.

A month later, Bob Wise and I were in New York again interviewing children. I called Dick Rodgers, who said he had just finished the second of the two songs we had asked him to write and would like us to hear them. We went to his luxuriously appointed suite of offices on Madison Avenue. I was as impressed as I was when I first met Cole Porter. The comparison is apt because here again I had to judge the work of someone I admired enormously.

He played the ballad first. It was called "Something Good," and it was lovely. We asked him to play it again, and I played along on the upper keys of the piano. I liked it even better the second time. He then told us the title of the song he had written for Maria's journey. He called it "I Have Confidence in Me." A marvelous title, I thought. It described exactly how Maria should feel at the end of the song.

But then he played it. What a letdown! It was very short, only sixteen bars, and in a minor key. There was no joy in it. He had completely ignored (or overlooked) my letter about the content of the early part of the song.

I could never get myself to tell him all of that, so I did my best to hide my disappointment and said I would like to take the song back to the studio with me and work with it. Then Bob and I "registered great waves of enthusiasm" (to quote Cole Porter) about "Something Good" and left.

When I got back to the studio, I wrote Dick a letter. I stated my objections to his song as diplomatically as I could. I was crazy about his title, "I Have Confidence in Me," but didn't he think that it suggested a happier tune than the one he had written? Also, I was sure that probably because he was so busy with other matters, he had overlooked my suggestions for the early part of the number. I thought it might be helpful if I spelled out what that part should be about in more detail, although I was fully aware that there were many other ways of accomplishing the same purpose. The song could be roughly divided into three sections:

1. ABBEY AREA (Maria slowly walking away from the Abbey):

    Music is religioso. Choir singing hymn in background. Maria— apprehensive, frightened about leaving. But it is God's will so she must obey. Wonders what the future holds for her. Tries to overcome fears by singing—that she's always longed for adventure. Sings dejectedly, "What's the matter with me?"

2. SALZBURG AND AUTOBUS (Maria crosses main square and boards bus):

    Music is quasi-recitative. She sings that she *must* find the courage to face this new life. She will endear herself to the Trapp family by being stern but gentle. She gradually convinces herself that everything will turn out fine. She gets off autobus.

3. ROAD AND TRAPP VILLA (Song: "I Have Confidence in Me"):

    Music is bright and happy. She is now certain that she will be able to fulfill her assignment. She comes barreling down the road, totally uninhibited, swinging the carpet bag she has been carrying. As she sees the imposing entrance to the Trapp Villa, her spirts are momentarily dampened. She regains her courage, runs to the front door and rings the bell.

Rodgers's response to my letter was a completely new version of "I Have Confidence in Me," totally different from the one we had heard in New York. It was in a fast tempo, in a major key, and would serve for the last part of the number. But once more he had ignored parts 1 and 2.

I wrote back how pleased I was with what he had sent me. I mentioned, however, that I thought it would be awkward to have her break out into such hilarity as she approached the villa when the last time we had seen her she was dejected about having to leave the abbey. To show this gradual change in her attitude, we needed the early parts I had written to him about.

The phone rang at a quarter to seven in the morning. It was

Rodgers. He didn't understand what I was asking him to write. I went through it all again, slowly. He asked numerous questions, and we covered the same points repeatedly.

After a half hour of polite jousting, I came to a conclusion: Either he didn't want to write the new material, or he wanted me to offer to do it. If he was refusing to write it, he was cheating the studio. According to his contract, he was to be paid $15,000 for every new song he wrote. He could claim he had earned the fee by what he had already written, even though I considered it incomplete. I was determined not to write it myself because I am no Richard Rodgers. This was quite different from occasionally changing Cole Porter's lyrics. This involved writing new music, and no one did that better than Rodgers.

After talking on the phone for over an hour, I capitulated wearily: "Okay. I'll try writing it. I'll send you a record, and maybe that'll give you an idea of what I have in mind."

I yelled for Ernie. He came to my house, and we put together the first section of the song. I decided that although Rodgers wouldn't write it himself, I would use his music. I based the entire early section on the music of the verse of the song "The Sound of Music," which wasn't sung in the picture. Over the next several days, I finished what Ernie and I had left undone and wrote an extra chorus of lyrics for Rodgers's "Confidence" song. I played it for Ernie and Bob, and they were very happy with it.

While all this was going on, Julie periodically asked when she was going to hear her new song. I invented all kinds of excuses, from "There's really no hurry" to "As soon as Dick Rodgers completes a project he's working on—just a matter of a couple of weeks."

When the song was finally finished, I didn't want Julie to know that we were asking her to sing a song that had not been written by Rodgers. In any case, I had to get his permission to use it. I brought in Marni Nixon, swore her to secrecy, and had her record the number. I sent the record to Rodgers and received a telegram, something like "Prefer my version. Okay to use yours if that is the decision."

Postscript: Julie didn't learn of the saga of "I Have Confidence" until about two years after the picture was released when I felt it was finally safe to tell her.

When the script was finished, it was sent to Darryl Zanuck in New York for his comments and criticism. (He had assumed the presidency of Twentieth Century–Fox when Spyros Skouras had resigned two years earlier. When the film later turned out to be an enormous international success, they both claimed to have been instrumental in acquiring the rights to the stage play for the studio.) Zanuck wrote Bob Wise a long letter in which he enumerated the changes he suggested for the script.

Most were minor and inconsequential, but there was a major change that we found quite startling. He wrote that we would strengthen the ending of the film and heighten the suspense if a sequence was added in which Captain von Trapp, Maria, and the seven children made their way through the dense forest hotly pursued by the Nazis. The Trapps would reach the Swiss border in the nick of time.

Bob wrote a masterful letter in response. He said that the ending being suggested would undoubtedly work as a finish to the film. But the general feeling at the studio was that there was sufficient suspense in the cemetery scene and that the high shot he intended of the Trapp family crossing into Switzerland over the Alps should be most effective. However, he was grateful for all the suggestions. The incident is worth noting because it was the only comment from any member of the executive echelon during the making of the film. Except for the budget—but more of that later.

I hired Iwrin Kostal as music director at Julie's request. She had enjoyed working with him on *Mary Poppins*. I knew him well from *West Side Story*. As vocal coach, I engaged Bobby Tucker again. He had also been on the *West Side Story* staff. Our choreographers were Marc and Dee Dee Breaux, who had worked with Julie on *Poppins* and whom I knew when they were assistants to Michael Kidd. Because it was such a congenial group and we were working with excellent material, rehearsals were great fun.

Working with Julie Andrews reminded me of working with Judy Garland. They both learned music instantly, as if by magic. They both made songs sound better than you imagined they could. Both made suggestions about how a song should be sung, and if their ideas were rejected, they accepted the rejection gracefully. They had great objectivity about their own work and knew when they had done well. And they were very bright and fun to be with.

There were important differences. Their vocal ranges were quite different. And where Judy's voice had great emotion, Julie's has great clarity. When Julie performs, she is always in control and near-perfect every time. With Judy, there was always the worry that she might fall apart at any moment.

Although their adult lifestyles were completely unalike, it's surprising how similar their childhood years had been. They both toured in vaudeville with their families and were both juvenile stars, Julie on the stage and Judy on the screen. Their most important similarity, however, was their superb talent as highly accomplished and exciting performers who could do it all—sing, dance, act—everything.

The Sound of Music started shooting at the Twentieth Century–Fox studio in Hollywood On March 23, 1964. The scene is Maria's bedroom. She says her prayers and gets into bed. At that point, a violent thunderstorm breaks out. The oldest child, Liesl, climbs into the room through the window, soaked and filthy, having clambered up a vine during the height of the storm. The rest of the children, frightened by the lightning and thunder, run to Maria's room. They all get into bed with her. She sings "My Favorite Things" to comfort them and distract them from the storm. The frivolity ends when Captain von Trapp suddenly appears, stern and threatening.

During the rehearsals of this scene, every time the lightning flashed, we heard someone counting, "one-two-three . . ." until the thunder struck. Then the counting would stop. It turned out to be the script supervisor, Betty Levin, who was sitting at the foot of the sound boom. She had decided she wanted to know how far away the storm was, which can be determined by the time between the lightning and thunder.

It was the kind of happy set where one felt free to do nutty things like that. But when Liesl made her entrance through the window, Betty turned serious and insisted that her dress was too dirty. It was pointed out that she had just climbed a vine in the middle of a raging thunderstorm. Betty's reply was that she looked more like she had come out of a coal mine. It was obvious that this was true, so some of the dirt was removed from the dress.

Betty's morning behavior was something else. She would arrive on the set and burst into song. Unlike most people who sing to themselves, she really let go. One of the actors, Richard Hayden, described it best: "When Betty sings, it's like she's on the stage of the Radio City Music Hall." She often became annoyed with me. I enjoyed being on the set most of the time and particularly enjoyed being with the children. Betty accused me of being too noisy and thought of me as something of a troublemaker.

Marc Breaux and I left for Salzburg a week before the rest of the company. We had prerecorded two numbers ("Do, Re, Mi" and "I Have Confidence in Me"), which were to be shot on the streets and environs of Salzburg. Since we couldn't rehearse in the actual locations, we guessed at the distances between certain points and how much music it would require to get us from one place to another. We put both tracks on a portable tape recorder and flew to Salzburg where we did the numbers on the real locations to see whether we had guessed correctly. If the length of the music had to be changed, the studio could adjust the music tracks before the rest of the company left for Salzburg, bringing the new versions with them.

That Marc and I weren't killed is a miracle. Since most of the action we were checking took place on the streets of the city, we knew there would be a lot of traffic. We first thought it would be a good idea to start very early in the morning when the traffic would be lightest. We rejected that because we had to play our tape rather loudly. That would awaken the whole city, and we'd certainly be arrested for disturbing the peace. We had no alternative but to do it during the day and use the traffic lights as an ally.

We would both stand at the top of a street where the action was to start and wait for the traffic light to turn red. The moment it did, I turned on the tape, loud, and Marc would go dancing down the street. Unfortunately, the lights had no regard for the length of our playbacks. Often they would turn green before our music ran out. Then it became a matter of dodging the traffic to stay alive. The onlookers thought we were crazy. A policeman finally asked us what we were doing. I speak some German, but I doubt that I could have explained our activities to a nonprofessional, even in English. In any event, the policeman neither stopped us nor helped us. He humored us with a crazy-Americans smile, shrugged his shoulders, and walked away. We went back to waiting for the next red light.

Salzburg and its inhabitants seem to have been created for a "Mitteleuropa" operetta. Its baroque architecture and its elaborately decorated furniture have been copied for works by Romberg, Lehar, and others, but one never expects to see them anywhere but on a stage. And the people dress like operetta actors. The women wear gaily colored dirndls, the men mostly short pants with forest-green jackets and Alpine hats. Their native food is delicious and fattening. I don't believe I've ever seen a thin Austrian. Their restaurants are quaint, and one has the feeling that Johann Strauss, the elder and the younger, probably had a meal at the same tables and must still be there. Their folk music, with its mandolins, concertinas, and guitars, is heard everywhere. In many ways, Salzburg seems never to have progressed beyond the nineteenth century.

There are certain advantages in never having acknowledged

the twentieth century. Almost nightly there were chamber-music concerts of programs played in the halls where they had premiered. It isn't possible to describe the thrill of hearing a Mozart string quartet played by four excellent musicians in the salon where it was first performed. The Salzburg Summer Music Festival is justifiably world famous, but I prefer the intimate chamber-music concerts I attended in various baroque castles during the filming of *The Sound of Music.*

In the beginning, a group of about eight of us from the production would go to them almost nightly. Gradually, people dropped out until there were just two of us who attended regularly—Betty Levin and I. Naturally, as in an operetta, we fell in love. But no librettist could imagine the kind of idyllic courtship we enjoyed: long walks along the banks of the picturesque Salzach River, intimate dinners in romantic restaurants, delightful journeys to magical lakes and enchanted forests—all in and around a fairyland called Salzburg.

Again as in an operetta, I asked her to marry me. But I didn't propose until four years later because until that moment I had been a confirmed bachelor. I had been through the equivalent of two divorces, Sammy and Ethel, and I had vowed never to put myself in that position again—happily, a vow I didn't keep.

When production managers lay out shooting schedules for films, they never make adequate allowances for unfavorable weather on exterior locations. But there was no way they could have anticipated the catastrophic weather that befell us in Salzburg. The city is nestled in a mountain range where the wind directions are totally unpredictable. We received daily weather reports from two sources: the German Weather Bureau in Munich and the U.S. Air Force, based in the same general area. Often their forecasts were different. On several occasions they both refused to make forecasts because the winds were so erratic. I suppose their honesty is to be commended.

It isn't that it just rained. It often rained aggravatingly. For example, we would come down for breakfast at 7:00 A.M., the weather sparkling, nothing but blue skies above, the air refreshingly crisp. We would get into our cars and head for our location, happily jabbering away.

As we drove, a cloud would suddenly come into view. Then another—and another. Conversation would stop as though a signal had been given. By the time we reached our destination, we would be in the middle of a torrential downpour. We would sit around on location all day waiting for the sun to reappear. A few times it did, too late to start shooting. But the sunny days compensated for the waiting. It was all beautiful.

At the end of our schedule we were left with one shot for which we needed bright sunlight. We sat around on that location for two days and watched it pour relentlessly. Finally we decided that if it was not sunny the following morning, we would find a way to do the shot at the studio in Hollywood. Regardless of what happened, we were going to leave Salzburg the following afternoon. Luckily, the weather cooperated. It was brilliantly sunny the following morning, and we finished our location shooting without a hitch. But we were three weeks behind schedule.

When the film was playing in theaters, the studio received countless letters with the same message: "We enjoyed the picture and were particularly impressed with the beauty of Salzburg, so we traveled there on our holiday. It is beautiful, but it rained quite a bit while we were there. We must have picked the wrong time to go."

During my first week back at the studio I was called to a meeting in the office of one of the studio executives to revise the shooting and recording schedules since we were so far behind. After that was done, the executive asked me to remain after the others left. He said, "Do you realize that the picture is way over budget?"

"Of course I do," I replied. "But it's because we had so much rain."

"You shouldn't have kept waiting for good weather. You should have come home and shot what you didn't finish at the studio."

"But have you seen how beautiful the film is?" I asked.

"Yes, but what's important now is . . . do you think you can talk to Wise about shooting faster so we can make up some of the time?"

Without even blinking, I replied, "I'll try."

Although I said it, I hadn't the slightest intention of even mentioning the conversation to Bob, and I never have. He knew better than I how far behind we were. My talking to him about it would have accomplished nothing. Quite to the contrary, at one point I suggested he shoot close-ups of the children, which he hadn't intended doing. This lengthened the schedule by half a day.

That doesn't mean that attempts were not made to quicken our pace, but Bob's films were always so masterfully created that we mostly stayed out of his way. The film finally did finish considerably over budget, but history has since proved it to have been a sound investment, indeed.

None of us anticipated what a wildfire hit the film would be, particularly after it received mixed reviews from the critics. Bob, Ernie, and I had gone that route before with *West Side Story,* but it's not the kind of thing you get used to. The criticisms included "too saccharine"; "story as flimsy as cotton candy"; "Julie Andrews, an engaging performer, does as well as she can with inferior material." When the word spread and the film became a runaway hit, an important film critic who had written a negative review was fired by the magazine where she had been working for some time. They felt that her opinion was so far afield from their readers' that eventually her reviews might lose them subscribers.

American film musicals had come on hard times in European theaters. One of the reasons for the sharp downturn in business was thought to be that while the dialogue was dubbed in another language, the songs were left in English and subtitled in the other language. Having to read subtitles annoyed audiences and detracted from their enjoyment of the film. It was decided that for *Sound of Music* the songs and dialogue both would be dubbed in various languages. I was sent to Paris, Barcelona, Rome, and Berlin to supervise dubbing the songs and to reproduce the drive, energy, and spirit of our original sound tracks.

But first the lyrics had to be translated, which turned out to be no small feat. The song "Do, Re, Mi," for example, presented almost insurmountable obstacles. The scale *do, re, mi* . . . etc. exists in all languages, so it had to be retained. But the English lyrics start with "Doe, a deer, a female deer." While *doe* means a female deer in English, it doesn't in any other language. Not only did a substitute have to be found in each of the four other languages for every note of the scale, but it had to be in synch with what Julie and the children were singing. Thanks to four extremely patient and talented foreign lyricists, it was finally accomplished. They needed infinite patience because I insisted on having precise English translations of everything they wrote.

The film was a success in most foreign countries, but there was never conclusive evidence that it was due to the translation of the songs. The picture was a dismal failure in two countries, Germany and Austria. The Austrians never understood why we were making another film about the Trapp family, since the Germans had already done one. But the primary reason was that the last third of it dealt with their Nazi past. They didn't like to be reminded of that period. In fact, Fox's German manager took it upon himself to delete the last third of the film, which eliminated the Nazis completely. The studio learned about it very quickly, fired the manager, and had the film restored to its original length.

At Academy Award time, *The Sound Of Music* was nominated in ten categories. Among those nominated were Bob, in two categories, Best Picture and Best Direction, and Julie for Best Actress. Bob was in Taiwan at the time wrestling with the formidable difficulties of shooting his next film, *The Sand Pebbles*. He wrote and asked Julie to pick up the award for him if he should win for Best Direction, and he asked me to accept it if the film won as Best Picture.

It was a truly memorable week. Judy and Hal were in Hollywood for the opening at the Music Center of *Fiddler on the Roof,* which Hal had produced. It opened during the same week as the Academy Award presentation. I invited Julie to both events, and the Princes joined us for the Academy show. We were picked up by a limousine sent by the studio and headed for the Santa Monica Civic Auditorium where the Academy festivities were to be held.

As we neared the auditorium, we waited in the usual line of limousines unloading celebrities. We could hear the fans yelling in the distant grandstands but paid no attention. We finally arrived at the entrance. I got out first, then helped Julie out. There was such an ear-shattering screech from the fans the moment they saw her that I was literally stunned motionless. I don't believe I've ever heard a more terrifying sound in my life. Julie, accustomed to this kind of reception and ever gracious, smiled through it all as we walked into the theater.

We took our seats and waited for the torture to begin. The awards Bob had been nominated for weren't given until the very end of the presentation, so we had a long, nervous wait ahead of us. We were also concerned with the other eight categories for which the film had been nominated. We felt that if we did well in those, Bob would stand a good chance, because often a very popular picture sweeps most of the awards. The first award was for Best Sound. We won it, so that was encouraging. But soon came the Best Costume award, which was won by *Doctor Zhivago.* Not too long after that *Doctor Zhivago* won the Best Art Direction and Best Cinematography awards, and we were worried. By this time, we were clutching each other to hide our nervousness. The hardest thing was to appear like good sports and smile in the face of all this adversity.

When Julie lost out to Julie Christie for her performance in the film *Darling,* I was sure all was lost. But then Bob's name was announced as Best Director, and Julie walked to the stage to accept his award. She got an enormous hand from the audience.

It was their way of expressing how much they admired her performance in *The Sound of Music* even though she hadn't won the award, which she had won the year before for *Mary Poppins*.

The last winner announced was Best Picture. I was now sitting alone; Julie didn't return to her seat after accepting Bob's Best Direction Award. I was a basket case. I was getting ready to feign my forced loser smile when I heard Jack Lemmon announce, "The Best Picture of the year is *The Sound of Music*."

I made my way to the stage—and suddenly realized that I hadn't prepared an acceptance speech. I was in a panic. What was I going to say? A simple "thank you" is inadequate for the most prestigious of all Academy Awards. I accepted the Oscar, walked up to the microphone, and said the first thing that popped into my head: "If Bob Wise were here, I'm sure he'd thank everyone connected with the picture and the Academy membership for voting him this Award. Instead, I'm going to take this opportunity to thank him for making the filming of *The Sound of Music* such a rewarding and stimulating experience."

It was easy to say that because it was true. I had now been through two long films with Bob and admired him enormously. Technically, there is nothing he doesn't know about filmmaking, and working with him was an education for me. I've often watched him make a dull scene exciting in an editing room. His byword was always "Make it play."

On the set he is the most accessible director I've ever worked with. He is always open to suggestions from others. Most important, he is a man of taste, and that is evident in all of his films. When his talent as a director is added to his great generosity and loyalty, it's easy to see why working with him is so stimulating and rewarding.

The film won five awards in all. In addition to those mentioned above, it won for Best Editing (William Reynolds) and Best Scoring of a Musical. Irwin Kostal, Oscar in hand, came up to me and said, "We should be sharing this. I don't know why you didn't hand your name in along with mine." I explained that

I had made a decision years earlier that on films where I received any kind of producer credit, I would forgo a music credit even though my contribution might have merited it.

My theory is that while most creative directors and producers are knowledgeable about every phase of filmmaking, they are usually particularly adept at one element. Some are especially creative guiding writers, others imaginative about casting or editing, and so on. My area of expertise is music. Just as the others usually don't take credit for their special contribution, I decided, I wouldn't. The irony is that during those years when I should have been given the awards, I wasn't. Yet here was a time when it was mine for the asking and I refused it.

Postscript: The huge commercial success of *The Sound of Music* prompted the other studios to resume making large, expensive musicals again. They were all failures.

Chapter 21 ■ While we were still in postproduction on *The Sound of Music,* Bob and I began looking for another project to do with Julie, which I would produce. Ernie was not included in our search because he was busy writing and producing *Hello, Dolly!*

After months of reading everything that held the vaguest promise and finding nothing, Bob's story editor, Max Lamb, suggested we read a biography of Gertrude Lawrence. Her background was so similar to Julie's that it seemed a perfect vehicle for her. She and Gertrude Lawrence were both *Star!* British, from middle-class families. They had both begun performing while they were still children. They both achieved stardom in the theater doing musical comedies and were as famous on Broadway as they were in Piccadilly.

Max wrote a short synopsis of Lawrence's life, and I gathered as many of her phonograph records as I could find. The list of hit songs she introduced was most impressive: "Limehouse Blues," "Do Do Do, "Someone to Watch Over Me," "My Ship," "Someday I'll Find You," "Jenny," and quite a few others. She had also made some records with her closest chum, Bea Lillie, and her lifelong confidant and mentor, Noel Coward.

Gertrude Lawrence was one of those rare personalities who could neither sing nor dance well but whose shortcomings went unnoticed when she performed. But I had to present her to Julie on records on which her voice was thin, out of tune, and unsteady. I had forgotten that Julie already knew what Lawrence sounded like, so I needn't have been apprehensive. In any case, after I told her briefly of Lawrence's life and played the records in their proper sequence, Julie was pleased with the project and agreed to do it.

Richard Aldrich, Lawrence's last husband, was the author of the biography. He wrote of the Gertrude Lawrence he knew. But major portions of her early life were omitted. In an endeavor to learn as much about her as we could, we sent Max Lamb to New York, London, and Paris to interview all her old friends and coworkers he could corral. We carried on similar interviews in Hollywood. Amazingly, almost everyone we approached was willing to talk about Gertie. Not willing—anxious. We were astounded at how much intimate and unflattering information was offered unhesitatingly. "Off the record," of course.

More than thirty people were interviewed. They represented her entire career, from the time she was a child in Clapham, a London suburb, to her last performance on Broadway in *The King and I*. They included actors, costume designers, directors, and business associates. Among the comments from these "friends" were "cold, reserved, and unfeeling," "aloof," "not intelligent—shrewd," "a reality onstage, an unreality offstage," "extremely egotistical," "bored and unhappy with Richard Aldrich," "hid her daughter for fear it might reveal her age."

There was a consensus that she was the epitome of chic, charm, and glamour, and a most skillful, talented, and accomplished performer. But even her decorum onstage had its detractors: "would tire of doing the same role night after night and begin clowning," "undisciplined as an actress," "jealous of dramatic actresses," "unpleasant to other actors in her early years."

Because these remarks were made in strict confidence, I do not feel free to reveal their sources. However, these ground rules do not apply to Noel Coward. He always talked about Gertie freely and wouldn't have minded being quoted. In fact, I think he'd have enjoyed it: "She could wear rags and look ravishingly beautiful. She was irresponsible. Magical but quite mad. Exaggerated her humble beginnings. Lonely offstage. As a performer, she needed great control. Wonderful sense of humor. She had many affairs—with just about everybody. Treated her beaux abominably. Made everything around her seem platinum-plated."

Noel and Gertie were notorious for their monumental rows. This tends to confirm what we were told by an intimate of theirs. They had a love-hate relationship.

Other than Noel, Gertrude Lawrence's closest friend was Bea

Lillie. We had every intention of portraying them both in the film. But Bea Lillie's manager, a most unpleasant man, refused to allow her to have anything to do with the movie unless she played the part herself, which meant she would be playing a teenager, although she was past seventy. Her part would have to be equal with Gertrude Lawrence's. Both requests were too ridiculous even to discuss.

Noel, on the other hand, was most cooperative. His only conditions were that he have the right to approve of the way he was portrayed and that he be paid for allowing himself to be represented in the film. We accepted his conditions and agreed to meet with him when we had a script.

We hired William Fairchild, the English screenwriter, and started putting the pieces together. After preliminary meetings during which we developed a rough version, Bob took off for Taiwan to shoot *The Sand Pebbles.* I remained at the studio where I worked with Fairchild on the script and investigated the availability of costume designers, cameramen, and other key technicians. I also educated myself in early English music hall songs, about which I knew nothing.

As we finished sections of the script, we sent them off to Bob, who wrote back his reactions. It was a long, drawn-out process because Bob was having more than just the customary problems with *Sand Pebbles* and couldn't get to the material we sent him as quickly as we would have liked. After several months, a first-draft screenplay was complete.

Bob fell further and further behind in Taiwan until it became clear that the start of our film, *Star!,* would have to be postponed. Fairchild went back to London to write the next draft of the script, and I took a summer vacation.

When I returned to the studio, Fairchild's second draft was waiting for me. It needed further revisions, but I sent it off to Bob, still mired down in Taiwan. He agreed the script needed work, but he was obviously more concerned at the moment with

Sand Pebbles. Each day brought new unanticipated problems, and he was falling further and further behind. He was sure that *Star!* would once again have to be postponed.

Julie agreed to a further postponement, and the studio had no choice. One thing became clear, however: Bob would have to plunge right into *Star!* the moment he returned from Taiwan. To implement this, it was decided that I should go there to meet with him to discuss script changes, cast, schedule, et cetera.

I was greeted at the airport in Taipei by the publicity man for *Sand Pebbles* and a photographer who took pictures of me as I deplaned. As we were walking toward the terminal, we were stopped by two uniformed men. They confiscated the photographer's camera, and after removing the film, returned the camera to him. It seemed strange behavior until I recalled having looked down before we landed and spotted a dozen rusting American bombers off to one side of the field. Evidently that was classified information, and on the vague chance that they might appear in the blurred background of one of my pictures, all the film had to be destroyed. It was rather odd, because the planes were not the least bit camouflaged and were plainly visible from any part of the airport, including the terminal.

I could not schedule regular meetings with Bob. I had to grab him whenever I could—between setups, during lunch breaks. Waiting around made me restless until I found a way to make myself useful. *Sand Pebbles* took place in China during the twenties. There were quite a few scenes in cafés and streets where the popular music of the day would probably be heard. Since no such music was available in the States, I researched it in Taipei.

When Bob Wise returned from Taiwan, we sent for Bill Fairchild and developed a final script for *Star!* We sent it off to Noel Coward, who invited us to discuss it with him at his summer home in Jamaica. Bob, Bill, and I flew to Montego Bay, Jamaica, where we were met by Cole Leslie, Coward's secretary, and Graham Payn, his oldest friend. They had chartered a plane, which flew us to Ocho Rios, the closest landing strip to where Noel lived in Blue Harbor.

He and a manservant lived alone on top of a mountain that had an unobstructed 360-degree view of everywhere. It doesn't seem to be generally known, but Noel was a better than average amateur painter. His house, with its ever-changing views and solitude, was perfect for him. Access to the house was by way of a road so full of boulders and loose rocks that it was virtually impassable. Only Cole and Noel's manservant could navigate it. At the bottom of the road were several small cottages in which Cole, Graham, and Noel's guests were housed.

Noel invited us to lunch the following afternoon. We were picked up by Cole, who drove us up the precipitous road to Noel's aerie while we sat holding on for dear life. As he drove, Cole told us that the road was kept impassable to keep strangers away. I thought to myself that it probably kept a lot of friends away as well.

Noel was there to greet us when we arrived. He apologized for the rough trip, then led us to the patio. Stretched out before us was a vast expanse of blue water as far as the eye could see. It seemed to blend into the cloudless sky. In the distance a few sailboats moved lazily across the horizon. It was breathtaking. No travel poster could have done it justice.

Lunch was charming, and Noel lived up to his reputation as an amiable host and brilliant conversationalist. I reminded him that we had met ten years earlier in Gene Kelly's living room at a party Kelly had given in his honor. I was flabbergasted at his total recall of that evening. He recited the guest list of about twenty people and then not only mentioned that I had accompanied him but also listed most of the songs he had sung.

I was most flattered when he said, "You're the chap who played those marvelous insides while I sang." He was referring to the harmonies and musical figures I had played as accompaniment.

I somehow neglected to thank him for a plug he had given a

song Sammy and I wrote, "Please Be Kind." In 1942, Coward was given a special Academy Award for his film *In Which We Serve*. His acceptance speech included "This is my first award, so *please be kind*." What was perhaps most striking about him, however, was his faculty for putting his guests at ease immediately. The lunch was like a get-together of old friends rather than a first meeting.

After lunch, we adjourned to another room to discuss our script. What crossed my mind was what Cole Leslie had pointed out to us on our flight from Montego Bay. He claimed that Noel Coward had contributed more to the British theater than anyone else. He had enjoyed great success as a producer, director, actor, song and dance man, author, librettist, lyricist, and composer. And this was the man who was about to sit in judgment of our script.

He liked it. He was pleased with the way he had been portrayed and had only one comment, which he made directly to Bill Fairchild. "You have me saying too many 'dear-boys,' dear boy."

The evening before we were to leave we were invited up to Noel's once again, this time for dinner. The table was set out of doors where the air was balmy, and the sky was so ridiculously full of stars that it looked like a corny stage set. During the course of our conversation, Noel asked whom we had in mind to play him. We told him we hadn't thought of anyone yet but that we were planning to go to London to search for the proper actor. He suggested that we see his godson, Daniel Massey, Raymond's son. We would be getting an actor who knew Noel extremely well and would be able to capture his character rather than do an imitation of him. We all agreed that an impersonation of Noel was to be avoided.

After seeing dozens of actors, we did eventually hire Massey to play the part. He was excellent in the film and received an Academy Award nomination as Best Supporting Actor.

My fondest recollection of the time we spent in Jamaica, however, is of something that happened after dinner. We were led to the music room for brandy and coffee. It happened to have two pianos. Naturally, Noel and I gravitated toward them, and before long we were playing together. It was about 10:30 P.M. when we started, and we played everything. We did songs by Rodgers and Hart and Hammerstein, Gershwin, Kern, Berlin, Youmans, Loesser, and Bernstein. (Noel was an admirer of *West Side Story*.)

We did them in the style of Mozart, Debussy, Tchaikovsky, and every other classical composer we could think of. It was one of those rare sessions where we each anticipated what the other was going to play. But what was most unusual about our recital was that Noel knew and played so many songs by other writers. Songwriters as a group are usually not that generous. They may know many songs but play only the ones they have written.

The only other songwriter I ever met who had such high regard for his colleagues was Cole Porter. In fact, he and Noel were much alike in many respects. They both wrote words and music. Porter didn't have Coward's quicksilver mind and keen wit. But they were both overly generous in their opinions of others and were stimulating conversationalists with an intense interest in all the arts.

Of less importance was that they both reacted to my first name, Saul. I was told that before we met, Noel referred to me as "the chap with the wonderful biblical name." And Cole once told me, "I love the sound of the name Saul, and you know I'm very sensitive to the sounds of words." As for me, I could never understand their reactions. "Saul" always sounds too formal to me and that's why I am usually called "Solly."

To get back to my stint with Noel at the two pianos, we played without stopping, until dawn. At sunrise, Noel got up from the piano and said, "There. That should hold them for a while." The "them" he was referring to were Bob, Bill Fairchild, Cole Leslie, and Graham Payn.

It was just as well that we stopped when we did. We had a plane to catch in several hours. On the flight home I realized what a wonderful few days it had been and how much I had enjoyed playing with Noel. I decided then and there that when I returned home, I was going to buy a second piano. I did, and I've enjoyed having two pianos in my living room ever since.

Back at the studio, I researched the songs to be used in *Star!* There was no problem choosing the songs that Gertrude Lawrence had introduced. It was just a matter of obtaining the rights to use them. What I could not find out from all my research was the names of the early music hall songs that Lawrence and her family used. I went through dozens of collections of old English music hall songs and found several they might have used.

Gertrude Lawrence was supposed to have been a member of an eight-girl singing and dancing group called The Daffodils. She was so inept (it might have been on purpose) that she was fired. I needed a song for The Daffodils in which we could show what she did that got her fired.

What could be more logical than for a group called The Daffodils to do a number about flowers? I recalled once having seen a bad vaudeville act in which the girls played different flowers, but I could find no published song to fit this situation. I resorted to the only course left. I wrote it myself. It's called "In My Garden of Joy."

Star! required a title song. I instructed the studio to hire Sammy Cahn and Jimmy Van Heusen. They were topflight songwriters and I had enjoyed working with them on *Robin and the Seven Hoods*. Lionel Newman, the head of the studio Music Department, called me. "I spoke to Sammy. He'd like to write the song with *you*."

I was surprised and very tempted. I might have enjoyed writing with Sammy again. But I replied, "No, I'd rather he did it with Jimmy."

For one thing, I was too busy during that period to write a song. But that wasn't the real reason I turned Sammy down. Somewhere inside me I still felt a residual pain from our broken-up partnership. I also recalled how upset I got on the few occasions when Sammy wrote songs with someone else while we were partners. Even allowing for the strong likelihood that Jimmy Van Heusen would not have reacted the way I did, I wasn't willing to risk it. They had been a successful team for a long time, and I wasn't about to do anything that might interfere with their collaboration.

Star! was a most difficult film to make because of the concept we had adopted. Instead of telling a straightforward biography, we telescoped parts of Gertrude Lawrence's life and presented them as though they had been photographed years earlier as newsreel footage. These sections were in small-screen black-and-white with scratchy monaural sound. The remainder of the film was in wide-screen Technicolor with six-track stereo. Because newsreel shots are always rather short, there were many more scenes than in the average musical. And Julie was in almost all of them.

She was inexhaustible. She was needed for endless fittings by Donald Brooks, who did the clothes; by the makeup and wig people; by Lennie Hayton, our musical director; me, for song rehearsals; and Michael Kidd for dance rehearsals. Of course, as always happens, everyone wanted her at the same time. There was so much to do that it was impossible to accomplish it before we began shooting.

To put it in clearer perspective, Julie sang sixteen songs in *Star!* In *The Sound of Music* she sang seven. For each of them, she had to wear something different, and for most she had a makeup and wig change since she aged over twenty years during the film. Each of the numbers had to be staged and learned. It was obviously inhumane to ask anyone to keep up this pace for very long. More than once we adjusted our shooting schedule so she could have several days' rest.

In the meantime, I was seeing Betty on a regular basis. I was getting worried. Our relationship was becoming too serious. I wasn't ready to make any rash decisions, like getting married. Before this, I had dated several other women but never had as much fun as I did with Betty. Then one weekend, while I was working on the postproduction of *Star!*, it suddenly hit me: That unpleasant feeling I had been experiencing for some time was loneliness. Not only loneliness—loneliness for Betty. I missed being with her.

On March 4, 1968, at about a quarter to four, I drove to the guest house she was living in and, after a friend who was visiting her left, I asked her to marry me. Luckily she said yes.

My timing was perfect. She had just about decided that if I didn't ask her soon, she was going to break off our relationship. It had been going on for four years, and that was long enough, she figured. Considering that I had been single for eighteen, four doesn't seem that long.

I was still deeply immersed in postproduction of *Star!* so we set a wedding date after I was scheduled to be finished. It goes without saying that I was with the picture for a longer time than planned. We didn't let that delay us, however. We were married on a Friday afternoon in a judge's chambers in Buena Ventura, California, more commonly known as Ventura.

We spent a glorious weekend at the Bel-Air Hotel and on Monday moved back into the house I had been living in. I then went back to work. Two weeks later, when I was finally finished with *Star!,* we departed on a long honeymoon all over Europe. We arranged it so that the last city we would visit would be London to coincide with the world royal premiere of *Star!*

The royal premiere of *Star!* in London was a triumph. The audience adored the picture. A preponderance of the reviews were out-and-out raves. There were a few exceptions, but there always are.

The one sour note was that Julie didn't attend. She was shooting another film, *Darling Lili,* and Blake Edwards, her director (now her husband), couldn't readjust his shooting schedule to give her enough time off to attend the premiere. The London newspapers made much of her absence. In several it was headlined on the front page along with pictures of Julie. She was, after all, their star portraying another of their stars and had been away for too many years already.

The following week we premiered in New York with not quite the same results. The audiences seemed to like the picture, but with nowhere near the enthusiasm the British did. This was reflected in the reviews, which were mainly good, but there were no raves like those we had received in London. Business was excellent the first weeks, but grosses immediately started plummeting during the weeks that followed. The same pattern was repeated all over the country. The studio tried everything from a new advertising campaign to shortening the picture. Nothing helped. Eventually they shortened the film considerably, gave it a new title, and rereleased it. I have never seen that version.

The picture was a flop, and I took it hard. I had never been so closely associated with a failure. I was consumed with trying to figure out what we had done wrong. Yet I should have anticipated problems because of an unusual incident that took place even before the movie was released.

A year before the film was made, Fox took a two-page ad in the Sunday *New York Times* announcing that the makers of *The Sound of Music* were about to launch a new project. If readers were interested in receiving advance information about the film's release date and wanted preferred reserved seats, they were to fill out the coupon at the bottom of the ad and send it to Fox. Thousands upon thousands of replies were received.

During the year that followed, all the general audience knew of the film was what they read in feature articles about Julie as Gertrude Lawrence and pictures of both. There was a monumental advertising campaign. No one ever saw a foot of the film except those of us connected with it. When the picture was about to be released, Fox sent notification to the thousands of people who had sent in coupons in response to the ad a year earlier. Fewer than a hundred replied.

The astonishing disinterest could not be attributed to the quality of the film, since no one had seen it. The only thing they knew from all the advertising was the character that Julie played. Given these conditions, I concluded that at that time audiences would accept Julie only as the heroine of a fairy tale, *Mary Poppins,* or as the almost make-believe heroine of *The Sound of Music,* not as a real person.

Then the question arises: If Julie was so good in the picture, why didn't word of mouth make it a hit? I have an answer that satisfied me. From the start, we were aware that the character of Gertrude Lawrence in our script was cold and aloof. We wanted her that way because we had learned that that's how she really was. We relied on Julie's built-in warmth, so evident in *The Sound of Music,* to compensate for this deficiency. We took a calculated risk and lost. Audiences could not identify with the character, and even worse, disliked her.

Audiences—not me. I still believe it a meticulously directed film with a fine performance by Julie. It contained much that was innovative. I suppose I'll be haunted by its failure forever.

Chapter 22 ■ In the fall of 1971, Betty and I moved to Rome, where I worked on *Man of La Mancha* with Arthur Hiller. He had directed such films as *The Americanization Of Emily, Love Story,* and *Hospital.* It came about in the same way as my association with Bob Wise on *West Side Story.* Arthur had never done a musical, so Phil Gersh, my agent, arranged for me to meet with him and fill him in on what to expect. By the end of the meeting, it was agreed that I would work on the film as his associate.

Man of La Mancha & That's Entertainment, Part 2

We were the third "regime" United Artists (UA) had hired to make the picture. They first engaged the creators of the stage show. Mitch Leigh, the composer, was to be the producer, and Albert Marre, who had directed the stage production, was to direct the film. They made numerous tests of actors, sets, and costumes, and had a screenplay written by the original author, Dale Wasserman. After seeing these tests, UA was dissatisfied. They dismissed Mitch Leigh et al. and replaced them with the second regime, which was headed by Peter Glenville, the English director. He made more tests of different actors, sets, and costumes, and hired the English writer John Hopkins to write the screenplay. Hopkins did a fine job, but he eliminated most of the songs. Understandably, this made no sense to the UA people, who had paid an astronomical sum for the show *because* it was a hit musical. Peter Glenville and company were sent packing. The expense incurred by the first two sets of film-makers was reported to have been several million dollars.

Enter Arthur Hiller. He immediately hired Dale Wasserman. We used his original play script as the basis for a new screenplay. But certain elements of the film that had been contracted for by the people who had preceded us had to be retained. Two enormous sets, on which most of the action was to take place, were already being constructed when we arrived in Rome. The set designer, who also did the costumes, had already done months of research and purchased yards of expensive, rare materials in various colors. The look of the film was preordained by him. For budgetary reasons (I think), none of the dance numbers from the show were to be used in the film.

To insure its investment, United Artists engaged two top stars to play the leads, Sophia Loren and Peter O'Toole, but at what a cost! In addition to paying them their regular enormous salaries, UA agreed to finance a picture of their own that each of them was eager to make. The combined cost of both films was well over $2 million. Neither film returned its cost.

Casting Peter O'Toole as Don Quixote was a fine idea. He is an accomplished actor and his fragile physique and sensitive face made him perfect casting. Perfect in every way except one—he can't sing. And that was a particularly devastating deficiency; since there were no dance numbers, the singing became most important. Peter, like so many other actors, thought he could sing well enough to record his own tracks.

To his credit, however, when he heard the playbacks of his voice, he admitted he wasn't good enough. He flew off to London and returned with a singer who he thought was a perfect voice double for him. He was wrong. The man, an excellent singer, sounded nothing like Peter. But using him would not be doing irreparable damage to the picture, so we recorded him. As usual, we found a proper voice dub for O'Toole and replaced his vocal tracks after the film was finished.

The results, however, were not completely satisfactory. The part of Don Quixote in *Man of La Mancha* is a heavy singing role. He sings the most important songs in the score, and several are quite difficult and require a professional singer to do them justice. But that kind of sound coming from Peter would have been unbelievable, so we had to sacrifice quality in the interest of credibility.

Working on the film was less than enjoyable. To begin with, I found Peter O'Toole very bright but very unpleasant. Offscreen he played "star" to the hilt, aloof and demanding. Although he never drank on the set, we were occasionally heirs to his hangovers. He often treated the people around him rather shabbily, and I made it a point to avoid him whenever I could.

To compensate for him, there were, thankfully, Sophia and James Coco. They were wonderful. They showed infinite patience in dealing with Peter. Lunch hours were the best time of the day; Sophia made pasta for all of us in her dressing room. Getting back to work was always a little difficult.

Sophia Loren did her own singing. Her songs called for more acting than singing, and she's a wonderful actress. She's extremely musical, a joy to look at and to be around. She's another dramatic actress who had always longed to be in a musical and was excellent in our film.

Man of La Mancha was not well received by the critics. It was not the film it might have been, and curiously enough, part of the blame must be borne by the people who preceded us. They had dictated the look and principal casting of the film. Were it not for that, a totally different concept might have emerged.

Not long after I finished working on *Man of La Mancha,* Dan Melnick, the production head at MGM, invited me to see one of the early versions of *That's Entertainment,* a compilation of some of the best musical numbers MGM had filmed. I flipped. There were clips in the film of twelve numbers that I had had a hand in. It was like watching part of my past being unfurled before me.

Betty and I were invited to the international premiere and supper party at the Beverly Wilshire Hotel. Not since the demise of the studio system had so many former MGM stars been assembled in one room. It was a truly happy, festive night, heavy with nostalgia.

As part of the impromptu entertainment, Gene Kelly was called on. He announced that he was going to do a number he had done with Judy Garland, "You Wonderful You." He then asked me, as one of the writers of the song, to come up and play for him. After that, he introduced Judy's daughter, Liza Minnelli, for whom I also played. She chose to sing "You Made Me Love You." When I asked her about a key, she replied, "The same as Mama's." I suddenly flashed back to the time we were all in London doing *I Could Go On Singing,* when Liza, then a teenager, had learned all the arrangements I had made for Judy. What a different Liza this was. She was now a star in her own right.

MGM then invited Betty and me to the New York premiere of the picture. I was asked to organize some entertainment on a much smaller scale for the supper party that followed the screening. It coincided perfectly with a trip Betty and I were planning with Judy, Hal, and their children to Paris, then on to their mountaintop home in Majorca.

In New York, I immediately got together with Betty Comden and Adolph Green, who had written eight very successful musicals for MGM, including *Singin' in the Rain, It's Always Fair Weather,* and *On the Town.* We prepared what they would do. Nothing else was rehearsed, but as luck would have it, there were several MGM alumni at the party who were only too happy to perform. It turned out to be an entertaining evening.

The following night, Betty and I went to the Russian Tea Room after the theater. As usual, there was a long line waiting for tables. We were about to leave when Dan Melnick invited us to join him. We talked about what a joyous film he had made. At the end of our conversation, I said, almost as a throwaway, "If you decide to make a sequel, I'd be interested in doing it." Dan immediately extended his hand and said, "You're on. We *are* planning a sequel." We shook hands, and for the ensuing two years I was involved with *That's Entertainment, Part 2.*

When Betty and I got back from Europe, I reported to the studio. Dan and I met as often as he could to devise a format for the film. We worked very well together. Although I had known

Dan socially for some years, I had no way of knowing what he would be like in a work situation. We had always had good times together and I knew that that wouldn't change, but I was amazed to find him so creative. One doesn't usually expect that from a studio executive.

I looked forward to our meetings, and before we were through, we had come up with at least a dozen formats for our film. We finally hit on the one we wanted to see the most and would be the most entertaining and novel: We were going to reunite Gene Kelly and Fred Astaire—they had done a number together in the film *Ziegfeld Follies*—as performing masters of ceremonies to introduce the segments that would make up our film.

Deciding on an idea is one thing, but getting it activated is something else altogether. It was not easy to convince Gene and Fred. Not that they didn't want to work together, but Gene had other commitments and Fred was semiretired again and about to leave for Ireland to visit his daughter. I worked on getting Gene, who eventually consented to do the film, and he convinced Fred to join him. In fact, Fred would do anything Gene asked of him. Incidentally, they were each other's number one fan.

Fred had one irrevocable condition that was impressed on us over and over by his agent and by Fred himself. Under no circumstance would he dance. He would withdraw from the film if it was even suggested. At our first meeting, when I demonstrated the opening lyrics they were to sing, Fred said, "Gene, what about doing sixteen bars of dance after the first chorus?"

Gene didn't say it. I didn't say it. *Fred* said it! I sat at the piano, motionless, lest Fred change his mind. He didn't. They danced in the picture—not once but three times.

Although the number of times they danced was few, Gene, as choreographer, faced an unusual problem. His style of dancing is so different from Fred's that he had to find a happy choreographic medium they could both execute comfortably. He accomplished it admirably. But the most fun for me was watching these two giants, who had totally reshaped the American film musical, work together. There were obvious similarities between them. They were both perfectionists and hardworking. It was not uncommon to see Fred go off in a corner of the rehearsal stage to practice a step. At the same time, Gene would be at the other end of the stage creating new choreography.

Only once did Fred register anything in the nature of a complaint, and then he addressed it to me, not to Gene. He said it as only Fred could. Referring to a tiny section of one of the numbers, he asked me, "Do we look good doing that?"

I watched the next rehearsal and thought Fred was right. I mentioned to Gene that I, not Fred, wasn't sure about the section in question. His reply was "Good. I'm glad you told me because I wasn't sure of it either. I'll change it."

Since Dan Melnick was also running the studio, it left him no time to look at complete films and choose clips to be included in our picture. The modus operandi was this: I ran all the films and chose sections I thought worthy of consideration. When I had amassed about two hours of clips, Dan and I spent evenings screening them. We then chose the best clips and set the others aside. I also benefited from the fact that he had been through a selection process on the first *That's Entertainment* and knew of numbers I might have overlooked.

By the time I had finished, I had screened over 250 movies, some of them more than once; looked at parts of over 100 more; saw about 75 shorts and a similar number of trailers. There were times when it became almost unbearably tedious, but then I would discover something that made up for the tedium. For example, I was running a 1929 film called *Untamed* when I noticed that Joan Crawford was doing the same savage-native-girl dance that she had done as a Broadway personality in *Hollywood Revue of 1929*. Maybe that was her dance for that year.

Also, every major dramatic star did at least one song in a picture during his or her career at the studio. Jimmy Stewart, definitely a nonmusical personality, played the lead in a musical called *Born to Dance* and was assigned the difficult task of singing "Easy to Love," one of Cole Porter's rangier songs, tough even for pros to sing. Stewart got by on his charm. In general, however, the level of creativity demonstrated in the musicals was truly remarkable.

The first version of *That's Entertainment, Part 2* ran about four hours. After juggling many elements, we finally cut it down to two hours with much pain and sorrow at having to lose some of our favorite film clips. At that point, we had the obligatory screenings for friends and opinion makers.

You don't have to be in this business very long to learn that a large part of the audiences at these screenings devoutly hopes your picture is a failure. The competition in Hollywood is so fierce that many wish for no one's success but their own. Yet you receive only congratulations after the picture has been shown. What is most difficult to learn is conquering the temptation to take all of these compliments seriously.

Knowing all this, the obvious question is, why hold these screenings at all? Because after some experience you can tell whether the audience is enjoying your film despite itself. And should they sincerely like it, the good word of mouth spreads over Hollywood the following morning like wildfire. This favorable reaction reaches the critics and a certain segment of the public very soon thereafter. Judging from the applause and laughter at our screenings, we knew they liked our film.

The first public showing of *That's Entertainment, Part 2* was at the Cannes Film Festival of 1976. A junket was organized: Gene Kelly, Fred Astaire, Cary Grant, Bobby Van, Marge Champion, Kathryn Grayson, Johnny Weissmuller, and a group of top MGM executives.

Weissmuller did his Tarzan yell as we departed from Los Angeles and didn't stop until we returned a week later. As though that weren't enough, Kathryn Grayson tried to top him by singing higher and louder. Unfortunately, he accepted the challenge. It was nightmarish. Eventually, they became aware of the effect their screeching was having on the rest of us and stopped. Ironically, the fans asked for Weissmuller's Tarzan yell everywhere we went. He yelled. We cringed.

Our reception in Cannes was insane. The streets were lined with hordes of people as our limousines made their way slowly toward the Palais Du Cinema. The entire gendarmerie of France must have been there to hold back the crowds. As our stars stepped out of their cars, it was as if the pins on hundreds of hand grenades had been pulled. There was the kind of high-pitched shrieking that makes the noise at a rock concert sound like a slumber party. They had never seen the likes of Gene Kelly (he is virtually an honorary citizen of France), Fred Astaire, Cary Grant, or the rest of our stars before, and they went wild with appreciation.

Their enthusiasm carried over to the film. I've never been part of a more excited audience. Almost every number was applauded, often cheered, and every joke laughed at. When the film was over, it was given a ten-minute ovation.

The screening was followed by an all-American dinner given at the Winter Casino for about a thousand invited guests. Steak, baked potato, apple pie, and California wines. (A French connoisseur said of the California offerings, "The white wines are excellent, but the reds lack soul." I wish I knew what he meant.) The big goof on the menu was corn on the cob. In France, that's cattle feed.

Soon after the film went into general release, the letters from viewers started pouring in. A vast majority of them were complimentary, but complimentary or not, they almost all posed the same questions: "How could you leave out _____?" (They would then name a favorite number of theirs.) "How could you include _____?" (A number they didn't like.) Other complaints were that the numbers or sequences were too long, too short, too loud, too soft. But these were in a minority. What amazed me was how many obscure numbers were mentioned. So many were suggested that to satisfy all the requests, the picture would have had to run half a day.

The other question asked most frequently was "Why don't they make pictures like that anymore?" The questioners should be grateful that they didn't have to sit through some of the pictures from which the clips were extracted. They assumed that because the numbers or sequences were fun to watch, the entire pictures would be as well. Unfortunately, that is not always the case. Sometimes they were so bad that viewing them made me almost suicidal with boredom. But suddenly a wonderful number or scene would appear that would make the wasted hours worthwhile.

The main reason MGM-type musicals aren't made anymore is costs. No films represented in either *That's Entertainment* picture cost even close to $5 million, an impossible budget by today's standards. To illustrate, the *American in Paris* ballet cost $500,000. The entire film cost a little over $3 million. Today the ballet would cost about $8 million, the entire film about $30 million. As a matter of fact, the average MGM musical during the golden age cost between $1.5 million and $2.5 million. Such budgets are nonexistent for musicals today.

■ When I made my first vocal arrangement for a grossly untalented female singer almost half a century ago, I found that the hardest part was the ending. Since then, I've learned that everyone has had to deal with this problem. Puccini solved it by introducing a new aria at the end of an opera. In today's stage musicals, it's known as the "eleven o'clock" number. In classical music, the ending is even given a special name—coda.

I have now come to the end of the book, and I am once again faced with the problem. All that is left to be told is the surprising

Epilogue

changes that have taken place in me while writing these pages. It has been a purifying experience, like a postgraduate self-analysis. I find I feel quite differently now about the occasional injustices I endured than I did when they were happening. Then I might have been upset, but I eventually rationalized why they were being done. Now I feel great resentment toward Harry Cohn, Al Jolsen, and the others who took advantage of my naiveté and, I suppose, good nature. I would react quite differently today. I think. I'm sure.

Also, looking back, I feel lucky to be living when I am. Never has show business undergone so many changes: vaudeville, radio, musical theater, musical film, and television. I've been lucky enough to have been involved in all of them.

And I witnessed the changes in music from ragtime to Dixieland to the period of the crooners—Rudy Vallee, Russ Columbo, and the early Bing Crosby. They were followed by the swing era, with its big bands and vocalists, which somehow led to rock 'n' roll.

I am not a fan of rock and the other music fads it has spawned: heavy metal, hip-hop, and so on. They employ harmonies that are too simplistic and uninteresting, and I find the ear-splitting cacophony offensive and depressing. What I loathe even more is rap. To begin with, it isn't music, which by definition connotes a tune of some kind, even if it's as primitive as hitting two different-size logs with a stick. I won't comment on the content of the lyrics except to suggest that a good rhyming dictionary would be useful. Rap is rhythmic talking. Period.

The state of today's film musicals is lamentable. They are few in number, and most are not very successful. They differ drastically from the musicals of the golden age in ways besides the sound of the music. In earlier musicals, the filmmaker's aim was to make the musical numbers look as much like live performances as possible. Therefore, there were very few changes in camera angles for a musical sequence. Today the camera angles change every ten or fifteen seconds. They say it creates excitement. Perhaps. But it sure detracts from the continuity of a performance and destroys dance numbers. That's really unfortunate because some of today's young dancers are wonderful.

Also, the integrated musicals of the past, in which the numbers either advanced the plot or enhanced a moment in the story, have been abandoned. Numbers now seem to appear for no discernible reason, probably because the filmmaker has to make certain that he has enough musical sequences for the release of a sound-track album.

The only studio where traditional musicals are being produced is Disney. The success of *Beauty and the Beast* and *Aladdin* has been attributed by producers to the fact that musical cartoons have always enjoyed a certain popularity. They refuse to recognize that both films are hits because they have singable scores.

I am optimistic that the style of film musicals will change again. It always has. I hope the next phase in the development of movie musicals will combine what was outstanding about the earlier films with the best features of today's, including the startling new audio and visual technologies that are constantly being developed. Musicals will then rightfully reclaim their former glory.

In the meantime, there is an enormous audience out there waiting.

blank page 252

Appendix

FILMS

Below is a partial list of films in which I functioned in one or more of the following capacities: songwriter, vocal arranger, arranger, pianist, music director, associate producer, producer.

Argentine Nights
Rookies on Parade
Time Out for Rhythm
Go West, Young Lady
Sing for Your Supper
Two Latins From Manhattan
Ever Since Venus
Eve Knew Her Apples
Honolulu Lu
Cowboy Canteen
The Thrill of Brazil
Kansas City Kitty
The Countess of Monte Cristo

Cover Girl
The Jolson Story
You Were Never Lovelier
You'll Never Get Rich
Down to Earth
On the Town
Summer Stock
*An American in Paris**
Lovely to Look At
Two Weeks With Love
Three Little Words
Everything I Have Is Yours
Give a Girl a Break

*Academy Award.

Pandora and the Flying	*Merry Andrew*
Dutchman	*I Could Go On Singing*
The Last Time I Saw Paris	*Can Can*
Teahouse of the August Moon	*West Side Story**
Kiss Me Kate†	*The Sound of Music*
Seven Brides for Seven	*Star!*
Brothers*	*Man of La Mancha*
High Society†	*That's Entertainment,*
Les Girls	*Part 2*

Partial List of Published Songs

"Rhythm Is Our Business"	"Savin' Myself for You"
"Rhythm in My Nursery	"You're a Lucky Guy"
Rhymes"	"Tell Me Why"
"Rhythm Saved the World"	"All My Love"
"Shoe Shine Boy"	"Prosschai"
"Until the Real Thing	"Just a Simple Melody"
Comes Along"	"I Could Make You Care"
"If It's the Last Thing I Do"	"Bei Mir Bist Du Schoen"
"Posin'"	"Joseph Joseph"
"Dedicated to You"	"Please Be Kind"
"Wait Until My Heart	"The Anniversary Song"
Finds Out"	"You Wonderful You"

*Academy Award.
†Academy nomination.

Index